time to mend

time to mend

release the death grip

Rita Esterly, Ph.D.

TATE PUBLISHING & *Enterprises*

Published by Tate Publishing & Enterprises, LLC
127 E. Trade Center Terrace | Mustang, Oklahoma 73064 USA
1.888.361.9473 | www.tatepublishing.com

Tate Publishing is committed to excellence in the publishing industry. The company reflects the philosophy established by the founders, based on Psalm 68:11,
"The Lord gave the word and great was the company of those who published it."

Book design copyright © 2009 by Tate Publishing, LLC. All rights reserved.
Cover design by Lance Waldrop
Interior design by Joey Garrett

Published in the United States of America

ISBN: 978-1-60799-969-0
1. Self-Help / Death, Grief, Bereavement
2. Family & Relationships / Parenting / Child Rearing
09.09.08

Dedication

I dedicate this book to the best father a little boy with cancer could ever hope to have, my husband, Chuck Esterly. His compassion, his sense of humor, his courage, his medical knowledge, his tender guidance, his brave spirit, his impeccable timing, and his warm heart gave Wes what he needed when he needed it most. Saying *yes* to Chuck's offer to be my life partner was one of the best decisions I have made. For his understanding during the long hours it took me to create this book, I am thankful.

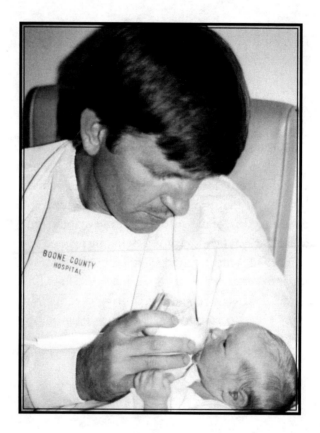

Nurtured

Kite Flying

Golfing Instructions

Fishing Moments

Snow Fun

My Family Sandwich

Acknowledgments

Many people have helped this book to become a reality. I want to acknowledge and thank the people who walked with me on the journey of sharing my story, my experience, and my knowledge. They have been angels in my pathway, placed strategically where they needed to be when I most needed to hear the message they had to share with me on my journey. Additionally, I want to thank the friends who graciously allowed me to include their writings, artwork, and song to enhance the story. Finally, I appreciate the three people who took time to read the book and give me feedback before I created the final product. They also helped me promote the book. For all of these contributions, I am thankful.

My dear, lifelong friend, Johanna Corn, who is an astrologer, kept telling me on a yearly basis that the universe was telling me to write not "for the masses" but "from me." I tried to ignore her for years by writing self-help books, articles, and audio tapes that were what I thought people needed to know to maintain a positive perspective on life. She kept telling me that my destiny was not to write "for the people" but to write "from my heart." Her words were my message. See how easy it was for me to ignore what was put right at my feet? Discernment is a tricky skill. Johanna hung in there with me year after year. I am thankful for her presence in my life.

After I realized I was destined to write the story of my experience with my son, I was having difficulty making my disconnected thoughts come together. I constantly debated back and forth about how to assemble my thoughts. Through a series of coincidences, I met a woman who took me out of the fog so that I could see clearly how the book was to be written. Rhinda Shearl Fairless got me unstuck. Rhinda believes that death is just another form of life. Rhinda said two things to me that allowed the book to become a reality.

First, she told me that even before Wes was born that Wes and I colluded to take this journey together, so Wes was fine with me writing the book. At first, I was very angry about that. What mother would ever make such a pact with her child to watch him suffer and die? But the more I thought about it, the more everything in my life seemed to make sense. Things I had thought, things that I had done, things I was puzzled about all made sense.

Secondly, she merely stated that the book was already written. I went home and pondered that for weeks. Before long, I realized that the book was written. I dusted off the journals that I had written during those years that Wes lived. There was the story. I went to my Web site, and I reread what I had written about optimism and resilience. There was the self-help piece for the book. The book was to be a self-help book on grief using my story to make it credible. All I had to do was mesh the two together. Thanks to Rhinda for clarifying the journey.

Once the book was written, my dear friend Carol Collins, a retired high school English teacher and voracious reader herself, did the editing for me. Her endeavors have allowed me to feel secure that the book is not only readable, but also well written. Then Hannah Tranberg from Tate Publishing made the best edits even better.

Additionally, I want to thank those people who allowed me to use their words about Wes. Monsignor Michael Wilbers gave the homily at Wes's funeral. Reverend Patrick Shortt gave a testimonial at Wes's funeral. Chris Rozier, Wes's best friend, wrote a poem about Wes when Chris was a sophomore in high school. Bobbie Prenger, a friend of mine, wrote a poem about Wes that was used on the funeral program. Lisa Dulle, a long-time friend, wrote an e-mail to me on what would have been Wes's twenty-first birthday, telling me about her thoughts of Wes. Pat Lock, Wes's fourth and fifth grade teacher, wrote about what made Wes so special in her life. Ali Esterly, Wes's sister, wrote a story about her relationship with her brother when she was a sophomore in high school. Tony Esterly, Wes's brother, made a comment that Wes was his hero. For each of their contributions, I am grateful.

I want to thank Gary Delamatre, the fantasy artist, for allowing me to use his amazing illustration of the boy and the fairy. He calls it *The Healing Touch*.

Thanks go to Charlie Stokes, who is a fund

raiser and excellent musician, and his son, Matt Stokes, who is a professional actor/singer and holistic nutritionist, for allowing me to use the song they wrote for Wes for his funeral.

Tom Durkin, an actor, playwright, and teacher served as my interviewer for the live teleconference launching/interview/reading done on October 17, 2008, which was the fifteenth anniversary of Wes's death. For his contribution in helping me promote my book, I am thankful.

Valda Stroesser, a middle school teacher, and her husband, Ed Stroesser, a journalist who has a successful strategic communications firm, both read my book in order to be interviewed about their reactions to it. I thank them for their support and feedback.

Nothing is ever a coincidence. Needing someone to cover my private practice in my absence, I contacted a previous graduate student of mine. She came to my office one day so we could talk over her responsibilities while I was gone. Our conversation stuck in my mind. I had written some lyrics that went with each chapter of the book. I sent the lyrics from chapter three and five to her. I told her that if the spirit moved her to put some music to the lyrics. She wrote the music and contacted a friend of hers who is a singer for a band. This friend and her husband decided to record the song. Kudos to Janese Neher for her musical ability and networking skills.

Making musical notes and lyrics come alive is what Lloyann Akers, a school teacher, and her husband, Chris Akers, a barber, do with their musical talents. They took the lyrics that I wrote along with the music that Janese wrote and made the essence of my book come alive. For their passion and talent in taking words and transforming them into feelings, I am thankful.

Many thanks also go to Lola Rice. Lola was my children's caregiver as they grew up. She became my office manager in my private practice. Through her nurturing, her devotion to my family, and her loyalty to me, I was able to accomplish my goals. In particular, without her, my dream of becoming a psychologist would never have come true. For twenty-nine years, she has been my anchor. For her friendship and devotion, I am grateful.

Ali Esterly, Wes's sister, an advertising art director, suggested that the book cover include the original drawing that I did with Wes when I told him he was going to die. For her creativity, her support, her encouragement, and her marketing ideas, I am thankful.

Table of Contents

Introduction

"For I know the plans I have for you," declares the Lord (Jeremiah 29:11, NIV). Little did I know that those plans would be an eight-year roller coaster ride and another fifteen years of wandering until I finally told the story of that ride. Each of you has had your own ride. Each of you has wandered, trying to make sense out of the path that life laid out before you. While the path may be treacherous, it is the attitude with which you face it that makes the journey manageable or miserable. A satisfying life is a matter of how you embrace the journey and those who cross your path.

My son Wes very wisely said to his sister something that I want to share with you on your journey. Here is what I wrote in my journal. *One day, when Wes and Ali were playing with their Duplos this past summer, I heard Ali say, "I'm so sad. I have no friends."*

Wes said, "Of course you always have a friend, Ali. Jesus is always your friend." He quickly added, "You know, you also have another friend. Yourself. You are your own friend." With Jesus beside you and you as your own friend, nothing can stop you from managing your adversity.

The intention of writing this book was not that it be a scholarly piece. It is definitely not based on research. The object was to tell my story and the things that helped me through my grief. I love sharing what works. For some of you it will fit. For others it won't. I offer it to you as an opportunity to try behaviors and thoughts that have the potential for getting you to the goal of weathering your grief in a resilient way. It is up to you to choose to apply what you learn from this book. My best wishes to you in finding among these pages a small nugget of help to make your grief process at least slightly bearable.

Heartache of Discovery

A child that loses a parent is an orphan.
A man who loses his wife is a widower.
A woman who loses her husband is a widow.
There is no name for a parent that loses a child
for there is no word to describe the pain.

Author Unknown

While there is no single word to label a parent, there are many words in combination that describe the pain one endures concerning the loss of a child. I probably described the pain best on the tenth anniversary of my son's death. Here is what I wrote.

The greatest sorrow as a mother that I endured was to hold my lifeless child in my arms, his body beginning to stiffen as I rocked him, tears flowing as I had never cried before, like a flood in the desert, raining on his hallowed body. No thoughts, no images, only the emotions flooding my senses and feeling his body growing cold. My heart, for the fourth time, ached. I sat silently, weeping from the depths of a broken heart. The spirit of that joyful child had gone, and I knew I was only hold-ing the shell that housed what once was my son and all that he was about in his life. The golden, feather-haired child with the long eyelashes and genuine smile was on a heavenly journey. No longer would he have to endure the pain, the shots, the treatments, the medi-cine, and the surgeries. Although in all of that, he still was joy filled. He endured so much better than I. No matter what he had to do, he just accepted it as part of the tasks of normal life, for that was all he knew and that was normal life to him. God gave him a special gift of being present to the moment and never wishing for anything else. Perhaps he could enjoy the moment because he knew he had no future; so he could just enjoy the present, each day as it came. He taught me so much about living for today and being content, no matter what life brought to him. He was a truly unique and unbelievable child. I marvel that God allowed me to be his parent. He was such a special gift, and I have been blessed to be his mother.

This book does three things. It describes the pain, the feelings, and the struggles a parent endures when dealing with a chronically or terminally ill child. Second, it describes ways to cope when liv-ing with such a child. Third, it gives techniques for mending the resultant broken heart that a parent has over the loss of a child. These three are revealed through my own story. At times you will want to put this book down because you will believe you cannot read another sad word. At other times you will be unable to put it down because you want to learn how to heal. My hope is that you can persist to the end of this book so you can learn ways to choose to make your life more satisfying despite the loss of a child. Let's begin.

This is the story of a unique little boy and my journey with and without him. The celebrating priest at his funeral stated, "Wes was really a unique child, a unique individual. There were many in the parish who knew him … Wes taught us that even in the midst of pain and suffering there really could be a smile." Additionally, at his funeral, another very special priest who stood beside me on this journey said, "His story may never be written in a book, but it's written in my heart, and I think it's written in the hearts of a lot of people." After years of discernment, I have chosen to write my story about the journey of being his parent.

My story is the story of millions of parents who stand by helplessly as the doctor informs them that their child has a chronic or terminal illness. The scenarios may be different, but the feelings are the same. The experience is like having a lead weight hanging on your heart while at the same time, it is struck by lightning. Then your heart just rips in two because of the pain and the heaviness. Those of you who have had this experience know exactly what I mean.

What else is it like to discover that your child has such an illness? Have you ever had one of those falling dreams? You are falling through space, and nothing can stop you, and you are wondering what in the world is going on.

Have you ever felt as though you were being sucked into a black hole of oblivion? You are rushing through space at the speed of light, and you are reaching out time after time to grasp something to stop the nothingness but are unsuccessful at each attempt.

Do you know the feeling of standing in the middle of the road on the darkest night of the year with an eighteen-wheeler's headlights headed straight for you? You want your legs to move so desperately, but the more you try to move them the more they feel like lead weights.

Have you ever awakened in the middle of the night and heard unfamiliar noises in the house and lay frozen in your bed? You want to get up and get a baseball bat, but your limbs won't cooperate with you.

Have you ever been stranded on a deserted road because your car broke down, and you don't know where you are or how you got there? All you know is that there is nothing for miles around and you are alone.

All of these reflect fear. The fear all parents have when the discovery is made that a child has a chronic illness, especially a terminal illness, has so few words to describe it. For me it took two forms: one was the fear of the unknown, and the other was the incredible fear of the lack of control over the process. What resulted from these two fears was constant anxiety.

When I learned that my child had a brain tumor, I feared what I did not know. I was totally clueless about what those words meant. I had no idea it would mean seeing my child cry out in pain, spending days in the hospital, having unending visits to doctors, watching many MRIs, quitting a job to drive somewhere for five weeks for my son to get a procedure, waiting in waiting rooms for doctors to bring good news, and being hopeful time and time again. There was always this constant fear that something was about to happen, so I was always in a state of readiness, creating constant anxiety.

Not being able to control the process of my life or the lives of my children was incredibly fearful, let alone not being able to control the process of what was happening to Wes. His life was in other adults' hands, not mine. How scary is that for a mother? I had watched over him and taken care of him. Now others watched over him as they performed an operation, as they gave him treatments, as they chose procedures for him. His life process was out of my control. Fear reigned in my life, and again, I was always in a state of readiness, creating constant anxiety.

What happens when a person is fearful? One of three things usually happens. First, a person might respond with the intense need to control. That was my response. Second, a person might respond by retreating. Third, a person might respond by being so overwhelmed that one is paralyzed in thought or action. Let's go over each so you understand common responses.

Control

In response to fear, I seek control. I am a firstborn child. As a first child, I like to be in charge. So my response was to try to control every aspect I could. What did this do for me? It reduced my anxiety so I could function.

There are three areas of control upon which one begins to focus. The first is the need to control time. That has to do with when what happens. I took control of the schedule as much as I could. I scheduled doctor's appointments, tests, procedures, etc. When I had a say in when these events would happen, I felt more peaceful. When I was told when to be where, I responded like a teenager by being oppositional and passive aggressive. I would call and reschedule or be late. Having that ounce of control was maximally important to me in order to survive.

The second is the need to control space. Three kinds of space are prominent to us. We have personal space around us that we need to be in control of. For example, when we were in the doctor's office, I often sat at specific spots where no one would be too close, invading my or my son's personal space. We also have physical space that we need to control. If there was a play area in the doctor's office and no other children were around, I would rearrange it to suit the needs of my child. When we went to the hospital to stay for a week, I would arrange the room and bring things from home to create a safe space for my child and a familiar space for me. The last area of space is emotional space. I kept my child really close emotionally so that I was the conduit through which his emotions were channeled. I was hypervigilant about all these areas of space to the frustration, at times, of many nurses and doctors, I am sure. This was the only way that I had of holding on to my own emotional survival.

The third area of control is how energy is spent. What I did when I was in a place I did not want to be in, such as the hospital, was paramount to my survival. So what did I do? I kept both my son's and my mind occupied by watching as many movies with him about winning as I could. I always brought VCR tapes to the hospital with me because at that time there were no DVDs to watch. I must have watched the *Star Wars* trilogy a million times.

A second thing I did was occupy myself when he was asleep. I took many pictures of my three children, so when I went to the hospital, I used the time to create one book of pictures for each child for each year of their lives. So the silver lining in this case was that in my library I have eleven photo albums for Wes, eighteen photo albums for Tony, and eighteen photo albums for Ali. I never would have had these had it not been for being captured in the hospital, needing to put my energy to good use. We will later discuss finding the silver lining in adversity.

Controlling the activities of the children so that their needs were met and at the same time ensuring that Wes was safe and as healthy as he could be was a full-time job. I ran my world with every moment controlled. The difficult part about adopting this response is that when that need is no longer prominent the behavior pattern is established and a new behavior pattern needs to be learned for more adaptive responses, in my case, after my son died.

Retreat

Retreating is another response that a person might have to the shock of learning that life will never be the same. Retreating can take several forms. One response is not dealing with things, and the other is dealing with things but retreating from people.

The paradox is that people retreat but expect friends and family not to forget them. They essentially set themselves up to fail because they put themselves in a double bind. On the one hand, they don't want people around and let that be known, but on the other hand, when people don't come around, they think people don't care.

When difficulty arises in any system, the system draws the boundaries in very close and regroups. I could elaborate on systems theory, but all you really need to know is the following concept about a family in crisis. The family cuts off external sources to regroup when a crisis develops. That means family members might not participate in as many activities as usual. They might not socialize as much. They stay close to home and each other. After adapting to the crisis situation, the family slowly reopens the family boundaries to others. At first, the boundaries are open to the outside sources that can provide help for the crisis. Eventually, the family allows more interactions with people. The family energy is needed to focus on the crisis situation.

Let me give you an example of this. At first, when I learned that my son had a brain tumor, I disconnected myself from several service organizations, volunteer groups, and social functions. My energy was needed to focus and concentrate on my son. When my family began to expand the boundaries again, we connected with the resources that could provide help. Where once my energy was spent on service, volunteer work, and having fun, my world became trips to hospitals, doctors, clinics, and treatment centers. Where once I had gone golfing and shopping with friends, they began to bring me meals and take my children to their activities. Where once we went to family gatherings, we began to celebrate holidays at home because of low blood counts. My whole world changed at first. The boundaries of our family grew smaller, and only when needed did we expand these boundaries. Once we adapted to the situation, we were able to expand the boundaries so that all of us were able to get our needs met, and we remained happy, even in the midst of our crisis.

This experience is common at first. The maladaptive issue here is when the closed boundaries stay closed instead of reopening. After the initial adjustment to the crisis, then the expansion of the boundaries is necessary if the family is to continue to be happy. It is a progression of steps. First, the boundaries are expanded to resources that can help a family with the crisis issues. Second, the boundaries are expanded to close family and friends. Third, the boundaries are expanded to the community organizations with which the family has attachment, such as schools, churches, and civic groups.

The family that does not expand the boundaries risks decreased happiness. This is why: The research on happiness tells us that the number-one correlation with happiness is to have what is called a "rich social network." This has nothing to do with finances. It has to do with having many people around you who care about you so you feel valued. Everyone needs to be valued by others. When the boundaries are closed, it is harder to get the emotional support that others have to offer. So expanding the boundaries when the family has adapted to the crisis is crucial to mending the heart.

Indecisiveness

Overwhelmed, therefore, paralyzed in thought and action is a very common response. From being paralyzed one becomes indecisive. In the beginning, dealing with all the responsibilities of scheduling doctor's appointments, procedures, treatments, and the resultant insurance paper barrage that comes from the former, one thinks that it is like looking up at a giant mountain bewildered about reaching the top. Knowing you have been challenged to reach the top and not knowing even where to start or how you will ever make it one step, let alone to the top, is totally overwhelming at first.

So you begin to attempt to do what you know you need to do, but you cannot make up your mind when, where, how, and with whom. You go back and forth in your mind. You are given options by the doctors, yet you keep debating back and forth. You cannot decide, because what if you decide the wrong thing? What if you don't have enough information to help you conclusively decide? What if, what if, what if?

In Barry Schwartz's book *The Paradox of Choice: Why More Is Less*, we learn that decisions are now so complex that one is forced to invest time and energy into a decision that creates self-doubt, anxiety, and dread. His idea is that when people have no choice they are miserable. As the number of choices increase, a consumer develops autonomy, control, and liberation, resulting in a positive feeling of power. However, as the number of choices grows, the consumer becomes overwhelmed, and debilitation results. In other words, with too many choices, a person feels overwhelmed and may shut down and possibly not be able to make a decision.

So you struggle to consider what is "good enough." At this point, you are not satisfied with just good enough because this is the life of your child. You need to make the "right" decision. The paradox here is that no one knows what the right decision is. Your mind-set at this point needs to be one with which you can live. My husband's and my mind-sets were that we would do everything that seemed reasonable but nothing that was far out, such as taking him out of the country for drastic treatment or using other than medical treatments or psychological treatments that would help him.

The basic fact still remains that you have absolutely no control over the fact that your child has a chronic or terminal illness. What you do have control over is how you respond to that situation. For me, the fear of not having any control over the process was like I described earlier: that of standing, frozen in the middle of a highway with an eighteen-wheeler coming at me full throttle. Seeing my son suffer without being able to do anything to relieve it was the most out-of-control feeling in the world.

What I did about having that feeling was to jump to the side, as I would if a truck were about to hit me. I took myself out of the middle of the highway. I stood on the side. I became the coach on the sidelines. I did this because with my personality I needed to have control. I called the plays, and Wes was my star quarterback. We worked as a team to respond to this situation. We never knew what the opponent (cancer) would do, but we had our playbook, ready to respond to anything. All quarterbacks have a style and something they just naturally do well without much effort. Wes's style of response was being present to the moment. So that's what we capitalized on during his short lifetime.

For instance, if Wes had to go to the hospital, he went and took his games, movies, and other things to occupy his time. If Wes was well enough to go to school, he went and enjoyed the interaction with his friends. When he had to be tutored at home because his blood counts were too low to be out in public, then he stayed home and enjoyed getting his work done with his teacher for two hours and then played with his Legos for the rest of the day. He was just present to the moment, no matter what had to happen. He was peaceful with whatever he was doing. That was his life. It was the only life he knew, and he accepted it for what it was.

Conclusion

No matter how a chronic or terminal illness affects life, there will be feelings. There will be struggles. There will be change. There will be thoughts. There will be decisions. You will be put in a position in which you never ever want to be put. However, there is a bottom line to the heartache of discovery. I probably put it best in my random writing in 2003.

As I watch the ice storm pelt its droplets on the window and hear the stilted click of ice upon ice, I am reminded of how my body seemed frozen for years as I endeavored to live through the time that I watched my son suffering with his cancer. I remember I would often be studying on my bed and he would climb in to cuddle up with me, I suppose just to have comfort and take the fear or loneliness away. I cradled him in my arms, and when he felt reassured, he lay there sleeping as I picked up my book again.

What allowed me to concentrate on my studies instead of totally giving in to the utter sadness of the situation is a mystery to me. I suppose we merely try to maintain a normal state in order to overcome the depths of weariness that sad suffering for others' pain brings us.

Shall we talk about a mother's pain? The worst pain for a mother is to see her child suffer. I felt helpless to relieve his pain as I could do with a minor scratch with a Band-Aid or a kiss. To be so helpless renders you to complete nothingness, as if you have no power, no hope, no control. All the love in the world for your child cannot ease the suffering. It can soothe him and reassure him that someone is there. Only that someone who is there cannot lessen the incredibly horrendous experience he faces daily. It is hard to even imagine what he is going through as he lies there in my arms. All I can do is pray that God will be with him to help him endure the sufferings and make at least parts of days bearable for him.

I constantly think: Was this my fault that he has to have such a life? What did I do? Was I not a good enough person? Did I get pregnant too soon after the miscarriage? Were my genes the cause? I don't want to have been responsible for that because it would be too much to endure, to even think it was because of me that he had to suffer.

So I would sit with him in my arms for hours, stroking his featherlike hair, when he had some hair to stroke, and would be thankful that I had him in my world for as long as he was to live with me. I would never give up, even though the experience of being in life with my son was difficult daily. No sacrifice of career, friends, social events, or success was too much to give up for the experience of being his mother.

In the next three chapters, I tell my story to set the stage and tell how I chose to mend my broken heart. Yes, it takes time. Yes, it's not easy. Yes, there are struggles. Yes, sometimes you feel like letting your heart stay broken forever. Yes, there are times when you feel as if you took one step forward, only to take three backwards. Yes, despite all of this, you can mend your broken heart. One way to do that is to believe in yourself. Believe that you can mend your broken heart. In each chapter that follows my story, I will remind you to believe in you. As you will find as you read chapter three, my son, Wes, told his sister Ali, "You are your own friend." Be your own friend and believe in yourself.

My Story

Life with Wes

When I first thought about writing my story, I wrote this sentence: *This is the story of one incredible little boy and the family that had the opportunity to live with him for eleven years.* Our family was very typical. Chuck and I were involved parents who gave the children a delicate balance in life. Chuck, a veterinarian, played with them, taught them sports, and supported them financially. I kept them organized, got them involved in the performing arts, and supported their dreams. Tony was Wes's older brother by two years. Wes was the middle child. Ali was Wes's younger sister by two years. We were a perfect family.

To differentiate today from long ago, I have placed in italics what I wrote in my journal in the midst of the trauma, during the years of being his mother, during the months following his death, and at intermittent times as I mended my broken heart. Those of you who have had this journey too will identify, and those of you who have not may come to better understand someone who has.

My son Wes was a typical three-year-old. He was all boy. He loved playing with swords because He-man was his favorite character. Swords would become a symbol for him in his life as he fought the dragon of cancer. When he was three years old, his preschool teacher alerted us to the fact that he seemed very lethargic and suggested we take him for a check with his doctor. He had been having headaches and clutched his head occasionally. He never complained, though, yet if someone else notices a change in your child, it is worth checking out. So we did. Our family doctor told us to take him to get a CAT scan that day. We did, and when the doctors read the scan, we were immediately put in contact with a brain surgeon, who told us that he had a brain tumor that needed to be operated on as soon as possible. He set up the operation for the next day. I am not quite sure why my husband and I left Wes all alone that night at the hospital. I suppose we were in so much shock we blindly obeyed when the nurse told us to go home and get some rest. After picking up the other two children from a friend who had kept them while we were at the hospital, we went home and just lay in each other's arms, bewildered that this was happening to him and to us. That was Halloween 1985.

We hardly slept. The next day, we hurried to the hospital. I am not sure how I let them take him to the operating room. We brought his Brave Heart Lion to go with him to the operating room. They dressed Brave Heart Lion in a surgery mask. Wes was sedated, and as they took him into the elevator, my heart was aching. I knew then what having a broken heart really felt like. It's truly a physical sensation. Chuck and I knew that we needed to lift him up to God. The surgeon had told us that the chances of surviving the kind of tumor he suspected it was were 20 percent. We held it in our minds that Wes would be included in the 20 percent.

Our many friends came to wait with us during the ten hours that it took to remove the tumor. Two dear friends bought us pillows with pillowcases so we could stay the night in the waiting room while Wes was in intensive care. Other friends brought food. I could not eat no matter how hard I tried. I felt nauseous. Days blended into days. Following in italics is my steady stream of thoughts as I wrote them long ago.

Discovery of the First Tumor

Operation Day: November 1, 1985

Day Four

The longer I am separated from it the better I can control my overwhelming urge to cry and have my thoughts speeding. Only now can I look back and ask myself, "How did I feel?" On day one when we found the tumor, I was scared, fearful, petrified of the unknown depths which we would be entering.

I started with denial and disorganized thoughts. Please wake me up from this bad dream, pinch me, please. This isn't real. I am going to wake up.

I can't eat. Nothing sounds good. I will throw up.

I can't stay at the hospital. I must go home and organize. We left him overnight. I feel guilty. He may leave us tomorrow forever. I should stay with him. I can't. I am in shock.

I cry big—big, huge, jumbo, crocodile tears. I have to see Father Pat to pray. Everyone pray. I have to go to Carol's and tell her I told her something somewhere was wrong—my dreams told me so. Cry. Wrenching my heart. Uncontrollable sobbing. Can't quit crying.

Poor little guy. It's not fair—he's only three—unfair for him to have to go through all this. Why him? Why us?

Pray—God is the only one that can save him. Does God want us to continue to care for him? Does he want him in heaven now?

What do I learn? What is the message?

Existentialism. We are born into this life alone and we will leave it alone.

Will he survive the operation? It's in God's hands—do we have to give him up? I don't want to give him up. I love him so much. Poor little guy. He's scared. He doesn't know what's happening to him.

Sleep—try to sleep. Aspirin—take some. You have been crying for eight hours steady. Sleep—try to sleep. He'll need you in the morning.

Four hours later—I can't sleep anymore. I have to get to my little boy. I love him. He'll be lonely—feel abandoned. It's a strange place.

What's happening? Yes, we know it's a tumor. Operation—tomorrow? Tumor—what does that mean?

Tell everyone—who to call? No, call Mom in the morning. Let her get a good night's rest. Pack—you'll be there a long time—pack, pack, pack—it's your nervous way of handling anxiety. Remember you packed three large suitcases to go home when Daddy died.

Die—no, he can't. I love him too much. I want to hold on to him—love him.

All the things we didn't do with him—the places we haven't seen—the times I wouldn't let him play in the mud or the dirt. Does it matter? He may be gone tomorrow. Poor little guy.

How will we tell Tony? Tony loves him. Ali's too little; she won't know what's happening.

Who can I count on? Who are my friends? Why him? Why me? Why us?

This is a bad dream. It isn't real. Denial—the first stage. Realization with crying the second stage.

On day two, we have to program toughness in. We rock all the time. I'm there. Three and a half hours. I play music tapes. I tell him he's a tough kid and he can do it. He asks me what's happening. I tell him the doctor is going to take a bump out of his head. He asks, "Will he cut me with a knife?" I respond, "Yes, right here." I touch his head. He begins to cry. I can't take it. He's so helpless.

Rock, keep rocking, and tell him he's a tough kid. Program his mind to come back to us. Let Chuck have a turn to hold him in case this is the last time we have with our little boy. Love him, squeeze him, let him know he is loved.

They come to get him. He's confused. He's riding in his bed to the elevator. He's crying. Why didn't I hug him more or let him play when he wanted to instead of taking a bath?

I'm a bad mother. Yes—no—I don't know? Would I do anything differently? No. What am I supposed to be learning?

Yes, we want to go with him. No, we can't? He's our kid. Why not?

Wait, wait, wait. Friends come. My sister stays all day, waiting with us.

Drink. Keep drinking. God can only rule the destiny. God, give the surgeon strength and skill to cure this evil in his head. Will God give him back to us?

Friends call. Friends wait. We know, now, who our true friends are. Support. Wait, wait, drama. When will they send word? We don't want to see the doctor too soon. Too soon would be bad—the longer the better. Get the tumor all out. Make it. Be tough. Hang in there.

Later and later and later—is everything okay, something's gone wrong. I'm worried. What if he can't walk or talk or move or think? No, please let him come out and come out okay.

He's out. Go upstairs and wait again. The doctor talks to us. No, no, no. Not the awful kind—radiation therapy. No, his hair will fall out. How will I help him cope? Will all this go away? How long do we have to keep him? Will he die eventually from it? Build us up to let us down.

Emotional highs and lows. Hopes up and plunge into despair. Can't cope. No food. Weak. Cry—keep crying—can't quit.

We can see him. Be careful. Not what you may expect. No! No! No! His eyes are rolling around in his head, he's calling out unintelligible words, he sounds like a baby. His mouth is pulled to one side, his face looks fallen and wan. No, no tell me he's going to be okay. I can't take this. Faint. I'm dizzy. I'm going to faint. Leave the room. Put your head between your legs. Nurses helping you. Get hold of yourself. Calm down. Sit in the chair. No, I haven't eaten much. Orange juice. Crackers. Okay. I can't, I just can't. I'll throw up. Force yourself to eat. Choke it down. Lump in your throat. Crying. Crying. No, no he has to be okay.

It's okay. Come back in after you eat and feel stronger. His eyes, why do they go crossed? His speech, why is it so slurred? Is it the anesthetic? Is it really? Are you just trying to calm me? What's wrong? Tell me what's wrong. Is he okay? I want to know. Wake, sleep. Wake, sleep. He's still responding the same way. I'm scared. Please let him be okay.

Be thankful. God sent him back to you. Another chance to do it right. Yes, thank you. Make him whole again—another demand. Accept. Just accept. Life changes.

What shall I do? Where is my path going? What journey am I on? Keep telling me that God is with me. He'll guide me.

Call people. Let them know. Friends come again. Support. Loss—a death of a way of life. A new path to follow. Where am I going? "His ways are not our ways."

I hurt. I hurt. My limbs are numb. My mind is racing. What will we do? What shall I do? Don't think of long term. Think only of this moment. Be present to this moment. Don't plan. We don't know.

Count on others. Use their support to be strong. Pray for him. Everyone pray.

Hold him. Rock him. His eyes—they are still that way. Talk to him. Make him respond. Can he think? Can he remember? He hurts. Be careful with him. He's still with us. But for how long? That doesn't matter. Make the most of today and now. Live in this moment. Experience holding him, loving him. Why him? Poor little guy.

Heavy heart. Hurting, hurting. Both of us in different ways. Get some sleep, sleep, sleep, sleep.

On day four I am worried about his depression. He seems like a hollow shell with no life—a shell left by a snail—the spirit gone. The fire quenched. His eyes still move. He speaks and thinks. Okay. Thought patterns are slightly off. Yet, he is coherent.

Going home. A new perspective. Seems like nothing is wrong. Things are normal. No, they are not. They will never be the same. People phone. I don't want to talk. I cannot handle explaining that my little boy is back with me now, yet I don't know for how long. That scares me and makes me sad. I don't want to think about that.

Coming back refreshed. A shower does wonders. I can make it. Send Chuck home. He must work all week. We need to be able to pay bills. Will I need to work? I don't want to take time away from him. Should I stay in graduate school? Can I concentrate? I don't know! I don't know. I can't predict. I'll just have to wait, attempt, and see what happens.

Pat helps. Rock him all evening. Doesn't want to sleep in bed. Why? Wants to sleep on the floor. Stuffed animals out of bed? Brave Heart with surgery mask on—perhaps an aversive stimulus. Take the animals out. Now will you go to bed? Yes. Hold my hand. Don't leave me. I won't. No, Daddy put me to sleep. Mommy puts you to sleep tonight. Remember we take turns putting children to bed. It's Mommy's turn tonight. Tomorrow it will be Daddy's turn.

Sleep, little baby, sleep. Heal your head. Heal your spirits. Heal, please heal.

Day Five
Refreshed. He's more enthusiastic about eating, yet just lies there with glassy eyes most of the time. Eats good

breakfast, yet just lies there. Helpless. How can I cheer him? I try to get him to talk. He rejects that.

Ask him to count. One, two, three, four, five, six, seven, eight, nine, three. No, ten. Angry. Don't want to do this anymore.

Tape player ran out of batteries. No stories or music. Call to have someone bring batteries. Depend on others to supply needs. Hard to do.

Feel I am soothing him. Move to new room. Different. Want to go home, Mommy. Want to play Go Bots. No, let's read. Okay. So we read. Want to watch television. Nothing good on. Maybe Sesame Street *later.*

How long will I have him? What do I say to him? I love him so much. Poor little guy. He's so fragile, so delicate, so vulnerable in this big, white hospital bed in this sterile room.

I prayed every night for God to guard, guide, and protect him from harm. Why Wessie? Why not some mean, rotten person? Why gentle Wessie who hasn't hurt anyone or anything in his life?

Evening despair. Not knowing if he's here to stay or may leave me soon. The unknown. Anxiety, stress, worry about tomorrow, yet I try to focus on the moment and be glad and rejoice in it. Prayers for strength.

Why can't this hospital stay be the end of it? Why do we have to come back to go through more stress, anxiety, and pain? There is no end. It will be a constant cloud hanging over my heart.

Even with sleep, I'm weary. Beginning to cry again. Why? Why? Why Wessie?

I want to go home too, Wessie. I want to be a family again.

Beginning to feel angry. Physical therapy not ready for him, made him wait. One in the afternoon? That's when he naps. *Thoughtless people. It's stress enough being in a hospital without having to wait. Not knowing what's going on when. Stressful.*

Day Six
His headaches return. No, not more fluid and pressure in his head. Another CAT scan possibly?

More tears because of the unknown. Heavy heart. Aching as I see my child lie there and not cooperate because he's angry or tired or spiritless. Is the struggle he puts up really his spirit surfacing in a different way than I am used to seeing? No. He always puts up fights when something is thrust upon him without being prepared for it. Is the struggle one for control over what is happening to him?

"His ways are not our ways!" What does that mean in terms of children and suffering? What way could allow such pain, both physical and mental, to be in our lives? Especially in the life of a three-year-old child?

Just watching him sleep is a hard thing. I am amazed at the richness life brings. His being here is a miracle, and yet I yearn for him to be able to run and play and be a normal, healthy boy full of curiosity and playfulness; carefree and without worry, pain, anxiety, stress, anger, frustration.

What is going on in his little mind? What does he think? What goes on in his heart? What does he feel?

When he sees a person in a white coat, what feelings well up inside? He cowers and doesn't talk and searches for security in someone's arms.

Day Seven
Eighteen hours out of the hospital revived my spirit. I think I can go on for a few more days. Fear, fear, fear is all I had yesterday afternoon as I drove home.

Hopelessness, despair, aching in my heart, wanting to go back to the life we had before when all was okay. Anger that this should happen to a child so young. Anger towards myself for not going with my gut feelings about there being something wrong with Wessie a year ago. Anger at letting the cancer get this far.

A hot bath, a meal, loving my other children took me away from the despair I feel at the hospital. I slept all night, dreamed an incredible dream involving another family and not my own. Is that escape? Is that the way my mind handles the despair I feel? Is that the release, to envision my life devoid of everyone I love? How odd.

With a new attitude, I faced today determined to act, to do some activities that Wessie needs to do. Ask him to go with me, hoping he would join once I was there and acting. That works when others don't join us. When a third person is added, he hibernates within himself and stops acting.

How to cope with his anger tantrums? I have just let him rage. Calm him down by teaching him to relax. Then we try to make choices. After a performance of his choosing, I reward with lots of positive feedback.

Maybe a reward system will work for him if we could figure out what extrinsic object or intrinsic state would motivate him to perform. I would prefer to have him inner-motivated. To want to perform for the inner good feeling that accomplishment of task brings him would be the best.

I'm avoiding talking about what the doctor said about radiation therapy. Since it was a medulla blastoma, the danger is that the cancer would not only be in the brain, but the central nervous system as well. I have a million questions. CNS? That's life, the totality of life comes from the CNS; movement, response, etc.

God, please let the radiation therapy eradicate all the cancer from his body. Heal him! Totally heal him so he doesn't have to suffer from this horrible fate.

Keep your mind in check, Rita. Don't despair. Go one day at a time. Give your all to every minute. Appreciate what you have now at this moment. Live in the present. Life is a process of moving through moments. Live life to the fullest every moment of the day. Be with Wessie the best you can. Draw energy from the outside to keep you going.

Just looking at him sleep tears my heart apart. I love him so much and I can't do anything to stop the awful things he must go through. God help me have courage, patience, and stamina to get us through all that will come and let me live in the moment.

Crying, I'm crying again. Tears never stop when you love someone so much. Praying, praying for him to be with us and live, and yet praying for him not to suffer if God's will is to take him from us to be with him.

The doctor said after radiation therapy, there may be chemotherapy depending on what the CAT scan says. The CAT scan can tell us if it is anywhere else in his body.

Should I worry now about Tony and the feelings I have always had about things not being right with his stomach and intestines? Should I worry about Ali's bump on her back? Should I worry about the pain under my arm?

I had a dread all through the summer and into the fall that Chuck would be in a car wreck and leave me. I worried when he wasn't home on time. I called an old friend to find out if he was okay because I had a dream of him being lost in a forest. I had dreamed Wessie had drowned in the country club swimming pool. I had been dreaming that someone close to me had something wrong with him/her. There was an aura of sickness somewhere that I perceived, yet it was like a cloud hanging around and not quite knowing where to land. It was more vague than the essence I got that night before my daddy died; more pronounced and clear with the smell of his aftershave in the air. This was a funny dread, a fear, an ambiguous, yet salient essence of something awful coming into my life.

How quickly things can change. What will our lives be like with or without him? What will this do to my other children? What will it do to Chuck's and my relationship? What will it do to the person that I am? Will I be different? Will I change? What lies ahead?

Day Eight
Long talk with Chuck last night. I needed him to psyche me up to deal emotionally with this, to encourage me, to support me, to listen to my fears, concerns, dreads. All he said made sense. I wanted him to take care of me, to assure me all was okay, and that we could make it together through this horrible nightmare.

He's looking at the positive. He said to look at what happened. Wessie didn't have seizures like some children do. He had quiet headaches and throwing up (choke up as Wessie says). They could operate right away and got everything they could see. Our friends came to surround us. They prayed. People have visited us to show how they support us and care about us. All positive things happening. He was out of ICU and Step Down; each requiring only one day. He has improved and can laugh again. All positive. People kept commenting when we were waiting during his operation, "I have a really good feeling about this." One good thing for me is that it has shown me Chuck's true belief in God and that he does pray. Maybe all of this was meant to happen.

I asked Chuck to help me be positive, to quit worrying, and to take each day and live within it. He said that Wessie is only one person with an all or none chance to beat the statistics. He will or he will not. We have to think that he will and act accordingly. Give each day to him and put the worrying behind us. Smile, make my words positive, act like he will live and be with us. If I don't, Chuck says that it is as if I have given him up for dead, and that's not fair to Wessie.

So last night I asked God to guide my path, to allow me to put worry aside, and to be positive. I asked for the Holy Spirit to give me strength and support. And this morning I asked the Blessed Mary to guide my mother love, to be strong so that I could support my child, no matter what happens.

I feel better this morning. I look at Wessie sleeping, and I think how beautiful it is to be in this day with him for one more moment in time, no matter what happens tomorrow. I love him and will give my all today and every day that he is with me.

Day Nine
At peace, strength from God, lifted spirits, feeling positive. I look at Wessie, and I am sure that no matter what, I am going to be in this moment with him and do my best to help him through this difficult road that he is on.

The radiologist talked with us yesterday. He said that this is a terrible tumor and its treatment is not without risks. He will be shorter in stature from waist to neck because of radiation therapy on his spine to get the seeding cancer from his CNS. His hair will fall out. His head, back, and ears will be sunburned. His throat will hurt. He might have diarrhea and nausea. He will be duller (his words for not as intelligent) than he *would have been because they have to radiate the entire brain. His hearing will dull for a time, then return. It won't affect his eyesight. These are the things I heard. There may be other side effects that I just didn't want to listen to or didn't want to hear. I realized I had my arms crossed, as if blocking his communication with me, because I didn't want to hear what he said.*

I again asked God to guide my path, letting me know where he wants me to be, to show me more clearly my mission, and how I am to accomplish that. I asked for strength and to not worry about tomorrow, but to be present to today.

I pray that the damage to his brain will be minimal so that he will function at least at an average level of intelligence. Just let him be happy with his life. I love him so much and want to help him to live life without pain and with a truly happy attitude. Don't make him angry and bitter. Make him happy, God. Allow him to be the best and be happy in what he does. Let him be a self-fulfilled person from within. Give him peace. I love him so much.

Day Sixteen

I'm angry today. I'm at the "why" stage again. Why did this have to happen to Wessie? Why did this have to happen to my family? Why did this happen to me? Why couldn't this happen to someone who doesn't love and care for their children as I do? Why me? Why do I have to go through this? Why does this have to disrupt my life?

Then I begin feeling sorry for myself, poor little me. We waited so long to get a house. I struggled with C-sections to have children. I struggled to get into the doctoral program. Now all of this can be snatched away from me. Why? I finally felt that I almost had my chil-

dren out of diapers and eating by themselves. No more bottles, no more wet beds. We could begin going on family trips together. Just think of all the fun we could have. And now, back to getting up during the night, wet beds, feeding my child, carrying him. Not knowing what will constitute a normal family life for us. Why?

Day Seventeen

Depressed. Pits of despair. I finally realized the tumor everyone keeps talking about is really cancer. Cancer has a whole different meaning than tumor. My child has cancer. Despair. Why Wessie? I'm crying today for what could have been and not what is. I feel a sense of loss of normalcy in our family, of the lives we could have led.

Wessie is getting so chubby and swollen. My heart just aches for him. I love him so much and don't want to see him suffer physically or mentally. God give me the strength to help him keep a positive mental attitude and to beat this cancer that has invaded his body.

Chuck, my mom, and I talked a long time this evening about the positive things that have come from this situation. Chuck says, "Just think of all the people who know us and about Wessie who are probably hugging their kids more." We realized who our real friends are. We've experienced different sides of people. Chuck keeps saying that he has a chance. With some cancers, you don't even have a chance. With his, there is a chance he can survive. We have to believe that he will so we can keep going for him. Be positive and smile. Don't cheat him of any happiness he can have today because we are worried about tomorrow.

Day Eighteen

I woke up with a positive attitude. We laughed and smiled on the way to get his radiation treatment. He *was anxious and scared, but he was a real trooper. I would not let them sedate him. I told them he would stay real still. He stayed real still. It scares me to think that if they radiate overlapping areas, he can be paralyzed or have brain damage. The alternative is sedating him every day, and I don't want him to have to be listless on a continual basis.*

The side effects as described are skin changes, hair loss, possible decreased intelligence, slowed bone growth, possible hormone problems, possible nausea, sore throat, difficulty swallowing, and fatigue. Chuck says that we can stand a shorter, less intelligent child if we can just have him with us. Chuck says we have no alternative. We have to give him radiation therapy to get all the cancer that may have seeded throughout his brain and CNS.

Last Thursday, on day fourteen, I sent Chuck to go through the MRI with Wessie because I didn't want to find another tumor anywhere. It was as if the MRI was an aversive stimulus to me. They told us they could see no visible tumors in the brain. The spine was fuzzy, so they want to do a myelogram. So we go back to the hospital. Wessie is frightened and upset. We will probably lose the trust we had built up in him and will have to work again for days to calm him down so he can stay still for the treatments.

Prayer groups bring food to us. I am thankful. It has been invaluable. I don't have to think about preparing food. That is such a relief.

Day Twenty
Back to the hospital and feeling so out of control. Calmer now so that I can think to ask the questions that my fear prevented me from realizing to ask when I was here before.

Wessie is accepting this much better than I figured he would. He cried a small amount of time when we were waiting in admissions, but since we have arrived in the room, he has been fairly calm and not anxious.

It sounds as if they will sedate him, but not totally put him to sleep. He will need an IV again. I watch him sleeping contentedly now and pray that he'll not have to suffer at any time. I love him so much and my heart is heavy to know that such a little one has to go through so much. Maybe this is the same way my own mother felt when I would have asthma attacks. She would sit on my bed with me as I gasped for air. I am sure she felt as helpless as I do now. What and how do you communicate to a three-year-old about what is going on with his body and brain?

He seems to be happier this time when people ask him to do things. He even smiled for the doctors instead of crying and screaming when he saw them.

He resumed his life as a normal little boy after his operation. He continued his participation in preschool and then attended the Montessori School at age five with his sister, Ali. He played t-ball until age seven, when he started baseball. He began piano lessons at age four and participated in recitals. He started golf lessons at age five. He began playing soccer and basketball at age six. He began tennis lessons at age seven. He flew kites. He participated in both school talent shows and children's theatre. He skated on ice and participated in the ice shows. He played video games. He rode horses. He played in the snow. He was a cub scout. He sang in the children's church choir at Christmas. But most of all, Wes loved to do two things more than anything: he loved to swim, and he loved to put together Legos.

Brave Heart Lion

Trusty Sword

Favorite Sport: Swimming

Loving Legos

Discovery of Second Tumor

Operation Day: May 2, 1989

Oh, God! They want to do the dye technique. This is not a good sign. They aren't saying anything, and yet they are saying so much. He won't let them do it. He doesn't want an IV. He's panicking. I'm panicking. My thoughts are racing. My heart is heavy.

The doctor takes a long time with the MRI. Oh, please, no. Don't put him through this again. Not just at the point at which we thought he was safe. I can tell by the expression on the doctor's face that it's serious. He looks at me and says, "It doesn't look good." "Good!" What does that mean? Are we talking operation? Death? What? Give me the bottom line here!

He shows me the MRI pictures. Not good. A tumor in the left frontal lobe! How could it have grown so fast? He had a clean scan in July! He replied that when these cells begin, they just take off and grow rapidly.

Now I feel guilty for denying the problem. We could have caught this two months ago when he first started to throw up and have headaches. I let myself believe that perhaps it was sinuses or allergies. Yet I knew the symptoms: the headaches, the vomiting, the low level of focusing. I was too scared to act on this. Oh, Wessie, I'm so sorry. I feel so inadequate now to help you when you are hurting. I should have known immediately!

I have to tell Chuck. Let me keep it together until I can drop Wessie off at the babysitter so I can tell Chuck alone.

When I arrived at the clinic, Chuck was just arriving from a large animal call. He looked at me as he sat in his car and I told him. His first response was anger and then helplessness and then tears.

I could not stand still. I kept walking up and down

the sidewalk saying, "Oh, God, it's not fair to make such a little boy go through all of this again." I knew the reality of it, and yet I still didn't want to believe it. I was dreaming. It's like one big, waking nightmare. Please wake me up. Tell me it isn't true. He doesn't deserve to have to suffer and hurt again.

Keep it together. I can't! I cry! I fall to my knees in tears and anguish. Then I panic. I want to run away. My mind races. I get up. I can't stop moving. I don't understand. I need strength from God, yet I don't understand why God is letting this happen to our Wessie again. Give us all strength.

I feel sick to my stomach and my heart is very, very heavy. My heart aches for him. My heart is breaking. I love him so very, very, very much.

Keep things light for the children. We need to keep them unaware until Saturday and then we'll tell them all together so that Wessie can prepare. He's a little boy who needs to be told the score; told what is going to happen so he can prepare himself.

We took some pictures and then went to have pizza. The children had such fun playing the video games and eating pizza. I couldn't eat at all.

Operation Day: May 2, 1989

They came to give him a shot at five thirty a.m. He was more cooperative today. He was still scared, but his fear showed in the small, high-pitched, tense voice when he said, "Okay." He has such a strong will, and yet when he needs to adapt, he can and does.

As I watched him sleep, he looked like a cherub. His golden hair shining under the light reflected powerful courage. As I talked to him about his courage, he asked how long he would have to stay at the hospital. I told him that would depend on how well he cooperated. If *he does what the nurses and doctors tell him to do and believes that he will get well quickly, then he will get to leave the hospital soon.*

My throat has a lump in it and my eyes are misty. I love him so very much and yet there is nothing I can do to help but to show him that love. I feel out of control and yet his courage gives me peace.

Every so often, he opens his eyes to check to be sure I am still there, and I am. I don't want to leave him, and I don't want him to leave me either. He adds so much joy to our lives. He is strong-willed and fights for his rights. Although that strong will is frustrating at times as a parent, I admire it in him because that strong will can certainly be an advantage today.

I don't want to take my eyes off of him. I want to savor the way he looks, the way he smiles, the way he speaks, and the way he makes our lives so happy. So again, I read to him the story I wrote to help him through his operation.

I wrote the story "Wes's Dragon." The story was about Wes on a journey, using his magic sword of courage and light that gave him power to destroy the dragon. Wes had a sweet friend that mothered him at his preschool. She and her older sisters made a huge card that had a sword with light shining all around it. It said, "Get Well Soon." This card hung in his room after this operation so Wes could continue to remember that he had the power to heal.

Wes again resumed his life. This time, he had to undergo more radiation and then eighteen months of chemotherapy. For a week every month, he went into the hospital and received treatments. Despite his treatments, he remained involved in baseball, golf, piano, cub scouts, soccer, theatre, and swimming. However, much of the time, he played with his Legos.

Fall Fun

Pinewood Derby

Petting the Cat

Baseball

Lola: Companion & Friend

Autologous Bone
Marrow Transplant

August 7–September 12, 1990

My son went to a hospital in the eastern part of the United States for his autologous bone marrow transplant. They would harvest his own bone marrow, dose him with chemotherapy for a week, and then put his own bone marrow back. I am going to relay this in feelings not necessarily in a chronological storyline to illustrate that my story may be different from yours, but the feelings are the same.

Anxious

Anticipation brings anxiety. I was afraid of what I did not know. Since we had to go to the East, and we lived in the Midwest, I drove, as a plane trip was costly. One of the struggles that is prevalent when a family has a child with cancer is paying for all the trips to all the places that a child must be taken to get the necessary treatment he needs. We left a day early because I wanted to give Wes a tour of the monuments in Washington, D.C. We spent the night in Pennsylvania and then drove in to Washington, D.C. He was able to see the Lincoln, Jefferson, and Washington monuments. He saw the White House. He saw the Air and Space Museum. Then we saw the changing of the guard in Arlington. I remember an amazing picture I took of him with the Washington Monument in the background. My anxiety mounted as we came to the end of the day and headed to the city in which Wes would get his autologous bone marrow transplant. The following is what I wrote during that time.

August 8: I was frazzled by the time we got to our destination because the fun was over and I knew the next day would be stressful. By the time we got to the motel, the pool was closed, but I talked the manager into letting Wes dunk in for a few moments before going to bed.

I had taken with me a traveling companion who was Wes's caregiver, Lola Rice. She kept Wes interested and busy on the long trip. She kept me from being overcome by my emotions multiple times by her quiet way.

August 9: Lola kept me calm as I became anxious in traffic. As we walked into the building, my body was as tense as a drum. When we entered the children's admitting area, I could have cried, but I took a few deep breaths and sat down to register. We waited to be seen until I had reached my limit. I had tears in my eyes and just wanted to run away. I asked the receptionist if anyone was going to acknowledge our presence. She was nice, saying, "You don't have a nurse yet? Well, that could be stressful. Let me find you one."

Assertive

I knew what would affect my child. I tried to avert a crisis of Wes being fearful when he was introduced to the doctor. Parents know their children well: what scares them, how much they can handle, when to push, when to stop. I knew the name of the doctor who would be working with Wes. The doctor shared the same name as the bad guy on a video game Wes played. I knew that would result in Wes being fearful of the doctor. So knowing that helped me avoid a crisis.

August 9: I spoke with Wes's doctor before he saw Wes. I explained to him that the bad guy on the video game Wes played had the same name as the doctor and that scared Wes when I had mentioned the doctor's name. So I asked him if we could do something about the name. We decided that Wes could call him Dr. Joe. This doctor later wrote to the company and the company sent Wes a new handheld game and some game cartridges that kept him occupied and happy during the hospital stay.

Trusting

August 9: Our nurse, Michelle, was so bubbly and sparkling that she put me more at ease than anything. She seemed efficient and organized. I had trust and confidence in her right away.

August 9: I am scared and I am angry and I am anxious all at once. My body is tight and stiff. My prayers can be none other than they have been during his last two operations, "I put him in your hands, Lord, and I trust that you will guide him through this and give me the strength to help him persevere."

Questioning

August 9: I looked at Wes as he went to sleep and again questioned, "Why?" Why did this have to happen to Wes, to our family, to me? Why do we have to spend money on hospitals and not on vacations and having fun with our children? Why do we have to be apart for so long? Why does Wes have to endure a life-threatening disease? Why couldn't we have a normal life?

Surprised

August 9: A doctor came in this morning to get my permission for Wes to participate in the study. What study? I was surprised because no one mentioned to me that he would be part of a study. My question is: If he is part of a study, then I have to be assured that he is not the guinea pig for any new experiments.

Reassured

August 10: An hour and a half after he had gone into the operating room, Dr. Joe and Nurse Nancy came into the waiting room with smiles. Nurse Nancy was cradling a bag of bone marrow as if it were a newborn baby. They said that things had gone well and they were pleased.

Alone

August 10: I waved good-bye after hugging my traveling companion. As I watched her walk towards the airport waiting area, I felt alone and weak.

September 1: I tried to get Wes to go to the garden today to get fresh air, but he was too tired. I was disappointed. I knew everyone at home was having a party at a friend's house for Labor Day, and I felt cooped up. I felt so alone and left out. That evening, everyone called from the party and talked to us. It uplifted our spirits.

Puzzled

August 28: Wes started crying in his sleep and started yelling some language that sounded like African. I asked him if he was having a dream, and he responded in this same language. I asked him two more questions with answers in the same language. I asked him if he could see me and he said, "Yes." I asked him if he knew he was speaking a foreign language and he said, "Yes." I asked him if he knew what language it was and he said, "Yes, baby." I said, "You're talking in baby?" He shook his head affirmatively. I asked how old he was and he said, "six." He is actually eight. I asked what he was dreaming, and he said that he was in trouble. I asked him who he was in trouble with, and he said, "You." I asked what he was in trouble for and he said, "I was supposed to get out of the way." "Of what?" I asked. He said, "Of the airplane." I asked if he did get out of the way, and he said he had. He then drifted back to sleep.

Helpless

August 11: He threw up ten times the first day of chemotherapy. His prayer that evening was that God would not let him throw up tomorrow. The next day he did not throw up.

August 20: Wes awoke every hour with stomach cramps. Sores have developed in his mouth. They say that the sores are probably all the way down his system. We are doing mouth washes and sitz baths. His temperature is up to one hundred and two. Fevers really scare me. When he felt better, we tried to get him up for a walk, but he cried so we had to bring him back to bed. It is very difficult to see my child suffering and in pain. All I can do is rub his stomach and let him know that we have to be strong these next few weeks until his body heals. I let him know that even through his pain God is always beside him, helping him to cope with every-thing. I tell him to put in his mind the sentence, "My body is healing quickly." Where do I draw the balance between empathy and motivation?

August 21: It is so very difficult to see one's child in pain. I love him so much and I feel helpless too. Again, I question why God lets children suffer like this. Why? It makes me cry!

Appreciative

August 7: My friend Kay gave me a book to write in and a blue night gown as a parting gift when we left to go to the hospital. It means a great deal to have such thoughtful friends. Thank you, Lord, for giving me a friend like Kay.

August 17: The day Wes got his bone marrow put back into his body, a famous baseball player visited the hos-pital. He gave Wes an autographed picture and one for Wes's brother, Tony, too. He is only one of many famous people who came by to visit the children. I appreciate these special people taking their time so that a child's day is a little brighter.

Hopeful

August 9: I guess the most important and significant thing that was said to me was, "Of all the children we have done bone marrows on in the last year, Wes is the only one that I am hoping for a cure, not just time." Although that was music to my ears and gave me hope, I still was scared because I knew all the things that could go wrong. Somewhere inside of me, a voice keeps saying, "He will live. He will live." I guess the only thing I can do is to have faith that God will work a miracle in his life.

August 17: Even though Wes got meds that were supposed to put him to sleep, they did not, so he was wide awake for the whole procedure of putting the marrow back into his body. Dr. Beth pushed it into Wes's central line. We took pictures and laughed. Wes made jokes. It took twenty minutes.

August 29: He is such a fighter. Yesterday, on his walks in the hall he kept saying, "I'm going to tough it out." He really does, too. He's amazing.

Depressed

I needed to remind myself often that "comparison is the basis of all misery." When I compared our situation to what could have been, it just made me miserable, so eventually I quit comparing.

August 18: Yesterday was really depressing for me during the late afternoon because I kept thinking that on any normal day we would be swimming and playing golf and cooking out and watching a movie as a family if we were at home together. I almost cried. Today it was Wes's turn to be depressed. He started crying. I took him for a walk to the patio outside, and we sat on the bench for a half hour, enjoying the breeze. He said, "I want to go home." I said, "What's second best to going home?" He said, "Watching the tape of Tony and Ali at the fair." They called shortly after, and he felt better.

Frustrated

August 19: Wes slept most of the day with a fever. I wanted to scream, "Pinch me and wake me up from this nightmare!" What would have been? I look at him lying there so pale and wan and I say, "Why him? Why my little boy?" I wish that we could go back and none of this would have ever occurred. I cry for the way it "might have been" for him. I mourn the life he and we as a family could have had without his tumor. And what good does this crying do? None. No one can go back. Life can never be relived. Nothing but how we are in the present counts. We create our own meaning in life, and it can be shallow and hollow or rich and full. What will you make of yours, Rita?

August 22: I cope okay when things go smoothly, but when things go with hitches, I fall apart. I look at him and just cry. Why did it have to be my little boy? What did he or we do to deserve this in his and our lives? He should have been an excellent athlete and a scholar. What will he be now? He won't be real good at sports, and he will be bright, but struggle in school. Why Wes? Why us? I don't understand!

September 6: The interns tried to take out Wes's central line. I told the interns that Wes never fell asleep with meds, so they tried to give him the maximum dose, but *when he saw the needle, he freaked and went bananas. Eventually, a resident came in and stopped them. We went back to the room. Personally, I don't think the rookies knew what they were doing. They could not get the cap around the end of the central line dislodged. I doubt whether they had done many before. I sat in the room wondering what next. They finally got an anesthesiologist and a surgeon to remove the central line. They knew what they were doing. The anesthesiologist talked to Wes and soothed him, and within twenty minutes, they had removed it, and Wes did wonderfully.*

Exhausted

August 21: Wes was up most of the night. I am exhausted. I feel so sorry for him. He wants me to rub his tummy to make it feel better. The nurse asked him on a scale of one to ten how bad the pain was and Wes said, "Ten, no, no, twenty." Does that tell you anything from a child who doesn't like to take medicine?

Awed

August 22, 1990: About 7:30 p.m., Wes's small catheter was blocked and the nutrients could not flow through, so the nurse put heparin into the line to unclog it ... They changed his nutrients to the larger catheter and it got blocked too. Fortunately, Tammy unblocked it quickly ... They tried all day to unclog the line; however, after three tries, it still would not clear ... They accessed Wes's two portacaths and are using them for his nutrients and meds… They x-rayed his chest. The central line was in place with no kinks.

August 23, 1990: Today they will x-ray his central line with dye in it to see where the blockage occurs. I pray that they get that part of the central line open so they can de-access his ports. They took Wes to x-ray at 11:15, and we finally returned at 1:45. They had decided to put in another central line if it could not be unblocked because the portacaths were beginning to block. They found a fibril sheath over the end of the portacaths.

I had been keeping Chuck up to date. I was scared. I did not want Wes to have to endure another procedure to put in another central line. Chuck, who is a veterinarian and very sensitive and kind, had on his schedule at one o'clock (two o'clock in the time zone Wes and I were in) a cat brought in by Carmelite nuns. The spiritual purpose of the Carmelite order is contemplative prayer. He did the work on the cat, and when they got ready to pay, he told them that instead of money what he was really in need of was some prayers to God to help his son. He explained the situation with the blocked central lines and ports. They told him that when they got back to the monastery that they would start praying for him.

Back at the hospital, the nurses and doctors were working hard to unclog the lines, but nothing was working. They thought it odd that three lines would get stopped up all at one time. They scheduled Wes to go to a surgery room. One doctor came in about two-thirty (one-thirty in the time zone where the nuns were praying). He said, *"Let's give it one more try!"* He pushed something into the small line and it unclogged. My words were *"Thank, God."* I did not know until later that night the story about the Carmelite nuns and their prayers for Wes.

Positive

August 25: Nurse Debbie came in for a chat. During our conversation, she voiced her awe at parents' coping abilities. I found that my mindset is one of having chosen to come to this hospital for my son to have an autologous bone marrow transplant, so I live with that decision. I was not forced to be here. I chose it. Seeing my decision as a choice helps my attitude. Everything, in fact, is a matter of attitude. I could choose to be angry, or I can choose to take this captured time in the hospital to learn from the books I chose to bring with me. I can choose to live in the present moment here, getting to know the doctors and nurses and other parents who occupy my world at this moment in time. I can choose to be present to the moment or not.

Unsure

I got used to being in the hospital and knowing someone was there to respond to anything immediately. When they began to talk about going home, I became very hesitant and unsure.

August 31: Nurse Michelle seems to believe that we will go home soon. I hesitate to hear or realize that as I don't want to get excited and ready to go and then be disappointed. And more importantly, I want Wes well when we leave. I don't want him to regress. What about his phosphate levels? What should his counts be? These are all questions which must be answered before I budge.

September 1: Nurse Tammy began to talk to us about what we needed to do when we left the hospital. I still have a cautious attitude about leaving. I want him eating and with high phosphate and blood levels before we move. I don't want him to relapse. Later in the day, the doctor came in and indicated that he may be able to go home soon. I told her I was in no hurry to get out unless it was safe and Wes was stable. She concurred and indicated she was happy with his progress.

September 5: I have real mixed feelings about leaving. I don't want to go too soon and have something happen to him, yet I want to go home as soon as possible. I want to be sure they give him all the platelets and phosphate he needs before we go so he won't get weak or regress.

September 5: I stayed up late. I wanted to hold on to the moment. I guess when I feel comfortable, it's hard for me to give it up and do something new, even if it is leaving the hospital.

Resigned

September 5: God has given us an easy time here, and I called on him many times to be by my side, and each time he was there. Each time Wes goes through a crisis, I give him to God, and thankfully each time God has given Wes back to me. I hope I am worthy.

After we left the hospital, we stayed with a family for a few days before we journeyed home. The family was extremely hospitable. They took us to a children's zoo, to an old fort, fishing for crabs on a big boat, and to a professional baseball game. How can I ever repay such kindness? I cannot. All I can do is pass such kindness on to others in my life who need such kindness.

I will never forget on our way home something that warmed my heart. On family vacations, I would always make the children get out of the car, to their chagrin, and take their picture by every state sign. This trip was no exception. As we drove home, I had Wes stand by all the state signs and took his picture. When we got to Missouri, I stopped to take his picture by the state sign that says "Welcome to Missouri." A policeman stopped and gruffly asked me what I thought I was doing. I told him that we had just returned from getting my son an autologous bone marrow transplant and that I had been taking pictures of him at each state sign along our journey. I was taking a picture of him now by our own home state sign. The policeman spoke to Wes. Then he asked Wes if he would like his picture taken with a policeman. Wes smiled and nodded his head. This big, burly policeman picked Wes up and stood by his police car. I took their picture with both smiling warmly for the camera. He told us to have a safe trip and put Wes in the car. Welcome back to Missouri.

When we returned home, Wes again resumed his normal activities. He played soccer, had friends over to play in the hayloft of the barn, was a ghost for Halloween, participated in the piano recital, played in the autumn leaves, played basketball, was in a musical, played in the snow, flew kites, made a pinewood derby car for scouts, hunted Easter eggs, participated in the school talent show, danced in the dance recital, swam, and played with his Legos. Life was good.

Soccer

School Talent Show

Playing the Piano

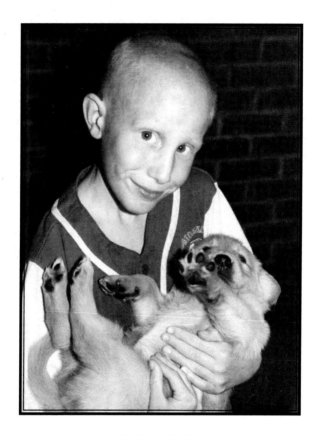

Holding the Dog

Discovery of Third Tumor

Operation Day: November 2, 1991

I have no recollection of this third operation. I did not write about it. All I have to remind me are the letter from the doctor and the photos that I took. The letter of September 24, 1991, stated that there was a small spot on the cerebellum and that more tests were necessary.

After this operation, again Wes resumed his routine. He golfed, swam, and played tennis. He participated in the talent show, ice show, and piano recital. He went to Big Shot and Six Flags. He played in the snow. He flew kites. He was the judge in the musical *Alice in Wonderland*. He went to Camp Quality, where he met an amazing musician who writes children's songs. His life was full.

As with most children who have terminal illnesses, Wes got his dream in 1992. The Dream Factory sent us on a trip to Disney World. We rented a van and headed for Florida on a nine-day adventure. While we were there, we stayed at a duplex at Kid's Village. We had free admission and food at Disney World, Epcot Center, MGM, King Henry's Feast, Gator Land, Sea World, Wolfman Jack's, Universal Studios, Hard Rock Café, and miniature golf. Of course, we could not be in Florida without participating in one of Wes's favorite activities, swimming. We swam in the ocean at New Smyrna Beach and Melbourne Beach. Wes had a wonderful time, and our family enjoyed the special time of togetherness.

My Story

Preparing for Wes's Death

The second worst day of my life was the discovery that Wes was going to die. I reflected about finding out and the events surrounding his death in a journal entry on January 11, 1994. Here is what I wrote several months later about what I remembered about that time period.

September 22, 1993, the second worst day in my life. The first had been on October 31, 1985, when we discovered Wes's brain tumor. Now we have been told that the tumors are throughout his brain and he may have two months to live.

Chuck and I had taken Wes for his MRI together, as I knew something was not right. Wes had been throwing up, he had a few headaches, his right eye had been giving him the impression of seeing double, and his lower back and legs hurt. A week before his MRI, I had called his neurosurgeon to let him know of my concerns. His balance was shaky and he had trouble playing the piano. Both were signs of tumor in the cerebellum area. His moods were swinging, and he had a problem seeing, both signs of frontal lobe tumor. The neurosurgeon said that he did not suspect a tumor could develop so quickly as his scan in June had been clean, yet the signs were there. I asked him if it would be appropriate to ask him to see Wes after the MRI. He gave us an appointment.

We had already scheduled an appointment with a growth specialist for hormone therapy for him so he could begin to grow. At eleven, he had the body of a seven-year-old. The doctor talked with him as if he were a grownup. He showed him drawings of what he would be doing to get him to grow. After our appointment with this doctor, we had him accessed through his port to have the MRI done with injections. Before we did, I put the medicine on his port to deaden the skin. Wes, as usual, lay quietly and did not complain. I always looked for the staff's reactions. If they were very quiet, that was a sign that all was not well. My heart was somewhat in my throat.

We then took Wes for an x-ray of his hand to see his bone growth for the hormone studies. After that, we ate lunch. Wes was always very particular about eating. He ate like a bird, but was eager to prepare food just right before eating. He could go for days without eating. I thought God might have been preparing him for some career in which he needed to go days without eating. At one time, I envisioned Wes being a priest in Peru who would work in ministry to help people. Maybe that's how God helped me to cope these eight years with a hope that made me believe he would survive to be a vital role of helping people. I trained Wes to be present to God at all times. I always trusted God to save my child from the cancer that overtook him.

We waited in the neurosurgeon's office after lunch. When he entered the room, I knew by the look on his face *that it was not good. He came over to me and grabbed my hand and quietly said, "It does not look good."*

We asked Wes to go to the waiting room to do his homework while we talked with the doctor. He obeyed immediately without question. The doctor told us there were multiple brain tumors throughout his brain and even on the brain lining and he suspected possibly down his spine. Chuck began to cry. He was not as prepared as I was because I had noticed the symptoms in August. But I was not prepared for them to tell me Wes would die soon. I had had flashes of graveyards and Wes in a casket for the past three to four weeks, but tried to ignore the forewarning.

Chuck asked how long he would have. The doctor said he did not know. It could be two months or it could be six months. Chuck said that the thing we wanted most was for Wes not to suffer. Whatever it took for him to be as pain free as possible, we wanted it. The doctor left us alone. I wish I had asked to see the MRI results. I am so visual; I guess it would have helped to see it in reality.

Chuck and I looked at each other, and we said that this could not tear us apart. That we could not let Wes's death destroy our love. We promised to get through it together and not to let it destroy us.

We then took Wes home. Chuck went immediately to the woods to cut logs. Wes walked through the woods with our new puppy, Elizabeth. I watched Wes walk on the path to the lake with his dog beside him and thought that this would be one of the last times I would be seeing him walking through the woods. My heart was in my throat. It was very strange, though, that at previous times I had felt as if my heart was broken when he had a tumor. It did not feel that way this time.

There was a sense of peace there instead. I called my mom and cried.

How do we tell him? When do we tell him that he is going to die? How could I help him die with the confidence and dignity he had always lived his life? I just prayed that God would give me the strength to help him through his death. That night, Chuck and I made plans. I tried to visit with our priest, but when I went to the rectory and office, both were locked, and the priest was out of town at a retreat.

The following day while I called the schools, Lola, the caregiver who watched Wes while I attended college classes, took Wes to the mall to play in the arcade and to buy a present at the toy store. I called Wes's elementary school and talked to the principal. I asked if I could talk with the teachers and counselor for both Wes and Ali, so I could share the news about Wes's impending death so they would be prepared. We set it up for the next day, which was Friday at eight in the morning. I then called the middle school to speak with Tony's principal. I asked to have a meeting with Tony's team of teachers and the counselor. I asked both principals to keep the content quiet; however, by noon that day, I had a phone call from the director of the special education telling me how sorry he was to hear about Wes. I knew we had better tell the children before they heard it from anyone else.

I had a big decision to make for myself. I had taken off six weeks from work to study for my psychologist licensure exam. My decision was whether to quit studying and spend all my time with Wes and not take the exam or to keep studying and try to do my best given the circumstances. This exam was very important to me. I had gone back to school nine years earlier to get my doctorate, get supervision, and take the exam to be a psychologist. The test was exactly three weeks away. How much time would I have with Wes? Should I devote it all to him, or pray that after my test he would still be with us for several weeks so I could devote every minute to him? It was a very, very difficult decision, yet I knew I had consciously already decided that I could not give up all the studying I had been doing since July first. To throw away three months of studying seemed fruitless. When Wes died, I needed something to keep me going. Achieving my goal of being a psychologist would keep me going. I decided I would study on the weekends, when his caregiver could be there to occupy Wes's time, and when he was asleep. The rest of the time I would devote to Wes. I prayed that God would give me two weeks with Wes after my test was over. It was not to be. I made Wes promise me that he would take me to lunch after my test on October 13. He promised that he would.

On Friday, I met with the elementary teachers. I gave them a handout on what behaviors could be expected from children who experience grief due to a death in the family. Then I explained that Wes was going to die within the next two months. I told them I believed that the children in his grade should know. Children get fearful and can make up all sorts of fantasies unless they know the truth. I asked that his class be told. At first, I got resistance from the physical education teacher that it was not a good idea. He questioned, "Why should kids have to know that?" I told him it was very unfair of us not to let them know. They had lived with Wes's cancer for five years. They were entitled to be able to process his death, not just be told he died one day. I respect children enough to know they should not be kept in the dark. We as a group finally agreed that the counselor would talk with each class on

Monday after calling the parents over the weekend to let them know she was going to talk with them. Then she would talk with Ali's grade on Wednesday when Ali was gone to the gifted program. (Whether they followed through with the plan or not, I do not know.)

I told the teachers that it was tempting to feel sorry for Ali, but that their job was to teach her, to be empathetic, but to expect her to learn and to do the work. I did not want Wes's death to stifle Ali from working to her potential nor cripple her emotionally. I wanted my other two children to grow up as good people despite the fact that they had a brother who died. We also agreed that Wes would attend as much school as he wanted to. I told them that we were going to plan each day for Wes the night before based on his desires and his capacity to function. If coming to school was part of what he wanted to do with his life that day, we would come for as long or as little as he could. We definitely would come for picture day to have his picture taken.

I then met with the middle school teachers. I essentially told them the same thing. I gave them the handout on behaviors to expect during each stage of grief. Then I told them my hope was that they would allow Tony to experience his grief in whatever way he chose to manifest it, but their job was to set boundaries on what was appropriate in their setting. I asked that they allow him to go to the restroom to cry whenever he needed to without making a big deal of him being excused and to let the class know whatever they believed was appropriate during this difficult time for him. They were all very complimentary towards Tony and promised to help him through as best they could. Several of them attended the funeral and then at Thanksgiving time, they sent us a copy of a book they had sent to the library of Wes's school in his memory. It was called, Tom's Remembrance. *The football coach told me to tell Tony he was going to make him the captain for the game that was to be played on Thursday. That was his way of trying to help Tony through a very difficult time.*

Upon leaving the middle school, I went to talk with the mother of Wes's best friend, Chris. I told her I had something to tell her about Wes, and I wanted her to know so she could prepare Chris before he heard it at school on Monday. I told her what the doctor had told us and that Wes was going to die. She cried, and I cried too. Together, we just cried and said that it just could not be true.

She asked me how this was affecting my faith. I told her that without my faith, I would feel very scared and helpless. With my faith, I thanked God for the eight additional years I got to spend with Wes after his first tumor was discovered. I am not angry that God is calling him. I am thankful he let Wes stay with us for so long.

When I finally got home that day, a little after two o'clock, I asked Wes to join me in his room. I wanted to let him know that God would be calling him to heaven soon. I wanted him to know before he was told by others. I tape recorded my telling him that he was going to die because I wanted Chuck to be able to know what I had told him.

He was sitting on his sleeping bag on his bedroom floor. I had drawn a picture of our house with a tree in fall colors and clouds over the house with lightning coming out of them, but with sun shining over the clouds. Chuck had actually noticed this symbolism from Wes as he described Wes saying that it was sometimes stormy on Earth, but beyond the clouds, it was sunshiny. I used this idea for the symbolism of his death.

We on Earth were experiencing the gloomy day while he would be experiencing the sunshine of heaven.

I asked him to describe the picture to me. He did and thought it was a funny picture to be dark on earth and have the sun shining above. He acknowledged that the house looked like our house. He said the house needed a chimney, but instead of drawing a chimney, he drew three red hearts around the house. We talked about the love in our home. I asked if he thought anything was missing. He said that the rain was missing and he wanted to draw it in, so I gave him the markers. He began to draw raindrops and acknowledge that they looked more like tear drops. How perceptive of this eleven year old.

I then began to tell him that he knew he had been feeling bad lately and that the doctors had found more tumors in his head and he said, "Do I have to have another operation?" I told him that the doctors could not operate, and that meant that God would be calling him to heaven soon. He said, "You mean, I'm going to be the first to go?" I said that when God called him, he needed to answer God's call and go with him. We didn't know when that would be, but that it would be soon.

He then drew a rainbow from our house up to the sun, symbolizing our connectedness with him when he gets to heaven. I told him how much we loved him, and that he would need to help me get through this time. I began to cry, and he got up and went to find some Kleenex for me as he always did. He always took care of me. At first, I thought I was teaching him about God, but what I realized was that right now he was and had been for a long time teaching me about faith and about God.

Whenever he had to do something in the past, whether it was going to the hospital, going to school, or staying home from school, he'd always say, "Okay." He was so congenial. This was no exception. When I told him God was going to call him to heaven, he merely said, "Okay."

After checking his feelings and how he was doing several times within our conversation, I told him that he would need to ask me for whatever he needed. I asked if he wanted something now and he asked to play the game Sorry. It was one of his favorites, and he knew it was my favorite. To me that was his message to me that he was sorry for what was going to happen. It was his way of comforting me by playing my favorite game. He was so very wise, beyond his eleven years.

I cooked his favorite meal that night. He loved fondue. After dinner when we were all gathered in the living room, I told Tony and Ali that the doctors had found tumors in Wes's brain, and they could not operate so that meant that God would be calling Wes to heaven soon. Ali and Tony began to cry. Wes just nodded his head as I told them, then he came over in my lap and said, "I don't want to die." He began to cry too. Chuck tried to reassure the children. Eventually, after many hugs, everyone went off to do their own thing. Ali and Tony played video games, Chuck read, Wes watched a movie, and I just watched my family respond to the most difficult situation we could ever experience.

Later that evening, as I put Wes to bed, he asked me, "Do you think I will make it to 1994?" I gathered him up into my arms and held him close and said, "I don't know, Wes. I hope so, but I just don't know."

We spent the weekend doing what the children liked to do. Wes watched Saturday morning cartoons. Tony had a yearbook meeting in the afternoon. Then we went to a movie as a family in the evening. We would *begin to sum our boundaries* (close off from the rest of the world) *and stick close for the next few weeks.*

On Monday of that week, I had a photographer take photos of Wes and me in the park at his favorite playground and of Wes at home. I wish I had been able to afford all the photos he took, but I picked the dozen that I could afford, and I still have the album in his room. Even though money meant nothing at this point, I knew I had to be reasonable. We got one eight by ten of him to hang on the wall in the kitchen as a constant reminder that he will always be part of our family.

I also took photographs of him. On September 21, the day before his MRI, I took many pictures of him. Internally, I knew he was going to die, so I wanted to capture as much of him as I could. I am sorry I did not capture more of him on my camcorder. I took three roles of thirty-six pictures each of him that day. During the weeks that followed us learning of his impending death, I would go with him to the parks he loved to play at and we would take many pictures. Sometimes he would say, "Just one more, Mom, and that's all."

We went to the toy store to buy Dungeons and Dragons Lego Castles. I bought three of them for him. Money for toys was no object at this point. Later, I would have to deplete his and my savings accounts both to pay for the funeral and burial. Money meant nothing at this time. I could always make more, but I could not always see my child smile as he built his Legos.

On Tuesday, Wes went to piano lessons for the last time. I had told his teacher the evening we found out that Wes was going to die so that she would be prepared. At his lesson, she played three songs for him. They would later be the songs she played at this funeral. Wes listened to all three songs as she played them and smiled. He knew. I cried, but tried to control my tears as best as I could. I took a couple of pictures of him with his teacher sitting together on the piano stool. She had been a big help through the years. She had given Wes lessons, knowing of his handicap in which coordination was often a problem for him. At times, he had trouble walking, but he seemed to manage to be able to play the piano at all times. After his death, she would send me beautiful cards, telling me how much she admired me. Many times they would come at a time when I felt most lonely and be at my lowest point. Tears would come to my eyes with each card she sent. Wes was very brave to continue to struggle to play the piano even after the doctors told us he would not be able to be that coordinated. They even told us he would not play soccer because of his spatial deficits, but he played soccer anyway. This music teacher knew he was an exceptional child, and she treated him as if he could do anything he wanted to do. He won three superior ratings at his piano contests. I am thankful that she allowed him to be her student despite his deficits.

On Wednesday, his grandma brought all the great aunts to visit, and they took Wes to lunch. He was still doing well, but was very tired. He would spend a lot of time in the next few weeks in his ninja turtle sleeping bag.

Each day, we had lunch at one of his favorite restaurants and then went to play at his favorite parks. We watched Wes progress downhill, getting weaker and weaker each day.

On Saturday, I had to begin giving him morphine as his pain was beginning to become stronger, and he was throwing up more. His appetite was still strong, though. I tried to study as much as possible when he was taking naps in his sleeping bag.

Sunday, October 3, his cousins came to visit him. In

the afternoon, Tony and Ali had a voice recital. Chuck took them. Wes's caretaker and I went with Wes on a plane ride. Interesting how wonderful things happen. A person who is a lawyer and also a pilot stopped by one of my husband's friend's office and mentioned that he had heard about Wes and wished he could help. The friend said that he could because he knew this person was a pilot, and he also knew that Wes wanted to ride in a plane so he could see what our house looked like from heaven so he would be able to recognize it. He also wanted to be able to see a thunderstorm with the sun above it. He did not get to see the thunderstorm, but we did get to see our house as we flew over it. I took my camera and took many pictures from above. Wes got to fly the plane. In his world of little control, to be able to take control of the plane was a great accomplishment.

One week later on October 10, Wes was able to see a concert which was a benefit for Camp Quality, a camp for children like Wes. I stayed home to study. Chuck took many meds with him as Wes was on Dexamethasone and morphine. Wes got tired at the very end, but was able to go on stage and to have this picture taken with the concert performers. That night started the first of what I suspect were small seizures. He would have to endure these for only one more week.

He came to my bedside about midnight with a bad headache. We had given him the maximum amount of the drugs. I held him close, and he rested. He would sit up in bed and scream out as if it hurt him, but he was not conscious. He would thrash about. I tried to calm him, but he would just scream out again and not be with us at all. We were up most of the night.

I had been at an afterglow party for the theatre until two a.m. the night before. Wes had emphatically insisted that he go also. He was becoming more and more demanding as his emotional mood became more fragile. Chuck and I decided he might as well go, as he should be allowed to do whatever he wanted to as long as it was safe.

He used all his energy to socialize with the other children who were there. People were amazed at him. A friend commented on his fortitude. Later, this friend would write me a letter stating that Wes was his hero. Wes was exhausted when we got home. He rested fitfully that night.

On Monday, I forced myself to stay up and study. Wes could hardly walk down the steps from his room to the couch. He could not make his legs work. They buckled under him. He was in and out of sleep most of the day with high doses of morphine and Dexamethasone to reduce the pain. We had called the priest to anoint him. He came and went through the ritual. Perhaps that was what gave him the strength to get through the next two days. Chuck slept with him in his room on a popup bed so I could get some rest as my test was on Wednesday. He would scream in the middle of the night and throw up.

The next day, Tuesday, Wes woke up early, popped out of bed as if nothing had been wrong with him the day before and announced that he was going on his class field trip to the historical society. His class had been keeping him up on all their activities. He had gone to school on the morning of October 6, the previous Wednesday, to get his picture taken and to stay for one lesson. Then I had taken him home.

Chuck rearranged his schedule to take Wes on the field trip. I could not have carried him if he was unable to walk. Wes seemed exhausted when he returned. He went straight to sleep on the couch, but woke up at meal time and wanted to eat. This would be the last family meal we would have with him.

One of my very dear friends, Cindi, had promised to stay with Wes on Wednesday morning while I took my test. I knew she was the only one I could trust to be present to Wes without any fears about his condition or without totally breaking down in tears. I am forever thankful to her for what she did that morning. She arrived and sent me off reassured that she would keep Wes occupied.

Two friends had sent me flowers wishing me good luck the day before. I had to be at the testing room at eight o'clock in the morning. For the next hour we waited to start the test. My anxiety was high enough already without the added wait of an hour before the test began. Finally the test began. I had a headache in the back of my head as if someone had hit me with an iron pipe. After fifty questions, I could not see. I had been crying a lot over the past three weeks and my contacts had been foggy from my tears. I finally took them off and wore my glasses. Even with my glasses, I had a hard time reading the questions. I guessed at most of the answers. I paced myself, fifty questions every fifty minutes. I took one break to go to the restroom after question 100. I finished with fifteen minutes to spare. I was totally wiped out. The pain in the back of my head was still prominent.

I walked out of the room, walked to my car, unlocked the car, sat down in the driver's seat, looked up at the billowy clouds on that beautiful sunshiny day and said, "God, please let me pass this test by at least one point!" Then I put my head on the steering wheel and I cried and cried. I had done it. I had taken the test knowing that my child was dying. What more could God ask of me?

Each time I had made an accomplishment in my life, Wes had gotten a tumor. When I got admitted to the doctoral program, Wes had his first tumor. When I passed my comprehensive exam and oral comps, Wes had his second tumor. When I had gotten my dissertation done and was ready to graduate, Wes had his third tumor. I told my post doc supervisor that I was afraid to begin preparation for my psychologist licensure exam as I feared Wes would get another tumor. Little did I know that in order for me to reach the final phase in my journey toward being a psychologist, I would see my son die.

Weeks before, Wes had promised to take me to lunch after my exam. Although he did not eat much, that tough child kept his promise to me. As soon as we came home, he rested on the couch. I often over those few weeks asked him how he was doing. He would reply, "I'm fine, Mom. I'm fine." How could he be fine? He was dying. That evening I went to a ballet class. Chuck told me when I got home that Wes had gone to his room about seven thirty p.m. after playing a game of cards with Tony and him.

Since my test was done, I was going to sleep in the popup bed in Wes's room so Chuck could get some sleep. I had told my supervisor at work that I would be going on family leave until Wes died so I did not have to go back to work.

That night, Wes began dying. He was having a hard time sleeping. He had been up four times to go to the bathroom. The Dexamethasone made him urinate frequently. The fifth time he got up, I asked him where he was going. He said, "To the bathroom." I let him go by himself as he had no trouble the previous times. I must have fallen back to sleep because I awoke with a start to a crash. I jumped out of bed. He was not in the bathroom. The light going downstairs and through the hallway was on. I called out, "Wes, where are you?" He was slumped over in a corner by the kitchen cabinets. I said, "Wes, why are you down here?" He said, "I have to find my pocket knife." This was at one thirty a.m.

He must have hit his head in the fall, and he began to groan with pain. I picked him up and Chuck was beside us immediately. I sat in the recliner and Chuck covered us with an afghan. He began to scream out, "Mom, I don't know, I don't know. Mom, Mom, Mom!" I could not help him. I felt helpless. I held him in my arms, and knew I could do nothing else for him. We debated about taking him to the hospital. I tried to quiet him, and Chuck tried to go back to bed, but Wes kept crying out with a moan that led us to believe the best thing to do was to take him to the hospital where he could get any help he needed medically.

We called a friend and neighbor who lived two minutes away to stay with Ali and Tony. They had woken up and were really scared for Wes. We did not want to traumatize them, so we spoke with them, and our friend stayed with them while Chuck drove us to the hospital. I sat in the backseat with Wes in my arms, his sleeping bag wrapped around him and his afghan over him and his white throw up bowl beside us.

We sped to the hospital at three a.m. Thursday. He calmed and would come in and out of consciousness. We had already scheduled a talk with the doctors and social worker about options concerning what might happen with Wes in the following weeks. We made the decision that if he regained consciousness and could medically handle it, we would take him home. We had to consider what Ali and Tony would be feeling, and we thought they would like us to keep him with us as long as possible.

I stayed with Wes that afternoon and night. At one point during the afternoon, Wes shouted, "I can't find him, I can't find him." I asked him who could he not find?" He said, "Oh, he's not important." I asked him if he knew where to find Jesus. He opened his eyes and stated emphatically, "I always know where to find Jesus. He's in my heart." Then he closed his eyes and was never conscious after that moment. Those were the last words I ever heard from my precious little boy.

Our priest came to visit that afternoon, and I shared with him the above story and others of how wise Wes was in his faith. I shared the story about Wes telling Ali that Jesus was her friend and that sometimes "you are your own friend." Many times Wes had to be his own best friend. No one ever made fun of him or ignored him, but very few people would take the responsibility of inviting him to their homes. Perhaps this was because I was so protective that they knew I would not let him go.

When we knew Wes would be entering school and have no hair, we met with the principal, instructed the teacher on how to demystify his cancer and allow him to be part of the group without the other children wondering about him or being afraid of him. We told her what to tell the class about why he had no hair. Wes stood by the teacher, and she introduced him and said that he had no hair, but that he was just a regular guy like anyone else. When you tell children the truth and tell them why, they don't have to dream up any fantasies to explain what they don't understand or find unusual.

By the next day, which was Friday, we decided that he was not going home. He was not doing well by early afternoon. He had what seemed to me to be a major seizure. His little hands and legs stiffened, his face contorted, and he kept moving about. I called for the doctors. They would not confirm a seizure.

I kept hearing the name of a mother whose son had been in the children's theatre group with Wes. Finally, I tracked her down. Her son, Nathan, who was eighteen, had been in a car wreck and had a head injury. All his teenage friends who also had been in the theatre group with Wes were at the hospital.

By two o'clock, Chuck arrived. Wes had another seizure. I began to panic. One of the adults who was visiting Nathan volunteered to drive me home. I wanted Ali and Tony to have a last good-bye in case anything happened. She drove me home to pick up my children from their respective schools. It was going to be more difficult than I anticipated gathering my children. When I got to Ali's school, she was somewhere with the girl scouts. I eventually found where they were meeting and whisked her out of there. I called a friend to drive us back to the hospital because I was in no shape to drive. I called the house where Tony was supposed to be at after school. No answer. We drove to the middle school. No Tony. We drove to the house he was supposed to be at and found him playing soccer on the street with three other boys in the rain. I told him to come with us. My friend dropped us off at home. Tony changed clothes.

My other friend was waiting at my house to take us back the thirty-five miles to the hospital. It would prove a difficult task getting back. That was the fall of 1993, when a hundred-year flood had broken the levees, so most of the area around the Missouri river was flooded. When we got to the bridge to cross the Missouri River (the only crossing point for miles), we noticed a wreck with traffic backed up for miles. We stopped at the Corp of Engineers building and asked if the road through Jamestown to Rocheport was open despite the floods. They said it was. It was now five thirty p.m. We headed towards Highway 179 to take the back roads. My friend drove as fast as she could and still be safe. I prayed that it would not be too late for the children to tell Wes good-bye. We got there by seven p.m. Wes had had another seizure in our absence.

I had held it together all this time. Two of Nathan's teenage friends walked into Wes's hospital room. The girl was one of the children's former babysitters, Bridgette. The boy, Matt, was someone who had always paid Wes special attention when they had been in musicals together. When I saw them, I just broke down and sobbed uncontrollably. They both held on to me, and we all cried.

Eventually, more teenagers showed up and more of our own friends. One dear friend, Charlie, had brought a guitar with him. He came about eight p.m. and asked if he could play some songs for Wes. We all sat or stood around while he played and everyone sang some songs. Ali stood at the foot of Wes's bed and sang "Castle in the Sky" for Wes. One day, I had asked Wes what he thought heaven was like, and he said it was like a big, big castle with a huge playground and rooms and rooms full of Legos.

After the singing, each young person and adult took a turn giving Wes a kiss and hug, and left the room, leaving our family alone. Tony said his good-bye first. He told him he loved him and thought he was the very best brother ever. He hugged him and gave him a kiss on the forehead. Ali was more reserved. She said merely, "Love you," and kissed him on the forehead. I hugged him tight, told him he was the most wonderful boy ever, and that I loved him very much. That would be the last time I would see him alive. Chuck and I hugged and he said, "We could not have asked for a more perfect ending for the children to remember Wes by than with all their theatre friends gathered around him singing."

The next day, Ali, Tony, and I went with another couple and their son to see Phantom of the Opera. Tickets to this production were my treat to myself for studying hard for my exam. Chuck knew that and said that if I could be okay if Wes died while I was at the theatre, then I should go because I deserved to have this special treat as a reward for my accomplishment. I pondered that question. I knew last night with the children singing to Wes and saying their last good-byes had been the perfect ending for me, so I could go to the theatre and be peaceful.

The day seemed endless. The two-hour drive to the theatre was arduous, as I knew I needed to make polite conversation. I was in no shape to drive myself, so I tried to put on my best social graces. The matinee was absolutely wonderful, as I knew it would be. The two-hour drive back home was rather silent. Somehow, I got through the day, but I can never hear the music from Phantom of the Opera without crying.

When we got home about nine thirty p.m. that evening, I called Chuck. He said Wes was breathing with such labor that they were trying to decide whether or not to suction him. They did not want him to drown in his own body fluids. I went to bed. At eleven thirty p.m., he called back to see if I agreed with some medical procedure. We decided not to prolong his life by artificial means. We would let him die in peace. I made Chuck promise that if Wes died during the night that he would call me. The friend that had played the guitar the evening before had spent another hour this evening playing for him. Wes's godmother had come to spend the *afternoon with him. So Chuck had someone during the day to keep him company.*

About two fifteen a.m., I was awakened by the phone, and I knew Wes had died. Chuck said that Wes was gurgling, and he had crawled up into bed with him, held him in his arms, and told him he was the best little boy in the entire world and that everyone loved him. Wes took one final gasp and died.

My Story

Life without Wes

I immediately called our friends who lived closest to our house. I asked one of them to drive me to the hospital and one to stay with the children. Later, the friend who stayed with the children told me that he was not much of a person who prayed, but he said he prayed that the children would not wake up so he would not have to tell them that Wes had died.

I cried all the way to the hospital. I wanted to hold my child one last time. My friend was so comforting. Halfway to the hospital, she said something to me that really made sense. She said, "You know, this was a good time for Wes to die. He was just getting to the pre-adolescent stage where his height, his physical features, and his capacity to learn would all begin to make a big difference for him, and he would be faced with lots of difficulties." She said it with a matter-of-fact attitude. She was right. He was having a difficult time with school. His small stature would set him apart from his peers. He was losing his hearing because of chemo drugs. Perhaps this was the right time for him to die, if he had to die in his youth.

We got to the hospital, and I sat down in the rocking chair, and Chuck put him in my arms, and I rocked him for an hour. He was already cold and stiff. I kept running my fingers through his hair and telling him that I loved him.

Chuck and I had prayed that he would not suffer. He only had three days of unbearable pain and unconsciousness. He was really a lucky little boy. He was vibrant until the very last. Chuck said that he had prayed that he would die at the last because Wes seemed to be in such pain. I know that on Friday morning, when he had gotten bad, I had told him, "Wes, if God holds out his hand to you, take it and go with him."

We laid him back on the bed and put the sheet over him and kissed his golden feather head good-bye. Chuck always called him "feather head" because when he had hair, he had soft, silky, golden hair. The funeral home had been called, and he had to be taken to the morgue before he could be given to the funeral home. I rode back home with my friend, and Chuck drove by himself. I was in shock and very numb.

About four thirty a.m. the funeral director called us to tell us they were on their way to pick up Wes. He would be by in the afternoon to make the arrangements. Chuck went to bed for an hour, but I stayed up and immediately found some poems to use at his funeral. Poetry has always been a great comfort to me. It's so succinct, yet so powerful and full of feelings.

I called the priest about six a.m. to let him know that Wes had died so he could announce it at all the masses that day. Then we called our relatives and dearest friends to let them know. At seven thirty a.m., we woke Tony and Ali and told them Wes had died. Tony sat on our bed and Ali was cradled in Chuck's arms. Tony said he was glad Wes did not have to suffer anymore. We told him that we agreed with him.

I told Chuck that despite the fact that everyone would be staring at us after the announcement at mass of Wes's death that was not going to keep me away from church that morning. So we all went to church together.

That Sunday was a whir of people. Food poured in. People called to offer help and condolences.

The Funeral

October 20, 1993

I wrote about what I remembered concerning the funeral in a journal entry on January 12, 1994.

The days that followed his death were an incredible time. People just volunteered to do everything. I sat at the kitchen table, which was my grandmother's, as friends arrived with what they wanted to do for Wes at his service. Things just fell into place. Singing and music was in the forefront of my mind as Wes loved music so much. He listened to a music tape each night as he went to bed. We listened to many of the Psalty tapes on our way to the hospital for his many chemo treatments. These were religious songs about a big, blue, singing songbook named Psalty. For the funeral, Wes's piano teacher would play the three songs she had played for him at his last lesson. The friend that played the guitar on Friday evening and again on Saturday in the hospital would play while the teenagers who had been at the hospital would sing. He and his son would end up writing a song to be sung at the gravesite, while the children released balloons. Another friend picked out a song called "Sweet, Sweet Spirit" to sing as the children brought Wes's favorite things to the altar during the service. His favorite things were his favorite college hat that he always wore, his Little Boy Blue hat that symbolized his love for acting, his cassette tape case that symbolized his love for music, his brown bear that symbolized his courage, his sword that symbolized his powerful spirit, his pillow that symbolized his peacefulness and security, his baptismal candle that symbolized his faith, and his Lego castle that symbolized his playfulness. Yes, his life was full of symbols.

Wes's counselor and teacher volunteered to stay at our house during the visitation and to have food ready for the relatives who would need to eat. The faculty at Wes's school sent food. The funeral director came by to get specifics for the paper. Later, we picked out the casket and vault. Two friends offered their homes for relatives to stay at while here. The priest dropped by so I could pick out several readings for the funeral. A relative took Ali to get an appropriate dress for the funeral. Another friend worked on developing a program when all the final choices had been made for the funeral. Another friend wrote a poem called "For Our Little Angel, Wes." I put that poem on the front of the program.

For Our Little Angel, Wes
With Love Always: Bobbie

If you'd ask me about Wessie,
I'd know not where to start,
But in his fragile body
Beat a courageous, golden heart.
A Ninja suit of armor
This little warrior wore,

To look at him you'd scarcely guess
The disease his body bore.
His loving eyes filled with wonder
As his precious family played,
Through the numbered days God gave them
Before He called Wes away.
"Mom," said little Wessie,
As he readied to depart,
"I always know where Jesus is,
He lives inside my heart."

Then the little details started to consume me. My friend Cindi, who had stayed with him while I took my test, came by bright and early that Monday and stayed with me until she felt it was safe to leave me. She helped me pick out clothes for Wes: black pants, pinstriped blue dress shirt, and a red and black striped sweater. Yes, I sent socks and underwear too. Not that it mattered. I had to choose a picture of him for the paper and one for the prayer card. I sorted through all the photos I had taken of him over the last three weeks, and chose one that was so very common of him. In the picture, he wore his favorite college hat and a sweatshirt with a great big smile on his face. That hat would later be put in the casket with him.

We had looked at burial plots two weeks before and picked out one that was easily accessible by the road and had a tree near. It looked warm and comfortable and peaceful there. Chuck confirmed our spot with the cemetery.

Tuesday, all the finishing touches needed to be done. All the readings, songs, and program copy were approved by the priest. The food kept pouring in. The calls kept coming. The people kept volunteering. I made three collages from all the pictures I had gathered.

It was all so overwhelming. I was virtually numb

by the end of the day. I ate little before going to the funeral home for the visitation. We had put his sword and Legos on display. We had family pictures and the collages of Wes scattered around the room. We had picked out red roses and white carnations for his casket. There were tons of flowers and plants. The one that made me cry was the single red rose from the little girl who captured Wes's heart in second grade. One day, I asked Wes what made him like Jennifer. He said, "It's not like. I love her. It's like when I saw her across the gym, it was love at first sight." I continued the conversation with the question, "So what makes you love her?" He replied, "She's pretty and smart and she'll make a good mother." And that was that.

All the relatives assembled at the funeral home. I cried and cried and so did everyone else. I hugged and cried with each person who came through the receiving line. The children that came wrote notes to Wes to be put in his coffin. I read every one of them. At the prayer service, our friend Charlie played his guitar and sang several songs. We left exhausted.

The next morning, my mother, who had stood in the line with us, had pain in her lower back. I went to the hospital with her. I was very calm. Eventually, I called my brother to stay with her so I could come home to shower and change.

People had gathered at the funeral home to say their last good-byes to Wes. We had a short service without my mother, but held the coffin open until she arrived. Everyone filed by the coffin and then hugged us. Then Ali, Tony, Chuck, and I went up to the coffin, and I hugged Wes and kissed him all over like I used to do when he would say, "How many?" I would say thirteen or twenty-three, and he would give me that many kisses back. No longer would my face be filled with kisses from him. Then, Tony put Wes's Lego knight and horse by his hands. My brother's children put in a baseball. Later, we laughed because we realized we should have put some Band-Aids in the coffin because Wes was always using Band-Aids, even on things that were not bleeding.

My mom arrived and said her good-byes from her wheelchair. Tony and Ali kissed Wes, and Chuck kissed him, and we all said good-bye. I gathered the children to me and told them that I never wanted them to be angry with God because Wes had died. God let us have him for eleven years, and for that, we needed to be grateful. They nodded. Then we left for the church.

When we arrived, the church was full of people there to celebrate Wes's life. Wes's godmother was on one side of me, and Wes's caretaker was on the other side of me, holding on to me as if they thought I might fall. Chuck had Ali on one side and Tony on the other side as we walked behind the coffin being wheeled into the church.

The service was beautiful. It was truly a celebration of Wes's life. As I listen again to the service, I cry; but I also have an inner peace that we did all we could for him and brought him up in a way that allowed him to be the amazing person he was, despite his limitations. Chuck said it all the day we found out he was going to die. He said that we had done everything possible to give him a chance for life. We never wanted to look back and say that we had wished we had done something we chose not to do. Yet at the same time, we did not want to do really crazy, desperate things that many people do. With each choice, we thought of him and his quality of life. We never wanted to put him through anything that would make him unsafe. At the end, when we knew he was going to die, we chose not to give him chemo. We chose to let him live as long as he could and do what he wanted to do each day. We have never looked back and regretted anything we did or did not do for Wes. We are content that we were good parents to him.

Another thing I am very proud of is how we treated him as a person, even though we knew there was a possibility that he would die. When he was three and had his first tumor, I can remember this day just as clear as anything. I had taken Ali and Wes to the grocery store with me. Wes still had his head bandaged from his brain operation. He threw a fit in the toy aisle because he wanted something, and I told him that he could not have a toy. I remember consciously thinking, "If this child survives, I want him to grow up as a kind, caring person not a demanding, spoiled child." It was hard not to give him anything he wanted. Often, I would say to myself, "Why not? He may only be here with us a little while." Yet I knew getting his way and getting anything he wanted was not good for him. I believe he grew up as normal as he could given his circumstances, because we did not let his cancer rule our house. Let me say that again. We did not let his cancer rule our house. We saw to it that Ali and Tony did whatever they could in their activities and participated in everything they wanted to despite Wes's illness. We never let his cancer keep the other children from what was important to them.

We treated Wes like a normal child. We expected good behavior from him. We expected him to participate in activities that he was capable of when he could. We expected him to accomplish something. He succeeded in meeting our expectations and beyond. I think he did because he knew we were always there to support him. We never left him alone except for that night when we *first discovered his tumor. Either one of us was always there at the hospital or one of us or his caregiver was with him at home. He felt secure in our love and could then venture out to succeed in his world.*

So when the priests cited his accomplishments and his fruitful life, I knew we had succeeded as parents. Reverend Patrick Shortt ended his comments about Wes by saying to Chuck and I, "We can't help but compliment, thank, and applaud his parents and his family for a tremendous job well done." Excerpts from both the homily by Monsignor Michael Wilbers and the testimonial by Reverend Patrick Shortt follow.

Monsignor Michael Wilbers
Excerpts from the Funeral Homily for Wes

October 20, 1993

In our Father's house, there are many rooms…

What is wonderful about childhood is that everything in it is a wonder. It is not just a world full of miracles, it was a miraculous world. We learned a lot from Wes. Children tell us of the miraculous beauties of life as they perceive them.

A child came running and said, "Look, look." He called and thrust into my hand a ladybug. I had stopped seeing ladybugs.

A child came running. "He's so soft," he whispered, then put my hand on the kitten's fur. I had stopped noticing how things really feel.

A child came running. I held him in my arms and offered thanks to God for my rebirth.

Wes was really a unique child, a unique individual. There were many in the parish that knew him … Wes taught us that even in the midst of pain and suffering there really could be a smile. Along with St. Paul, Wes tells us in the second reading of today although our outer self is wasting away, our inner self is being renewed day by day … To have such an insight as that, to be able to deal with pain and suffering, as we know that comes with a suffering such as cancer, and to be able to see beyond it is so very important. Wes, not all that old, could teach us how to be able to deal with the afflictions of life.

Reverend Patrick Shortt
Excerpts from the Testimonial to Wesley

October 20, 1993

Wesley and I came to this parish in the same month in 1982. He was born the very month I came to this parish. I remember a Sunday morning when he was three years old, downstairs in the Sunday school program, when he first went to the cross with Christ. I remember the Monday that followed when he brought this mom and dad that same cross. I remember that Monday evening, and I know Rita does too, because we burned the midnight oil trying to get logic and intelligence to help us when we turned and said, "The answer is faith." I remember that blue Tuesday when Wesley had his first surgery, and I was with Chuck and Rita in the hospital in Columbia for what felt like days. But I remember at one point in that day, we held hands and walked down the hall and down the elevators to the chapel in that facility, and went in and held hands together and celebrated Eucharist with the priest. For the last eight years, that has been one of my richest memories, because I feel in the depth of my heart that what we thought at that time was eight hours of fruitless effort and exhausted labor for surgeons has since turned into eight years of love and life.

I feel solidly that that day, Chuck and Rita, that we had our miracle. That's not all we were praying for and hoping for, but we had our miracle. This boy's whole life has been one walking, living, laughing miracle. I couldn't help this morning driving down here but think I have never so vividly looked at a life and seen the whole mystery of life, death, and resurrection lived so fully in eleven years. As Father Mike mentioned in his homily, it's incredible to us adult persons where this boy's faith came from.

Even in the worst of pain, he never lamented, he never cried out in any anger, he never had anything but a positive word to say, or a smile to share. I talked repeatedly with nurses that worked with him in the hospital, and they would all shake their head and say the same thing, "He's one powerful little boy." And that powerful little boy has given us horrendous memories, he has given us incredible hope, and he has given us joy beyond mention. He has especially given that to his parents and his brother and sister. And over the years, with all of his return trips to the same facility, each time had the same glow of hope that he always had in those beautiful little eyes that so much radiated a love that could not be described in words.

He loved to play. He loved to enjoy every moment of life that was in any way, shape or form enjoyable. That didn't surprise me because he came from parents who knew as the first reading says when to laugh and when to cry and when to play and when to be joyful. What a gift God gave to you parents and to his brother and sister and family. What a gift he gave to this parish family that has rallied around this little one who was the center of our focus and prayer and our focus in love. His story may never be written in a book, but it's written in my heart, and I think it's written in the hearts of a lot of people. Every trip that he made I thought brought all of us who knew him closely even that much closer to Jesus Christ and to understanding this mystery that we could not see contained in eleven years.

I stayed in touch. It's been incredible over eight years how many different directions communication to me about Wesley kept coming. I kept returning to the hospital and finding his name in the book and checking it out and somebody saying, "Oh, he's gone home again." And I'd check down here and find out, yeah, just as Father Mike said in his homily, he's either playing ball or he's gone to a play or he's doing this or doing that. He was way beyond my imagination each and every time.

Oh, I have other great memories too. I remember a great day when we celebrated Eucharist in your lovely home, shortly after it was built, and that child so thoroughly enjoyed, as did the other two children, that family having the privilege of being together as a family for Eucharist. One of the last times I drove out, and I mentioned earlier he learned his ability to laugh and enjoy life from his loving parents; the last time I drove out there, just as Father Mike did to see where Wesley was at and how he was doing, I didn't find Wesley playing, but I found Chuck playing with a four-wheel drive in a four-foot ditch with six inches of snow on *the ground. I couldn't help but think that this little boy inherited some of those traits of fun and joy.*

There is no way for me to describe how Wesley followed in the footsteps of Jesus as a child. But I saw him day in and day out as on that Sunday school morning eight years ago, constantly pouring out his little self right up until he gave the last drop of his life on Sunday morning. And how appropriate that he did that in the arms of his dad, who loved him so much, representing the love of the parents who loved him...

In our program this morning, we called Wesley our little angel, and that is truly what he has been to his family and to every one of us that has known him for eleven years. We don't need to wish Wesley any farewell other than his memory, but we can't help compliment, thank, and applaud his parents and his family for a tremendous job well done. God love you.

We included the children in the funeral mass. His closest friends began the funeral by bringing to the altar symbols that represented Wes's life. A dear friend of mine, Kathy, read the following as each one of Wes's special friends brought to the altar Wes's symbols of life.

As we remember Wes today, his friends will bring to the altar the symbols of his life.

Mizzou Hat: Those of you who know Wes well will recognize the Mizzou hat Jake will bring. Whether with or without hair, Wes always loved wearing his hat.

Little Boy Blue Hat: Sean brings another hat representing ACTPAC plays in which Wes was involved. This hat he wore as Little Boy Blue in Christmas in Toyland. *He was also the Door Mouse and Judge in* Alice in Wonderland *and the monkey in* Peter Pan.

Cassette Tape Case: Jane brings Wes's cassette tape case full of Psalty and Jim Valley cassette tapes, which Wes would listen to on his many journeys to the University Medical Center for treatments, and each night to fall asleep by. Music was a very important part of Wes's life.

Brown Bear: Michael brings Wes's brown bear that slept with Wes as his protector. When his mom tried to make more room in his bed by placing the brown bear on the floor at night, Wes would tell her that his brown bear protected him from all harm during the night.

Sword: Wes used the sword as an external symbol for his internal war against cancer. Lisa brings the sword representing Wes's battle.

Pillow: Ben brings Wes's pillow. This pillow, all ragged and torn, has been through many years of chemotherapy and radiation with Wes. It was always under his head, no matter where he had to lay it, just as his family and friends were always there for him.

Baptismal Candle: Chris brings Wes's baptismal candle. It symbolizes Wes's Christian spirit. The last conversation Wes had with his mother shows Wes's intimate connection with God. It went like this: Wes yelled out, "I can't find him. I can't find him." His mother asked him who he couldn't find. Wes said, "Oh, it's not important. Wes's mother asked him if he could find Jesus. Wes opened his eyes and said emphatically, "I always know where to find Jesus. He's in my heart."

Lego Castle: And lastly, Jennifer brings the Lego castle. The castle is not only a symbol of Wes's love for building things, but also a symbol of what he believed heaven to be like. Wes's mom asked him a week before he died what he imagined heaven to be like. He paused, and he thought for a moment and he said, "Heaven is like a big, big castle with a huge playground and rooms and rooms full of Legos." We know that Wes has found that huge playground.

A friend helped me pick out the scriptures that were used at the funeral. We decided on the following passages.

Ecclesiastes 3:1–8 (NIV)
There is a time for everything and a season
for every activity under heaven:
A time to be born and a time to die,
A time to plant and a time to uproot,
A time to kill and a time to heal,
A time to tear down and a time to build,
A time to weep and a time to dance,
A time to scatter stones and a time to gather them,
A time to embrace and a time to refrain,
A time to search and a time to give up,
A time to keep and a time to throw away,
A time to tear and a time to mend
A time to be silent and a time to speak
A time to love and a time to hate,
A time to war and a time for peace.

2 Corinthians 4:13–18 (NIV)
It is written: "I believed; therefore I have spoken." With that same spirit of faith we also believe and therefore speak, because we know that the one who raised the Lord Jesus from the dead will also raise us with Jesus and present us with you in his presence. All this is for your benefit, so that the grace that is reaching more and more people may cause thanksgiving to overflow to the glory of God. Therefore, we do not lose heart. Though outwardly we are wasting away, yet inwardly we are being renewed day by day. For our light and momentary troubles are achieving for us

an eternal glory that far outweighs them all. So we fix our eyes not on what is seen, but on what is unseen. For what is seen is temporary, but what is unseen is eternal.

Mark 10:13–16 (NIV)
People were bringing little children to Jesus to have him touch them, but the disciples rebuked them. When Jesus saw this, he was indignant. He said to them, "Let the little children come to me, and do not hinder them, for the kingdom of God belongs to such as these. I tell you the truth, anyone who will not receive the kingdom of God like a little child will never enter it." And he took the children in his arms, put his hands on them and blessed them.

Wes's piano teacher played the organ. A friend of mine volunteered to sing a song taken from 2 Corinthians 13:11 entitled "Sweet, Sweet Spirit." Several of Wes's older theatre friends who were with him in his hospital room on that Friday before he died, plus a few of their parents, provided the guitar music and songs.

We went to the cemetery, and Wes's coffin was put in the horse-drawn hearse that took him to his final resting place. It was raining. How perfect. Later that night, I called a friend and said that the day was perfect because it was as if Jesus was weeping with us, and that I knew that tomorrow God would make the sun shine because Wes would be happy in heaven with God. Sure enough, the next day dawned bright with sunshine.

At the cemetery, people gathered with their umbrellas. At the end of the service, our dear friend Charlie, who had played the guitar in Wes's hospital room along with his son, Matt, had written a song about sending balloons up to heaven. The funeral director had gotten balloons to let the children release and send up to Wes. The song was perfect. These are the words to the song that was sung at Wes's gravesite.

Wes's Song

By: Charlie and Matt Stokes

Way high up in the sky
These balloons take our message
Of love up so high
So please, Jesus, give Wes
A hug and a smile
And hold him
On your lap awhile.

As Matt and Bridgett and Charlie sang the song over and over, all the children sent their balloons up to heaven, and then each took a rose off of Wes's coffin as a keepsake. The rest of the roses were kept in order to make rosaries. I left the cemetery feeling worn out, but peaceful.

Days Following the Funeral

I continued writing the next day, January 13, 1994. I had converted Wes's bedroom into a quiet space with a recliner and a daybed. I sat in the recliner and wrote the following.

The day that followed the funeral would be pretty overwhelming to me in terms of people trying to help me get over my grief. All the plants filled my house. Every room looked like a garden. I tried to concentrate on writing thank-you notes. I cried while writing each one, because I wrote a special note in each. If a person takes the time to send something, then that person deserves a personal thank you, not just a signature or some nebulous statement.

Cards began to pour in at the rate of sixty to seventy per day. Each day, I would spend an hour opening them and crying. I did a lot of crying during the six weeks following his death. I asked for personal leave from my job as a therapist. I told my supervisor I would not come back until I knew that I was emotionally ready to help others. I knew myself well enough that I would sense the cues that would tell me I was ready to help others again. For the present, though, I just needed to let myself experience the grief. I didn't want to be depressed in two years because I had not allowed myself to deal with my sorrow now. My supervisor agreed.

The first week after his death, I started re-nesting from five to four members in my family. A friend helped me pick out new furniture for Wes's room. I bought a new bed, a reclining chair, and a table with a lamp. It was too much pain for me to pass by his room every day and see his bed. When I made his room into a sitting room with a daybed in it, I felt much more peaceful.

The next week, I went through Wes's closet and packed up all his things that I wanted to keep, and gave the rest away. Then I cleaned every closet and room. I even cleaned the basement. I had a tremendous need to put things in order and to rearrange.

The hardest thing for me was on Monday after the funeral. I was making supper, and I began to set the table. I had four plates but five chairs. I consciously asked myself, "Do I get rid of the chair or leave it?"

What purpose would it serve to leave it? It would only be a reminder of Wes's absence. So crying, I took that chair and put it in the library.

Earlier that day, Ali had to go to the orthodontist for the first time. The receptionist was taking a history. She asked me about any other children besides Ali. I looked at Ali, and Ali looked at me as if holding her breath to see what I would say. I said, "One other child, a boy thirteen." When we left the office, I talked with Ali about what I had said. I told her that the lady only needed to know how many other children I had who were alive. So I told her one, so that I would not have to explain about Wes dying. Ali seemed to understand. To this day, when I fill out forms and it asks how many children, I still don't know whether to put two or three.

Ali had not cried when we told her Wes died. She cried only when she saw him in the coffin at visitation. She cried a little before we closed the coffin at the funeral home, but other than that she did not cry much. She talks about Wes often. She mentions the funny things he used to say or do or what he would say or do if he were with us in a particular situation.

I think she coped with it symbolically. One day, she wanted to go to the mall to buy some jewelry. She had twenty dollars, and so we went to the mall. She had her mind made up that she wanted "one of those black and white things." Come to find out that she wanted the popular jewelry that had the yin yang symbol on them. She bought a necklace, bracelet, ring, and earrings. That was her internal way of externally coping with Wes's death.

I noticed that I had been wearing only two rings for months after his death. I usually wear three rings on each hand. The two rings I wore, I realized later, were the first ring my dad gave me and the ring Wes gave me for my birthday that year of his death. I still wear it today. I guess that was my way of keeping the two important people in my life who had died close to me. It is amazing how we do things unconsciously to take care of ourselves.

Tony coped very well after a few weeks. He had some real angry outbursts at first, but we knew what they were all about, so we tried to set flexible boundaries, but boundaries nevertheless. Tony expressed that he was glad that Wes died because he did not want to see him suffer. He had heard Wes's cries in the night and had woken up to become scared for him. He loved Wes very much, and Wes thought a lot of his big brother, Tony. I know Tony had a hard time saying that he would rather see Wes dead than suffering, but that just shows what a mature child Tony is.

It was hard when Wes's school pictures came. I cried. I put a photo in a frame for each of his two favorite people. Chris was his best friend and Jennifer was Wes's best friend who was a girl. When I was putting Wes's stuffed animals away, I kept putting two of them in the box and taking them back out again and again. Finally, Chris and Jennifer's names came to mind, so I said, "Okay, am I supposed to give these to them?" In my head, I heard, "Yes." So at Christmastime, I gave Jennifer a photo of Wes in a frame and a game I had originally bought for Wes for Christmas. I gave Chris a photo of Wes in a frame and a Lego set I had bought for Wes for Christmas. I only gave the presents after checking with the children's parents to see if it would be okay and not cause them any pain. Wes had sung a song called "Stuck on You" in a talent show and had a "Pound Purrie" stuck on him (among other things), so Jennifer got the cat because he was always stuck on Jennifer.

Another hard time was when the Ranger Rick magazine arrived in the mail. I just started getting it for him in the summer, so I guess until next summer I will be reminded of him in this way monthly.

After putting my journey into words, I felt relieved. I could go forward. The story was out of me and onto paper where I could put it away and not have the burden of the pure sadness prevent me from being present to the moment. Freeing myself of the words allowed me to function. When more words accumulated, I gave them expression so they did not become stuck inside me, causing feelings that would hold me hostage. Following are a few of the writings I did over the years.

Interesting Experience

December 8, 1993

I needed desperately to know that Wes was okay. A strange thing happened one morning, and here is what I wrote about the experience.

For the past ten days I have cried each morning upon awakening and each evening before retiring. I miss my child so much. Last night, I asked myself what was making me so sad or so unsettled. My answer came as I said to myself, "I just want to know that he is okay and in heaven with God, watching over and caring for him." I desperately needed a sign, a physical sign that he was in heaven with God and that he was okay. I prayed for a sign.

When I awoke this morning, I went in to Ali's room to close her door as I do every morning before waking Tony. I was drawn to her window by the beautiful sun-

rise. It was shades of purples and oranges and yellows and pinks. I closed her door gently and went to Tony's room. I woke Tony and went downstairs. I have been coming downstairs each morning for nine years, but this morning as I walked into the great room, the angel that was upon the television was outlined with sunlight in a large square. It looked as if it were sunlight reflected by a window, but there were no windows that small in this particular room. The angel was perfectly outlined with a square of sunlight around it.

I knew instantly that this was my sign. I sat down in my rocker and thanked God for giving me that sign. Then I looked to see where the light was coming from and could not detect from where the light reflected. I busied myself getting the children's vitamins set out for them. As I went back upstairs, I glanced at the angel. The sunlight square was gone. In my heart, I knew that was my sign that I did not have to worry about Wes and that he was resting peacefully in God's loving arms. I can let go now, and it is okay.

Resignation

January 14, 1994

Sometimes I just cry and say, "I miss you, Wes. I just miss you so much." In my head comes back in Wes's little voice, this reply, "But I'm happy in heaven, Mom. Heaven is a beautiful place, just like Psalty said."

I miss his hugs the most, the way he would pat me on the back when he hugged me. I miss holding him in my arms. I just could not get enough of hugging him those last few weeks.

Knowing your child is going to die is one of the most

frightening things ever. I was in a panic. How could I help him go through the process of dying? Could I hold up and be strong for him? Each time I have learned that God gives you the strength to go through a situation, no matter what it is. Sometimes I look back and say, "How in the world did I do that?" "I" didn't. God did. So God gave me the strength to be present to Wes and to take my test at the same time. He didn't give me those two extra weeks I asked for, but he gave me eight years with my precious baby. For that, I am thankful.

Sometimes I hear Wes's voice calling me in my head, and he tells me things. He comforts me when I'm sad, and I know that his spirit at first when he died was very close to me. As the time has passed, I realize the voice comes less and the feeling of his presence being close has grown dimmer. I try to rationalize that by believing that Wes was called to heaven to be someone's guardian angel so that he is needed elsewhere. He still knows when I need his comforting voice in my head to help me through the difficult spots. I know that I can always count on Wes to be there for me, to help me through whatever comes.

Sometimes I wonder whether we pushed him into death by telling him to take God's hand if he offered it and to go with God. We just knew we did not want him to suffer needlessly. We wanted him to be at peace. I know he is at peace, and he is with God and that's all that we could want for him, to be in God's loving arms.

Wes is so much better off in heaven with God. There he has no pain, no sorrow. He does not have to suffer. God knew he had suffered long enough and called him to heaven to be with him. I know he's in good hands. If he can't be with me, then God is the only other one that I would trust to care for my child as I do. To let him go is so difficult. I can hardly believe he is gone. I know it, and yet I don't know how he could be so alive one minute and gone the next.

Through the last few months, I have been awed by the friends who have tried to take care of me. I believe that some people called me to go to lunch out of caring, and yet also because they realized how lucky they are to have never experienced this kind of trauma with their children. Others may have called because of curiosity. One lady called because she had experienced friends forgetting her and that did not feel good to her, so she did not want to be one of those friends who forgot. Whatever the motive, I am happy they took the time for me.

However, after an influx of attention, I had to let people know that I needed a whole week just to be by myself to write, to listen again to the tape of his funeral, and to put the whole process of Wes's death in perspective. I needed to make a movie in my head. Then I needed to store it on a shelf in my mind. Once stored, I could choose to get it out and view it, or I could leave it on the shelf when other things in my life take priority. I knew I had to go through this process of putting all the bits and pieces of memory into a whole so that I could have closure on Wes's death. Once closure was obtained, I could move on to be a productive person.

So it was three months after his death when I could finally take a week to cry and to mourn and to reflect on Wes. Once the week was over, I felt as if I had a renewed spirit. My crying is less, and my sadness need no longer possess me. I can now open myself to the joyfulness of Wes's memory, instead of the tearful reflection of my loss. To remember him will fill my heart with the joy for life that was so much a part of his life. I love him, and his memory will always be a part of my own spirit.

And so, from time to time, I will sit down and write; but for now, my process is done. I love him, I miss him, and now I have put him in perspective. When I look at his picture, I can smile at the joy-filled life he led. His life was a gift. His presence in our family has been a true gift to all of us. I was his caretaker here on Earth, yet he belonged to God always. He knew and I knew, yet we had a most special relationship. He is with his heavenly Father now, and he is happy and at peace. What more could a mother want for her son?

Reflections

January 18, 1994

Wes had a good life. He had everything a little boy could have wanted. He had loving parents, an older brother who took care of him, and a younger sister who was his best friend. He went to school and learned. He played. He could run and jump and climb upon the playground equipment. He played soccer and baseball and basketball, although none very well. He danced jazz and tap. He acted and sang in four musicals. He was a cub scout. He took piano lessons and had three superior ratings at the contests he was able to attend. He took ice skating lessons, and he roller skated. He had boys and girls both that he could call friends. He had birthday parties. He celebrated many Christmases and Easters. He attended church and religious education classes. I took him to the theatre. Chuck took him to sporting events. He watched Saturday morning cartoons. We took him to the movies. He fished. He rode a horse. He rode four wheelers. He sledded in the snow, made snow angels, and threw snowballs. He rode in an airplane. He went to Disney World. He went to theme parks and water parks. He had his own room, a space to call his own. He did not miss out on anything in life.

We loved him, and he knew it. There is nothing more we could have given him to make his life full. He missed nothing and wanted nothing more. Wes had a good life. It was just very short. I am trying to convince myself that as his mother, I did everything to help make his life full of experiences and adventures. He may have been on Earth a short time, but he participated in many things so that his life was enriched. I just had to convince myself of that.

Reassurance

February 6, 1994

It's my birthday. All week I have felt sad. I have cried when going to sleep and again upon awakening. I miss him so very, very much, and again, I am so desperate to know that he is okay. I know God gave me the message that he is an angel in heaven and is okay when I saw the light around the angel on the television, yet at this moment in time, I need another sign of reassurance. I prayed last night that God would give me another sign on my birthday that Wes was okay.

It never ceases to amaze me how God does give me what I need when I need it the most. "Ask and thou shalt receive." On my birthday, a very strange thing happened that can only be interpreted as God letting me know that Wes is okay.

We came home from Tony's two basketball games

and were going to go to dinner for my birthday, but Chuck got an emergency call to take care of a cow, and so we told him we would meet him at the restaurant. Before we left the house, I got a phone call. Out of the blue, a child who I had done an educational evaluation on eight years ago called me and apologized for being mean to me during the evaluation. He told me that he was doing very well, and now as a young adult, he was in his third year of college.

I cannot interpret this any other way than two messages from God. First, that even though life is rough, it is okay now. He is in heaven with God, and he is okay. Second, eight years ago may have been a hard time (for us learning about his tumor), and yet the life he led was fulfilling and his outcome was good.

Many times I still ask, "Why us, why our child?" Could we have been so awful that God wanted to punish us by taking our child? Yet at the same time I believe that he was such a gift for such a short time. He was so beautiful. He taught me so much about enjoying the present moment. He taught me to relax and not let things bother me.

I miss his pats on the back when I would hug him. I miss his caring for Ali by telling her to buckle up her seatbelt. I miss him taking ten times as long to create his snack than to eat it. I miss his love for cartoons on Saturday morning all wrapped up in his sleeping bag. I miss his kisses at night all over my face. I miss his excitement when going to the movies or the arcade or the park. I miss his love for nature. I miss his love.

I know that he no longer has to endure life, which was very difficult for him, but it was all he knew. He knew pain and hospitals and struggling for life. He also knew the things that enriched life. I know that he is with God and he is whole and healthy. I know heaven *has opened up its arms to him and has embraced him. I know he has met my dad and Chuck's parents and they are helping him get to know the afterlife and that he is probably relishing it as he did his life on Earth.*

I hear his little voice often. I know he is with me always, in my heart and in my mind. It is hard not to be able to touch him, to hold him, to be in physical contact with him. I believe I am in spiritual contact with him because we were so close in life, but I still miss the hugs and kisses. I miss him, and I love him always.

The Dream

February 22, 1994

I wrote the following about a dream I had. I can only believe that this was my reassurance that Wes was in heaven with God.

I awoke at 12:20 a.m. from a dream. In the dream, I had picked Wes up to help him see out a window to look at some very tiny black and red chickens. Then, he was cradled in my arms, much like a baby. I was carrying him, and he was dying in my arms. All of a sudden, there was a tunnel; we were being sucked down. It was taking Wes away. He was still in my arms, but his spirit was going. A loud noise like a train was pounding and it got louder as the rush of light sped by us as we were whisked through the tunnel. Then, at the end of the tunnel, the fast motion changed into slow motion. Clouds appeared and then two angels appeared. Wes was taken from my arms, and the angels gathered on each side of him, gently taking him to God. Then I awoke.

Understanding

June 5, 1994

I wrote this about the realization that I needed to monitor my emotions so that I did not create misery in my life because of what I call "piled on anger" from the past.

I had been having an intense emotional reaction at Tony's baseball games, which I failed to understand. My emotions were out of proportion to his being treated unfairly. I realized some of it was due to my belief that Wes was treated unfairly in the world and now it was happening to Tony, too. But the overwhelming anger I felt was a million times worse than warranted. Tony's coach was not letting him play. His playing time did not reflect his ability and his batting average. Tony was weighing his options and was considering quitting. Chuck advised him to stay on the team for another weekend. Chuck had advised me also that if I could not handle my emotions, then stay home. For some reason, I wanted to go. Why I wanted to go was beyond me, but internally, I knew I needed to go.

There must have been a divine plan, and there was. I was so furious at the coach this weekend that my anger caused two startling revelations. Fortunately, this particular week, I had taken off work to handle another emerging spiral time. (A spiral time, which I describe in a later chapter, is when you again experience feelings that you thought you had let go.) *As I processed, two things became clear to me.*

First, I realized that with Wes, I had been traveling out of town for eight years, watching him suffer through his treatments, just as I was now traveling out of town to the baseball games to see my other son,

Tony, suffer emotionally by not being played during the games. The realization was that Tony's pain is not Wes's pain, and I needed to let go of Wes's pain and focus on Tony's pain, that was less intense and less life threatening. I do not need to see my other children's pain as the same, nor respond to their pains in the same way with the same intensity. Tony is realistically responding to his hurt feelings, and I am trying to respond to his hurt feelings like I responded to Wes's pain. I projected my angry feelings at the doctors and nurses who administered helpful but painful care, onto the coach who was hurting my other child emotionally. This was a great realization and helped me control my own emotions many times when I saw my son Tony disappointed.

Secondly, I fought for eight years for Wes so that he would survive. I was hypervigilant and ready to attack anyone who would threaten his health, emotionally or physically. I realized I did not need to play the same role with Tony. I can let go of that role now that Wes is dead. I played the role so well that I am trying to play an encore in Tony's life. He does not need me to play that role for him. He is capable of fighting for himself. I can give up the role. I can let go of it.

Thank you, God, for giving me the opportunity through the coach's actions towards Tony to work through and resolve the internal strife and loss of a role that I needed to let go of. I know that the experiences you give me lead me to greater understanding and wisdom. What else is life about than striving to understand existence and how we function therein?

What greater gift than a wise child could you send to me to teach me so many valuable lessons? I miss him, but I do know that he is in your loving hands and that you will take good care of him. Somehow, I know that, and if I have not accepted it yet, I am trying hard.

Please send me peace in my heart and mind. I know that Tony and Ali are my present and Wes is my past.

Conclusion

January 12, 1994

I cannot believe that a child is here one day and gone from us the next. I miss him so much. I miss his laughter, his smile, his caring for others, his little hand in mine, combing my hand over his feather hair, playing in the park, saying good-night prayers, watching him brush his teeth so fastidiously, seeing him snuggled in his little sleeping bag in front of the television, having him snuggle close to me. He was so soft and always smelled so good. I miss thinking about what things we could do to make his life happy and full. I miss having to protect him from the world.

I try to stifle my tears, and I get this burning sensation in my nose as if I had just sniffed pepper. When I cry for long periods, I finally begin to have deep, deep sighs. Each night before I go to bed, I hold his picture in my hands and put it up against my chest and hug it tightly as if hugging him and tell Wes how very much I love him and miss him.

Sometimes, I wonder how I could have helped him more to get through his dying. I wonder if there were things I should have said to him or done for him to make it easier for him. The intensity of love that I have for him is awesome to me. The great caring and the time I spent with him was such a gift. I can see how mothers can run into burning buildings to save their children. There is just such a love there that is so very different from the love of a woman for a man.

He was so beautiful in body and spirit and mind. His fair skin and fragile body made me want to care for and protect him, yet his spirit was so strong he did not really need my protection. He cared for others so intently. Likewise, children and even adults cared for him. It never failed that when we were in public that someone said hello to Wes and called him by name. In his short eleven years, he touched the hearts of many.

Why did God take him? Why was his time on Earth up? Did God need him for a heavenly mission? I often wonder. One thing I wonder is if Wes is someone's guardian angel. This may be very crazy, but an inner sense brought this idea to mind, perhaps to salve the hurt inside me and justify his death. I often think that Wes has been called to be the guardian angel of a new-born who will eventually become a priest. Awesome thought. See how one's mind will try to do anything to ease the pain the heart feels? Somehow, in my mind, I believed that Wes's body was not allowing him to do what God was calling him to do, and so God wanted to put his spirit to work elsewhere without the hindrance of the body Wes had. Then again, what, just what, if there is no life after death and Wes is just gone? I could not bear that thought. I know his spirit is somewhere. That's why I panicked that one week when I wanted a sign to let me know that Wes was in heaven with God. Remember, when the light shone on the angel in the great room? After I got my sign, I felt peaceful, as if everything with Wes was okay.

At Christmas Eve mass, I saw a banner hanging on one of the pews. I asked if I could have the banner. The person in charge asked the person who made it and it was given to me. I still have that banner hanging in Wes's room. It was black with two angels holding a cross. The writing said, "Heaven touched Earth."

That banner spoke to me about Wes's life. I feel that he was really a part of heaven that touched Earth for a brief period and then returned to heaven, where he knows the joy of the kingdom of God. Wes was rarely afraid. He had an inner strength and an inner peace. He always had the Lord right beside him. Sometimes I would come into Wes's bedroom and kneel by his bed and watch him sleep. He always looked like an angel, my little angel that was sent to Earth to bring intensity to our lives. He never quit. He never gave up. He worked at something no matter how long it took. He stayed with things to the very end. He always offered to help and did a good job in helping. When he finished, he asked if there was more he could do. He was thoughtful and kind, and yet tough enough to be a middle child who had to fight for his place in the family.

Sometimes I fear that with time, my memory will dim and I won't be able to remember him and all the little things he would say and do. That scares me because I always want to have him close to my heart. I want to remember vividly his little smile, his strong spirit, and his love of living life to the fullest.

Compared to him, I feel like nothing; as if my life has been pretty worthless and pointless. I have lived forty-three years at this writing, and what have I done? I keep asking God for a direction. What am I supposed to accomplish here on Earth? What path should my life take? I keep getting the answer: write. I have heard that for years, but when I have tried to publish, I have been rejected time after time after time. So why do I still keep getting the answer, write? I also get the words, be patient, all in good time. Patient for what? What time? Whose time? Patience is not one of my strong points. God's been trying to teach it to me for years, and I guess I have not learned that lesson yet. I am a high energy, highly motivated person. To be quiet and content is not my nature. I trust that whatever I am to do will unfold.

He was priceless. Do I regret having him? No, never. With all the pain and sorrow and sacrifices and struggle, I am still thankful that God gave me Wes to take care of for eleven short years. The experience of being able to be a part of his life was worth all the pain. I love him so very much. He will forever be in my heart.

So that is my story of the amazing son that I was fortunate to parent for eleven years. I know that each of you who read this has your own incredible story. I know that no matter how many years pass that I will still love him as you will love your loved one who died. Wes occupies a special place in my heart reserved only for him. My heart is big, though, and although it was broken several times during his short life, it has mended time and time again.

Isn't it time to mend your heart too? The following chapters tell you how I mended my broken heart. I hope that at least one of the techniques that I describe will help make your burden lighter, your days brighter, and your life more satisfying. I believe in you, and I know you can mend your broken heart just like I did mine. Good luck.

Prepare Siblings

There might be controversy about what I have to say concerning this issue, so please read and discern for yourself how you want to handle this issue. I know from my own experience that my children, who are in their twenties at this writing, developed into responsible, effective adults: perhaps because of how the illness and death of their sibling was handled.

My suggestion is fourfold for those who have a child with an illness. First, never keep anything a secret from siblings. Tell them what is happening on a level they understand. Involve them as much as possible with helping and supporting the sibling who has the illness. Second, at the same time, do not let the illness of the sibling interfere with the activities of the other children. If the other siblings have events in which parents need to participate to support them, and at the same time the ill child must be at the hospital, split duties or ask friends to help. When you use these two approaches, there are no secrets that cause anxiety and no resentment that all the family energy is focused on one child.

Third, do not get stuck in tradition. Be as flexible and adaptable as possible. Fourth, do not let the death of one child keep you from being a parent to your other children. Focus on the needs of your other children and create balance. Let me go over each and give examples.

First Suggestion:
Don't keep secrets.
Do be totally open with what is happening.

Secrets are never effective in a family where trust is a basic foundation. When everything is out in the open, each family member feels safe and comfortable. Why? The answer is because everyone feels a sense of belonging. Belonging is the very first, basic emotional need that a child must fulfill in order to feel a part of the family.

When a sibling hears adults whispering, is asked to leave the room while adults talk, or is told that the information is only for adults, the sibling feels left out, and the sense of belonging begins to decline. This creates anxiety in a sibling. When a sibling is anxious, he/she is more likely to act out. He may throw a tantrum. She may start wetting the bed. He may break things. She may hit peers. If a sibling is a teenager, he may not come home at curfew time. Her grades may drop. He may start drinking. She may try drugs. All of this may begin to happen because a child feels left out of the information loop in the family system. The sibling is not getting his/her basic emotional need of belonging, met within the family.

Let's take an example of this. My son was diagnosed with his brain tumor at age three. His siblings were one and five at the time. We let them know that Wes would be in the hospital, and he had a bump in his head that needed to be taken out. Mommy would be gone at times, but Daddy would be with them. Sometimes Mommy would be with them and Daddy would be gone. That was what they could understand at the time.

When Wes had to have another resection at age six, his siblings were four and eight. I wrote a story for them to explain what was happening and to help my son retain a positive, perceptual framework as he underwent his surgery. The story follows.

Wes's Dragon

Once upon a time, there was a brave, strong boy who had a dragon hiding in a cave in his head. The dragon caused the boy all sorts of discomforts. Sometimes the boy had headaches. Sometimes the boy threw up. Sometimes the boy was very cross and cranky.

The boy's name was Wes. He had a family that loved him very much. They wanted to help him to feel better. The only way for him to feel better was to go on a long journey inside his body. In order for Wes to go on this journey, he had to turn into a wee little person and disappear within himself. A magician was called to help with this magic trick.

The magician said some magic words, anointed his forehead with magic oil, made him prince of the Kingdom of Wesley, and gave him magical powers.

Then, the magician told him that he must select a dragon slayer that would be in charge of the expedition and help Wes to conquer the dragon that lived in his head. Wes knew of a doctor that slays dragons in children, so he went to see his friend, Dr. John, to ask him to go on the journey with him.

Wes's friend, Dr. John, was happy to help Wes on his journey. He suggested that they take his dragon-slaying team with them. The dragon-slaying team knew how to fight the dragon, so that the dragon would disappear from the cave. Wes agreed that Dr. John's idea was a good one. He knew when he allowed all the other people to become part of his journey that they would be in charge, and yet he wondered what his part would be, so he asked Dr. John. Dr. John told Wes that he had a very special part in slaying the dragon. He would be the team's scout. The scout's job was to find the dragon's cave and lead the team to it by shining a light on it so the team could slay the dragon. Wes agreed that he would accept the mission.

As Wes thought about this journey, he decided to call upon another friend to help him. He knew that no matter where he was, that he had one friend that he could always count on. He looked up to heaven and smiled at God. He asked God to be by his side as he went on this journey to slay the dragon within him. The sun shone brightly upon Wes. Wes knew God had replied that he was right there with him every step of the way. In his mind, Wes remembered the words to a song. The words said that when we are climbing a mountain, we can make it if we take one step at a time, with Jesus by our side. He felt comforted.

In order to prepare for his journey into himself, Wes needed to go to a hospital where he would be put to sleep so that he and the team could enter the Kingdom of Wesley. Wes felt like running away at first, because he really did not know what the journey would be like. But he knew no matter how far he ran, he would always have the dragon in the cave in his head. So he decided to stay and fight this dragon with all the strength and bravery he had within him.

At the hospital, there were a lot of people who came to help Wes prepare for the journey. They had swords and pokers and needles. All these things helped Wes to begin the journey. Even though he felt scared inside, he knew that these people were helping him to fight the dragon within him. They explained to him that one of the best ways to fight the dragon was to take big, deep breaths when he felt scared. He thought about the bravery that was discovered by the lion in the Wizard of Oz, and he puffed out his chest to show his courage.

When Dr. John had assembled his team, it was time for the journey to begin. Early one morning, Wes prepared to go within himself with the aid of the dragon-slaying team. In order to become a wee little person and go inside himself, he had to go to sleep. One of the members of the team came to Wes and gave him a shot to help start the journey. Wes's mom and dad let him know that they knew he was a brave and strong boy, who could fight the dragon with all the courage and strength he had. They wanted him to remember that when they were not with him that God would be by his side always to help him through any dark moments that he would come across on his journey. Wes took many big, deep breaths and as he fell asleep, he began his journey to slay the dragon.

As he started to drift off to sleep, he felt himself shrinking, and as if by magic, he was inside himself. He was now in the Kingdom of Wesley. He was a prince and the scout for the expedition to slay the dragon. He *looked around. What is all this grey, hilly terrain? Oh, yes. He was inside his brain, because the dragon lived inside a cave in his brain. As he peeked around the corner, he saw more and more hills. He had been given magical powers, so he wished for a flashlight, and one appeared in his hand. He took a deep breath and ventured one step towards a roaring sound that was coming from the darkness ahead.*

Wes wondered why he was alone, and yet he felt someone was right beside him. Then he remembered that, although he could not see God, God was at his side. Then he began to hear voices. It was his dragon-slaying team, preparing to help. He could not see them, but he knew they were there ready to help him when he shone the light on the cave. He ventured on toward the roaring sound. Slowly, one step at a time, he climbed the hills and walked through the valleys and squeezed through the tiny crevices. The roaring sound became louder as he continued. He also heard another sound. It was the sound of drills. He knew that his team was hard at work. As he rounded a great grey mass, he saw what looked like a river. Gazing around, he spied a boat. He pushed the boat into the river and set out in the direction of the drilling.

As he drifted downstream, he decided that he needed a sword just to be sure he was protected. He wished for a sword, and it was in his hand. A voice told him that this was the magic sword of courage and light. With God beside him and a sword in his hand, he felt more secure. Calmly, he relaxed in the boat as he drifted. Soon, along the banks of the river, he began to see people. They were waving their hands at him and shouting, "You can do it, Wes! You can slay that dragon! We know you can do it!" Then they cheered and cheered for him. Wes felt good inside. It gave him confidence to know that many people believed in his ability to slay the dragon.

Suddenly, the boat began to rock, and the waters became rough. The terrain along the sides of the river was moving as if an earthquake was in progress. Wes held tight to the boat. He knew that the dragon-slaying team was approaching the Kingdom of Wesley so they could get to the dragon in the cave. He reached for the sword of courage and light, held it up, and said, "I have the power and the courage to help slay the dragon." A flash of light spread through the Kingdom of Wesley, and Wes was filled with courage. As the light began to shine, he spied the cave. His light led the dragon-slaying team to the entrance. The dragon-slaying team assaulted the cave where the dragon lived. They used their mighty swords that gleamed and sparkled from the courage and light of Wes's powerful sword.

Breathing deeply, Wes held the sword high. The team of dragon slayers worked slowly and cautiously to remove the dragon from the cave. Wes watched as the dragon clung to the sides. That did not stop the team. The team carefully cut some of the cave away to be sure they got the whole dragon. It breathed fire at Wes and the team. This did not stop them. They increased their determination. Finally, Wes squeezed his sword and a lightning bolt from the sword flew through the air and struck the dragon. The dragon let go of the cave walls and tumbled to the ground. Wes watched as at last the dragon was captured and lifted out of the cave. Wes heard cheers of success as the dragon-slaying team disappeared with the dragon into the darkness. He felt a sense of relief. He knew that he had helped to take the dragon out of the cave by holding his powerful sword of courage and light in the air.

As the sword began to lose its light and he sat down

in his boat, he heard more cheers from the crowds along the river banks. He knew he had accomplished his mission. He sat back and relaxed in his boat. God bathed him in a cool spray of mist so that he felt refreshed and relaxed as he sailed further down the river. Soon, he fell asleep, and when he awoke, he was again his normal size and back in the hospital room with the dragon-slaying team by his side. He had made the journey inside himself. He was weak and tired, but felt a great sense of courage and power. His team smiled at him and told him to grow strong, for they had one more step to go.

The next step was to spray for the eggs that the dragon had left behind. They had taken the dragon away, but her eggs would hatch if they did not eliminate them. Wes knew that he must develop more courage for the next journey. He felt sure he could conquer the next step with his powerful sword of courage and light and with God by his side. He would take one step at a time. For now though, Wes fell asleep and rested easily, for he knew that he must become strong again in order to win the battle against the dragon that lived within him.

This story spoke to them in a medium that they were familiar with each day. At school, they either read themselves or were read to by their teachers. They seemed to understand and feel empowered each time they read or heard the story.

At the time of the third resection, Wes was nine, and his siblings were seven and eleven. By this time, it was not a surprise to them and was part of what their lives consisted of, due to having a sibling with cancer. We sat down at dinner one evening and told them that the MRI had shown that

Wes had another tumor, and he must have another operation. They asked questions, and we answered as best we could with the information we had.

The fourth time was when we were told that an operation would not be effective and that he would die within a few months. Wes was eleven, his sister was nine, and his brother was thirteen. We did not keep this from Wes. Nor did we keep this information from his siblings. I had someone stay with Wes while I had my meetings with the schools and with Wes's best friend's mom. After lunch, I sat down with Wes and let him know what was going to happen so he would be prepared when we told his siblings that evening. What I said was not perfect. It merely came from my heart and from all the knowledge I had about what children need when faced with the fear of the unknown. I turned on a tape recorder so that his father could later hear what I had said to him.

Telling Wes

September 24, 1993

I use drawings in my therapy with children, so using a drawing to talk to Wes about what was going to happen to him was natural for me. Thus, I brought the news to him through a symbolic representation in a picture that I drew for him.

I drew a blue house representing the sadness that I was feeling. Then I drew the sun with sunbeams streaming from it in the corner of the picture with only a fourth showing. This symbolized happiness yet not as much happiness as could have been present. I put three grey clouds overlapping in the sky, representing the three surgeries that always saddened us and blocked the sunshine from our family. I drew three lightning bolts, one coming down from each cloud, representing the shock that each of his surgeries had given to our family. I drew a tree with fall colors, representing the beauty of life and also the knowledge that life was coming to an end. I drew blue grass around the house, representing the fact that the earth would be blue without him.

We discussed the picture. He said that it was a weird picture because it was thundering and lightning and yet, the sun was shining. He acknowledged that the house looked like our house. He said the house needed a chimney, but instead of drawing a chimney, he drew three red hearts around the house. We talked about how the house in the picture was filled with love, just as our house was full of love. Then I talked about the symptoms he had been having and the fact that we had gone to the doctor recently. He said with a matter-of-fact attitude, "I'm going to have another surgery, right?" I told him that they could not do another surgery because of where the tumor was located. He quickly asked, "What are they going to do about it?"

My heart was breaking as I told him, "Like in this picture, sometimes we are down here on Earth with the rain and the storms. And then sometimes we go to heaven. So sometime, you're going to go to heaven, and you will have to leave us. God must be calling you to heaven with him." He merely said, "Okay." I asked if he had known this for a long time. With an uncanny confidence, he just said, "Um hum." I added that God was always in his heart and God would always watch over him. Then I broke down and cried.

His first response was to take care of me. He asked if I wanted a tissue. He got up and went to the next room to get one for me. I told him I appreciated him watching over me. I wanted to be sure that he understood, so I asked him what he thought I was saying to him. He said, "That someday I am going to have to go to heaven." I added, "That might be pretty soon. You will be going to heaven because God will be calling you. You will know when that is because you will hear God calling you. I want you to remember this picture, though, because you will be up in heaven, and we will be on Earth, thinking about you and loving you." I went on to tell him that lots of people really respected and admired him because he had courage.

Wes began to respond in a symbolic way. He redirected me to the picture. He said, "Where is the rain? That's another thing I noticed, no rain." I asked if he wanted to draw some rain on the picture. He said that he did. I asked if he wanted the color blue to draw the rain. He said that blue would be fine. Then came the symbolism. He said, "I can't make tear drops very good." He acknowledged that the raindrops he was drawing under each cloud were really teardrops and that he was sad. He drew them in three and then in five, and then three again and then five. I assumed that the three represented his belonging as a sibling and the five represented his belonging in our family.

Then I reframed the symbolism for him. I stated, "Sometimes it has to rain here on Earth to make the rainbow, doesn't it?" I then asked him if he wanted to draw a rainbow. He did, so we drew the rainbow together. He clapped when we were finished.

I wanted him to have some sense of control, so I gave him choices. I told him that we needed to tell Tony and Ali that he would be leaving us and going to heaven. I gave him some choices about how we could do that. He spoke very softly with his answer to the choices. He wanted me to make his favorite meal and, after dinner, gather in the living room and talk about it.

Then I sensed that he needed to be comforted, so I gave him the security of being in my arms. He gave a great big sigh. I asked him what he was feeling, but he could not express it in words. So I said, "Come here and let me hug you." He sat in my lap, and I hugged him and kissed him on his temple. I talked about something safe and pleasant for him. I said, "Remember those stories I used to tell you about walking through the woods? Maybe we can tell a lot of those stories. Maybe you can tell me some stories about walking through the woods too? You think?" When I would put Wes to bed, he would often crawl up into my lap in the rocking chair and ask me to make up a story. I would start the story by saying, "One day, I was walking through the woods and ... " Each time, I would tell him a different adventure about what happened when I was walking through the woods. We live on forty acres, so we had lots of woods, and he was familiar with walking through the woods.

Wes began to take control so he could remain powerful. He said, "How about let's change that." I said, "How would we change that?" He said, "One day, I was walking in the house, not in the woods." I said, "Well, we could do that." Then he changed his mind and said that he thought it should be "into the forest." Then I confirmed that would work. He laughed.

Next, I begin to build him up so he had the self-confidence to be resilient, even in the face of death. I said to him, "I want you to know that you are never alone. God is always right there with you. I will be here with you as long as I can, and you'll just have to reach out and ask me for help whenever you need it. You tried very, very hard to get rid of those tumors in your head. And you really, really fought, real good for so long, and I am very proud of you. You have great courage. We need to hang on to each other a lot, so Ali and Tony may want to hug you a lot more than usual, but they need to do that. They'll need to hug you because it will be hard for them to say good-bye to you and let you go."

He took another big sigh. I gave him permission to do what he needed to do. I told him that it was okay if he needed to talk about it, and it was okay if he needed to cry. I reminded him of the Psalty tapes that said that heaven was a wonderful place. He started to hug me tightly. I kissed him on the temple again. I redirected him to his big bear that was given to him when he was in the hospital for the first time. He took that bear and Brave Heart Lion with him every time he went to the hospital. We talked about how brave he always was.

Because fear of the unknown is the greatest fear, I give him another chance to ask questions. He had none. Then I turned control over to him to ask for what he needed. And he did. I said, "Well, if you do have questions, will you please ask me? Okay? And if there is something that you want to do please tell me so we can do it." He immediately replied with,

"Can we play a game of Sorry?" This was symbolic in two ways. First, I believe it represented the fact that he was sorry he had to leave our family. Second, he knew it was my favorite game. So I gave him a choice about where he wanted to play it.

So Wes added to my picture the hearts representing love. He added the raindrops, representing his sadness about leaving his siblings and his family. He added the rainbow, representing the connection between heaven and earth, and the hope that heaven would be a beautiful and colorful place for him. In Wes's world, there had always been love. The reality was that there had always been sadness too. There had been hope that he would get better and live a long, healthy life. There had been beauty because he saw the world as beautiful and accepted his life for what it was. There had been a brilliant array of colors in his attitude, his activities, and his ardor for life. He was an amazing little boy. It was unfortunate that he would not grow up to be an amazing man.

This was the most difficult task in my life with which I will ever be challenged. This selfless, amazing child responded to my sadness as I began to cry by getting up and going to Tony's room to bring me the tissue box. My heart was aching. We played our game of Sorry, read, went to the park to play on the playground equipment, took a walk, and finally, he took a nap. I sat by his side and watched him sleep, knowing that there would be only a few more days that I would have the privilege of watching him sleep.

That evening, we gathered in our living room after dinner. I sat on the floor with Wes in my lap. Because of all the radiation and chemotherapy he had endured, he was a tiny boy. His sister, at nine, towered above him. We told them that we needed to share something with them. I told them that within a few months, God would be calling Wes to heaven. I asked Wes to share what he told me about what he thought heaven would be like. He said that he thought heaven would be like a big, big castle with a huge playground and rooms and rooms full of Legos. He was a master at Lego construction. He could construct ships and buildings built from Legos in a very short time. A few tears were shed by all of us. We hugged each other and spent the rest of the evening playing games and watching a movie.

Secrets only make people anxious. Fear of the unknown is the very worst fear. It creates a helpless, hopeless feeling. I never wanted my children to experience that anxiety. So my first suggestion is that you let your child, as well as your child's siblings, know what is happening every step of the way. Be sure to do this at a communication level that each can understand, depending on the age of each child.

Second Suggestion:

Do not let the illness of one child
interfere with other siblings' activities.
Do let siblings live a normal life by
participating in activities that
build their self-confidence.

Before I start this section, I want you to know that you cannot do this suggestion alone. You need a mate and/or friends to make it happen. Do not try to do everything yourself. It is impossible. This is the time to let others help you. When you let others do things for you, you allow them to have really good feelings about themselves. So spread the good feelings by asking your relatives or friends to take on some responsibility for you.

Let me give you an example of letting friends help. My friend Peggy, who is one of the most giving women I know, helped more than I can ever repay. Even though she had three girls who were involved in many activities, she offered to take my daughter to ice skating lessons, piano lessons, and dance lessons. My daughter never missed an activity because I asked others to assist me in creating a normal life for Wes's siblings.

Sometimes it was necessary to send only one parent to an activity, and the other would stay home. If only one parent exists in the household, there is another opportunity to ask a friend to help and allow that friend to feel needed. This way the ill child gets his/her needs met, and the siblings get attention too.

Here is an example of keeping things normal. When I was away with Wes for five weeks when he underwent an autologous bone marrow transplant, my husband took Wes's sister and brother to the state fair and a rodeo. They took the camcorder and filmed their adventures. They sent the video for Wes and me to watch. Yes, Wes and I were many miles away, and I am sure we were missed, yet they kept their lives normal and at the same time, they shared their adventures with their sibling who was far away. Today with so many communication devices like webcams, it would be quite easy to keep in touch when the family is apart.

Third Suggestion:
Do not get stuck in tradition
Do be flexible and adaptable.

If you are a person who has to do the same traditional sequence of events year after year, then you will be unhappy most of the time if you have a chronically ill or terminally ill child or if your child dies. Sometimes it would be necessary to stay at home instead of visiting relatives on holidays, because Wes's blood counts were low and we did not want to expose him to germs that he would not be able to fight. We never knew when we could or would be able to visit. This taught my family to make our own fun, and, if all went well, we could also visit relatives. After Wes died, we made new traditions for our family to follow during holidays so we could be happy even without his presence.

I believe this had a great deal to do with how my children presently respond to planning in their lives. They want a structure, and at the same time, they want flexibility within the structure. They grew up living with that style of responding to their world. It made them adaptable.

Fourth Suggestion:

Do not let the death of one child keep you
from being a parent to your other children.
Do focus on the needs of your other
children and create balance.

I remember that I promised myself as I looked
at Wes in his coffin that I would never let his death
affect how I would be as a mother to my other children. I have often heard from parents who lose a
child that it is difficult to be a parent to the other
children because of the grief that they feel for the
dead child. What an unfair concept. As if it is not
enough for it to be totally unfair in life for a child
to die and a sibling to lose a sister or brother, it is
also unfair for the surviving siblings to get less of a
mother or father because of that death.

When children do not feel the value that a
parent's love creates, then the children are at risk
for acting-out behaviors. If I had focused only on
Wes's death, then Tony might have not felt valued,
and he could have turned to drugs or alcohol. If I
had focused only on Wes's death, then Ali might
not have felt valued, and she could have become
sexually active and gotten pregnant or dropped out
of school. I loved them so that each would feel valued. When children feel valued, they experience a
sense of self-worth. When children have a sense
of self-worth, confidence develops. At the end of
this chapter, you will see how Wes's siblings have
become successful young adults, due probably to
how they felt valued.

A Sister's Reflection

When my daughter, Ali, was a sophomore in high school, she wrote the following story for an English class. With her permission, I have included it. What it shows is that her childhood was normal, even with a sibling with cancer. She learned from her experience with Wes to be present to the moment, to spread joy to people, and to cherish each day.

My Precious Angel

By: Ali Esterly

November 21, 2000

"Are you two twins?" The department store lady asked my brother and me.

"No," my mom replied for us, "they are brother and sister, but they are two years apart." My brother and I just giggled and went about playing under the clothes racks.

"Let's go," my mom told us. So we followed her out with our white hair bouncing as we ran after her.

My brother, Wes, and I were the best of friends. We did everything together and rarely would you ever find us apart. We were definitely two peas in a pod. We looked after each other, and I never thought about what I would do without him. I did not need to because I thought we would be together forever.

When Wes was three and I was one, my parents found out that he had cancer, a tumor in his brain. The doctors were able to remove the tumor and said he was going to live. He did live, and we started growing up together.

I remember my first day of preschool like it was yesterday. I was going to Montessori school, and although I was happy about going, I was really shy. I was afraid of going to a strange place with strange people. Wes had already gone to Montessori for two years before me. He told me everything would be all right, and he would look out for me. I felt content then, and I loved going to school with him. We played together at recess, sang songs together, ate snacks together, took naps together, and, most importantly, looked out for each other.

During that year, Wes's cancer was getting worse. He missed a lot of school because he had to be in the hospital. So my parents thought it would be best for him to repeat kindergarten. This was all right with me because I did not want him to go to a different school. I did not know what I would do without him.

So we had another happy year together. We went trick or treating, played house, watched movies, played video games, read stories together, and went along happily with our lives. But soon it was time for him to move on to the first grade. I was a big kindergartner by then, and I could pretty much take care of myself. But I really missed him during the school day. It was just not the same without him. I could not wait until I was in first grade, and we could go to school together again.

Wes got along just fine that year and everyone in first grade loved Wes. He was a one-of-a-kind character. He was the sweetest thing you would ever meet. He was always ready and willing to help anyone out or give anyone a friendly hello. If you asked any of his teachers about him, they would always say with a smile on their face, "Wes has really touched my life." He was *a good friend and a good person. I did not think bad things could happen to good people.*

We grew up and grew closer. I could tell him anything and in return, he understood me. It is amazing how two siblings could get along as well as we did.

Wes had been in and out of the hospital through elementary school, but he always handled it very well. He would always have a smile on his face when I came to visit him, and he was never in a bad mood. He would make the best of being in the hospital whenever possible. He brought movies to watch, played games, and never got down or lost hope. He always told me not to worry, and he would be out of the hospital in no time. He always was. Well, almost always.

By Wes's fifth grade year his cancer was spreading immensely. The doctors had no control over it, and although they had done everything they could, that would not be enough. I was in fourth grade then and I did not understand death, and I did not want to.

My parents sat my family down one windy, October night and told us the bad news. Wes only had six weeks to live. Six weeks to live? I did not understand. How could one moment Wes be there and the next he would be gone forever? I did not want to believe them, and I told myself that he would get better. He had to. What would I do without him?

Those last six weeks were the hardest time I have ever experienced. I knew that everyday was one less day I got to spend with my brother, my companion, my best friend. I did not want to accept the fact he was going to die. What would I do with that hole in my life? That hole could never be replaced. Not by anyone, no matter how much I needed fulfillment.

I acted like everything was all right. I went about playing with Wes like we always had. I treasured every moment that we got to be together. I had to; what else could I do?

The end of six weeks was approaching, and Wes had to stay home from school. I did not want him to stay home and be bored and think about dying. I wanted to be with him to take his mind off it. But dying did not seem to bother him. He knew he was going to go to heaven, and he was glad to be going somewhere better. He was going somewhere he could run and play and spread his joy. He told me if I wanted to find God, he would always be in my heart. God was sure in his heart and he had spread God's love everywhere he had gone.

One dark, October night, Wes's cancer had gotten worse. My parents rushed him to the hospital. He only had a few days to live. No, I thought, how could this be? How could six weeks be over so fast? What was I going to do without him? I was brought with my older brother, Tony, to see Wes for the last time. My whole family and many friends were there and the hospital was chaotic. Everyone was crying and hugging each other. But I could not cry. I still thought he would be all right. It had not hit me yet that he would be gone in just a few hours.

I got to see him one last time before he died. I went up to his bed and saw that little boy I had gone to pre-school with just years before. I remembered how he made me laugh, made me smile, and now how he made me cry. Although he could not talk to me, I bent down, kissed him on the forehead, and whispered, "Goodbye, Wes. I love you." He looked so much at peace, and I know that is how he died.

My life has never been the same since that moment. I have accepted death, and I know Wes is as happy as ever. I have realized that life is precious and I cannot control what will happen. I have learned to live every day to the fullest and be the absolute best person I can be. Wes has taught me to spread joy to everyone and cherish each and every day.

I miss Wes more than anyone can know, but I have moved on with my life. I do not look back and cry. I look back and I am happy because I can remember all of the good times we shared. I do not even have a hole in my life because I know that he is always with me. He is looking out for me because he is now my precious angel.

A Brother's Praise

I recently found a biography Tony wrote on March 3, 2001, for a singing group he was in during college. One of the questions on the biography was: Who is your favorite hero and why? Tony merely answered it in this way: "My younger brother (deceased) because he showed me what courage really is."

Results

How did what we did with our children affect them? Did they get angry and ruin their lives? Did they give up hope? Did they blame God? No. They both attended a Catholic high school. They both went to college and did graduate work. Both children are now in their twenties. Tony and Ali grew up to be successful young adults. As I share the following about what my children have done with their lives, judge for yourself.

Tony

Tony went to a Catholic high school. In high school, Tony played sports and acted in plays. He played football in the fall, basketball in the winter, and during the spring he changed it up. His freshman and sophomore years, he played baseball. His junior year, he played golf. His senior year, he ran track. He also was in four musicals. He had the male lead his junior and senior years. He participated in choir and went to district contest as well as state choir. He was in National Honor Society. His senior year, he received the Father Helias Award for loyalty, service, and character.

In college, Tony participated in an a cappella singing group. He wrote a song for the group and received a national award for it at a competition the group attended. He was in a fraternity. He played lacrosse. He graduated magna cum laude. After receiving a degree in biology, he went to pharmacy school. He is now a pharmacist. He is married.

Ali

Ali also went to a Catholic high school. In high school, Ali played sports and acted in plays. She played golf in the fall. Her freshman and sophomore years, she was a cheerleader in the winter. Her junior and senior years, she was on the dance team that performed at halftime of the basketball games. In the spring, she ran track. She was in four musicals. She had the female lead in her junior and senior years. She was in National Honor Society.

In college, she was in a sorority. She graduated

summa cum laude. After receiving a degree in journalism, she attended a portfolio school, traveled, and plans to be an art director for an advertising agency.

I believe that allowing my children to be in the information loop about what was happening to their brother made them resilient people. I believe creating a normal environment in which they could thrive helped make them self-confident. I believe that creating flexibility around Wes's needs helped them to be adaptable.

Review

To help siblings weather the storm of the death of a sibling or the experience of living with a chronically ill or terminally ill child, do the following: Don't keep secrets. Do be totally open with what is happening. Do not let the illness of one child interfere with other siblings' activities. Do let siblings live a normal life by participating in activities that build their self-confidence. Do not get stuck in tradition. Do be flexible and adaptable. Do not let the death of one child keep you from being a parent to your other children. Do focus on the needs of your other children and create balance.

So my suggestion is that you not only think about the child who is chronically ill or terminally ill or who has died but also think about the siblings of the child. Your grief does not have to stop you from being the amazing parent you can be. I know from experience that it may be difficult at times to balance, but it is not impossible. You can grieve and still be the best parent to the children who are still with you. Believe in yourself. It's time to mend your broken heart.

Start mending by learning how to survive. Often it is like walking through a fog when you lose a loved one. How does one come out of the mist and see clearly? The next chapter will answer that question.

My Brother, My Hero

Hugs for Brother

Ninja Buddies

Soccer Support

My Buddy, My Brother

Shakespeare Nymphs
A Midsummer Night's Dream

Thumbs up for Sister

Dance Recital

Bedtime Stories

Christmas Hugs

Learn to Survive

What does it take to survive a broken heart? Questioning yourself will help. At first, you may want to curl up under the covers and never get up. You can do that, if you choose, for a short time. Then you have a big choice. Do I get up or stay in bed? Once you have made the decision to get up, there is another choice. Do I walk through the fog for a while or get back in bed? Yes, there will be fog. It is like living life in a gray mist where there are no colors. You know you are awake and walking through life, but all you see is haze. Things are not clear. Your tolerance of ambiguity and uncertainty will help you participate in your everyday life. If you tolerate the fog long enough, the fog will start to clear, and you will begin to see some colors in your world. They will be pale at first. Eventually, you will get back the rainbow colors of life. When you get the vibrant colors of the rainbow back, then you are on your way to mending your broken heart. So how do you go through this process? Let's talk about some things that may help.

Hibernating

Hibernating is helpful at first. When you experience sorrow, closing off the world at first to repair may be helpful. Your body is in shock. Sometimes you may feel suspended in air. Sometimes you may feel as if your world is moving in slow motion. Sometimes you may feel nervous, and your body may even shake. Sometimes you may have ringing in your ears from crying. Sometimes you may be confused. Sometimes you may stare off into space and lose minutes or hours. Sometimes you may cry uncontrollably for what seems like no reason. So at first, hibernating may be just what you need. Pay close attention to your own process of moving through the shock. Do not be impatient with yourself. The depth of your sorrow signifies the depth of your love.

However, you can take positive steps as you hibernate. A friend who lost his beautiful, loving wife at an early age told me that "busy is good medicine." He has a point. At first, you can choose to "get busy" doing anything. I remember that I redid my child's room. I made it into a guest room/ office for me/memorial. I bought a daybed with little angels on the ironwork so I could curl up and rest and it could be made into a king-size bed for guests. I put my computer desk there so I could work. I put a recliner so I could read. I hung all his baby pictures I had taken from his first five years of life. I hung a print of a picture of a guardian angel, watching over two children crossing a stream. I busied myself creating an atmosphere in that room that allowed me to find peace there. From there, I did other busywork. I just kept busy without thinking. Thinking was too painful. Just being busy worked. So one thing you can do is keep busy.

Keeping Busy with Purpose

Once keeping busy without thinking does not work any longer, you can choose to shift gears. One possibility you can choose at this point is to make the busywork purposeful. Redirecting your time and energy toward something that has meaning to you helps you get out of your own misery and focus on the outer world. What, in essence, you are doing is giving purpose to your time and energy.

One of the best ways to stop thinking about your own sorrow is to serve others, thus giving your time and energy purpose. You can choose to volunteer. In all communities, there are volunteer agencies just waiting for someone to help. Before volunteering, ask yourself, "What volunteer work would mean something to me?" Perhaps you love dogs or cats and want to volunteer at the local humane society. Perhaps you have loved ones who have heart disease, and you want to volunteer for your local heart association. Perhaps you love to work with children, and you volunteer at your church to teach Sunday school. Volunteer for a cause that has some kind of meaning to you.

I remembered that education was very meaningful to me since at one time I was a high school teacher. I volunteered to run for election to the school board of the private high school my children would attend. Fortunately, I was elected. I invested my time and efforts in the quality education of children in the community.

Keeping Busy with Passions

Another way you can choose to make the busywork purposeful is to do something that makes you passionate. For instance, I love photography. When I have a camera in my hands and am shooting photos, I am a happy camper. When I work with those photos to make an album, to design collages, to create a scrapbook, to give to friends and relatives, or any number of projects, I feel happy. I use my passion for photography to find purpose.

Here are some more ideas to get you thinking. You may love to act, so join the local theatre group. You may love to garden, so make a new garden that is different than you have ever made before. You may love to paint, so paint, even if it is a room in your house and not a picture. You may love to cook, so join a gourmet cooking club, or merely make food for neighbors. You may love to play sports, so join a local competitive team. You may love to sew, so make something and either give it to a charity to raffle or sell it on consignment. There are hundreds of things to be passionate about. Discover your passions.

The major purpose, other than filling time, is to be doing something that creates joy in you. So about what are you passionate? What really creates joy in your life as you do it? Discover that and then go out and do it. Do it for you. Do it because it makes you feel alive. Do it because it takes you from the gray area to the brilliant colors of the rainbow. Do it because it will help you walk out of the fog into the sunshine.

At this point, you are volunteering, you are performing a passion, yet you still feel really, really sad.

After giving your time and energy purpose, what's next? Next is opening yourself up to those who are around you. Yes, that is scary. You close yourself off emotionally to others in order to keep your energy for just staying alive. Volunteering and performing a passion has gotten you back into the world. Now, you begin to realize that there are other people in that world. Yes, you knew they were there, but you probably did not spend a lot of emotional energy on them. Now you realize that interacting could be helpful. So you begin to interact with others from a center-of-the-universe perspective.

The Succinct Speech

Most of the time, it is all about you when you first start interacting again. You will tend to think that people will feel sorry for you, and that is the last thing that you want them to feel about you. So many times you might avoid doing things when asked. That will not help you. People around you care enough to ask about how you are doing. You reply with something simple so you do not have to bother them with the real details about just how awful you feel. That is called "putting on your public face." You keep things at a surface level. That is totally fine at first for getting yourself integrated into the public again. You just need to get out there. If a person asks you to have lunch, go. Talk about what feels comfortable to you. Be honest. If you just want to talk about surface things, redirect the conversation when it gets to how you are doing. The most important part here is to just get out and interact with people. Yes, it will be hard at first. Just start. Then go from there.

I am thankful that three women asked me to go to lunch with them monthly for quite a while after Wes died. I felt like their special project, and I was happy to be the special project. They did not ask me questions about how I was doing. They just let me enjoy being with them in a social setting. Their caring enough to invite me spoke volumes to me.

The scary part is when you feel comfortable with others and then they tell you to stop saying you are okay because they really want to know how you "really" are. Interacting with emotions is like walking over a gorge on a swinging bridge. You need to go slowly and cautiously so you do not fall. Falling would be breaking down in some public place. Pretty scary.

Sometimes people who care will catch you off guard at odd places. They hit you with, "How are you *really* doing?" You know they genuinely care and are concerned about you, yet you still feel fragile. You do not want to break down and tell them in the setting in which they caught you. So here is a way to handle that.

One way to handle this is to have a condensed version of how you are "really" doing ready for those people who do care and who, unfortunately, address this issue in public. Make it a five-step comment that takes under one minute. Let's say you are in a restaurant having lunch with a friend, and she says, "Rita, tell me how you are *really* doing." Here is an example of what you might say. You are still in a stage of grief in which you could break down and cry any moment. You might say, "Sally, I appreciate you asking. I have times when I feel sad. I have times when I feel lost. I have times when my thoughts race. I have times when I just want my life to feel normal again. I know that eventually my joy will return. Just being here with you today having lunch helps that joy come back to me."

Let's look in depth at what you have done by saying these sentences. First, use the person's name, because it makes him/her feel that he/she is connected with you, and that is exactly why the person is asking. The person desires to feel connected with you. Second, show appreciation. Third, use "feeling words" because the person is really asking how you feel. Fourth, use an optimistic statement, because they want to know you will feel better eventually. Fifth, let the person know how he/she is helping you to feel better. When you let the person know how his/her friendship helps you, then it turns the focus of attention back on that person.

If you use this formula, you are less likely to feel as if you are going to break down in public. This may not be the formula you use when you are visiting with a friend at your home. You may want to share deep feelings and cry. In public, it is more effective to use the above formula. When you cry in public, it is less likely you will want to continue to go out to lunch with friends. So help yourself reenter the public arena by having your succinct speech prepared.

Let me give you a few other examples of the above formula when time has passed and you are traversing the steps of grief effectively. You are at a social gathering at a coworker's house, and a friend asks you how you are "really" doing. Say something like, "John, thanks for asking. My feelings vary between sad, lost, frustrated, and plain miserable.

However, I have more days that I feel happy than days that I feel sad. I know that those happy days will soon outweigh the sad ones. You help those happy days increase when we play golf."

Here is another one. You are at the grocery store, and a friend asks you how you are "really" doing. You are in the resolution stage of grief and are feeling much better. "Sam, thanks for caring. Although I still miss Wes, I realized that I needed to put some energy into being happier. I have always wanted a garden, so I rented a plot of land at the community garden spot and have planted vegetables. When I am messing with the dirt, I feel happy. I would love to bring you some tomatoes when they start growing. It would make me happy to see people I like enjoying what I have raised. I will call you when the tomatoes are ripe."

So the idea here is to be able to feel secure at being in public even when caring people ask you how you are "really" doing. When you have a formula for responding to people, you are more likely to continue to desire to interact in a social environment. I remember that I used to go to the grocery store at late hours of the night or early hours of the morning just to avoid people. Eventually, I knew I could not continue to do that, so I created this succinct speech to help me get back to doing things at a normal time.

Being Alone

So another real struggle is to deal with your grief when you are alone. You also have a choice here. Let's discuss ways to handle your grief at those times when the tears just attack you out of nowhere. First, remember to surrender to the attack. Allow it to wash over you like a wave. Think of being on a beach and a big wave comes in and rushes over you. Remember, a wave comes in and it goes back out. As the wave comes in, let it. It will eventually go back out.

But what if it doesn't follow that pattern and it stays? What will you do then with this untraditional wave pattern? You can choose to take charge. When the wave of sorrow comes in, it creates emotions in you. Once you get this emotional high, you can choose to distract yourself. Later in this book, I will teach you a longer method of de-escalation. Right now, though, you just want to survive in the fog. The opposite of being highly emotional is to be calm and tranquil. So what do you do to make that wave of emotionality go back out to sea? You relax.

After surrendering and letting the wave of emotionality wash over you, the second thing you do is calm yourself by creating a peaceful environment. Here is one idea among many to help you do that. Use your five senses to create peacefulness within you. Using the five senses in combination often helps you to weather a highly emotional mood. This idea may sound silly to you, but do try it sometime. Let me give you an example of how to do that.

Sound: Use music to soothe the soul. Put on a comforting music selection. I use the classics such as Bach or Mozart. Play any music that comforts you.

Smell: Light a scented candle and smell the relaxing fragrance. Your favorite smell would be most comforting. I use cinnamon because it is most comforting to me. Watch the flame flicker for a few moments.

Taste: Sip the delicate taste of something that

you enjoy. I do not recommend eating anything, just drinking something that you enjoy such as a cup of tea or a glass of lemonade. I enjoy a cup of cinnamon coffee. Just enjoy the taste of something.

Sight: Focus on an object that has meaning to you and just drink in the colors, the texture, the symbolism, the memories, or whatever comes to mind. I use a butterfly magnet. Allow yourself to be present to the object by focusing on the aspects of it in the present moment, then let it take you to memories, then let it bring you back to the present moment.

Touch: Put something in your hand to touch. You may choose to use a ball you can squeeze, a feather or a piece of furry material, or whatever feels comforting to you. With the ball, you can squeeze it as tightly as you need to, thus releasing some tenseness from inside. With the feather or something furry, you can stroke it for comfort as you would a cat sitting in your lap. If you have a cat or a lap dog, petting can bring great comfort. In the last fifteen years, the research on the therapeutic power of pets has suggested that animals provide a constant source of comfort and help focus attention on the present.

Do this until the wave has gone back out to sea and your emotional level has calmed. It may take a long time at first. After using this technique, you will notice that the duration of such waves will reduce.

Expectations Based on You, Not on Others

One helpful rule to live by is to base expectations on yourself and not others. It simply has to do with the fact that you control your own behavior. You do not control the behavior of others. You cannot control the fact that people will ask how you are doing. You cannot control whether or not they will feel sorry for you. You cannot control the fact that some people will not want to talk to you because they do not know what to say to you. You cannot control the fact that people might be afraid to talk to you because if you get emotional they won't know what to do. And, most of all, you cannot control the fact that someone very close to you has died. You only have the power to control how you respond to your situation. So when you think about venturing out to interact with others, you can choose to base your expectations on your own behavior and not the behavior of others.

What you do control is how you handle whatever happens to you, and that needs to be based on your expectation of you and not others. For instance, you might expect yourself to smile at people when you see them, instead of expecting them to talk to you first. You might expect yourself to ask how that person is, instead of expecting them to ask how you are. You might expect yourself to ask someone to go to lunch with you, instead of waiting for others to invite you. When you accept an invitation to lunch, expect yourself to give a brief statement about how you are feeling and then redirect your friend to other areas of conversation. Remember that the principle here is to base all your expectations on your own behavior. Do not expect anything of anyone else. When you do this, you decrease your disappointment in life.

Possibilities and Opportunities

Usually, when you think of being in a fog, you picture this gray mist of dismal, colorless aura-like ashes in the fireplace. After experiencing the death of a loved one, it might seem that all your dreams and hopes have gone up in smoke and left you with the ashes. I would like to help you see the gray area, or those ashes, in a new way.

Let's think of the gray area as a place between black and white, or between dark and light, where all the possibilities or opportunities exist. If you consider the gray area to be the land of possibilities and opportunities, then your mind is open to what "can be," and you have changed your thinking from negative to positive. Remember, you can choose to have different thoughts anytime you want to, because thoughts are under your control.

Here's an example of how to think about being in the gray area when you have lost someone. You are between the dark (losing your loved one) and the light (creating a picture of the world without that person in it). Do not just stay suspended in your own anxiety. Begin to create a dream for your life. Look for possibilities and opportunities.

The object here is to claim the loss of your dream with that person in your life and then look for the possibilities or opportunities so that out of the ashes you can rise like the phoenix. Never let anything get you down. You are in charge of your life. It can be as amazing or as miserable as you think it is. Trust your ability to recreate your life without that amazing person that died. I know you can do that. In a later chapter, you will learn how to revise your dream. Right now though, just learn to look for those possibilities and opportunities.

So choose to rise like the phoenix from the ashes by creating possibilities and opportunities for yourself. Let me help you by showing you how to create some possibilities. One possibility is to upgrade your areas of life satisfaction. Increasing the areas of life satisfaction can help you recreate the picture of your life without your loved one.

Creating Life Satisfaction

Let me go over the areas of life satisfaction first, and then I will explain each. First, develop pleasures in your life in two areas: mental pleasures and physical pleasures. Second, know yourself and be congruent. Third, create meaning in three areas: career, relationships, and volunteer activities. If you have these three areas balanced, you will begin to realize that, no matter who is in your life, your life is satisfying. You can then begin to recreate the picture of your life without your loved one.

Pleasures

So let's talk about pleasures. Pleasures are those areas in life that create joy, delight, and satisfaction. You can enjoy mental pleasures or physical pleasures. Mental pleasures are those areas that we usually think of as hobbies. The things that we choose to do with our free time that engage us are mental pleasures. The activities that give us mental pleasure are those that we can perform and time passes without us even knowing it. For example, I like to take photos, so, when I am engaged in the activity of shooting pictures, time passes without my really being aware of it. My mind is focused on the act of taking pictures. When I have something I am not really looking forward to spending time doing, I always see if there is an opportunity to take photos of whatever it is. This helps pass the time in a way that gives me pleasure. I take photos of fall trees, winter snow or ice storms, and beautiful spring flowers. I take photos of people during celebrations of birthdays, reunions, and vacations. I take photos of activities such as festivals, events, and competitions. When I can take photos, my time and energy is spent feeling joyful, delighted, and satisfied. So what can you do to get mental pleasure from life?

Physical pleasures are easy. Taking a warm shower, sitting in a bubble bath, relaxing in a Jacuzzi, getting a massage, taking aerobics classes, lifting weights, riding a bicycle, making love, swimming, running at the gym, walking on a treadmill, or whatever you choose to do to relax or work out can create pleasures of the body. When Wes died, I put a lot of energy into exercising. Exercising helps elevate the mood. The body releases endorphins, and endorphins elevate the mood. So exercising not only gave me pleasure, it kept me in shape. Eventually, I began to get massages. The experience gave my body great pleasure and was very relaxing. So what can you do to get physical pleasure in your life?

Congruence

The second area is to know yourself and be congruent. What we think of ourselves on the inside needs to match what we are doing on the outside. Let me explain. I consider myself to be a very social person who enjoys being with people and doing lots of activities. Later, I learned this is the strength in me called zest, enthusiasm, and energy. When I withdrew from being social because I was so sad, I was being incongruent. What I knew about myself did not match what I was doing. It was fine for a time period, but after a while, had I kept myself from being engaged in life, then I would have spun myself into depression.

One of the best ways to get in touch with who you are is to know your strengths. Marty Seligman and Chris Peterson, in their book *Strengths and Virtues: A Classification and Handbook*, suggest people have, in varying degrees, twenty-four signature strengths. The research by these two men suggests that when you are utilizing your top five signature strengths on a daily basis, you are a happier person. So by choosing to learn more about how to use the strengths you have, you increase your opportunity to be more satisfied with your life. If you would like to find out your signature strengths, go to www.authentichappiness.org and take the Values in Action Signature Strengths Survey. By using your strengths to weather adversity, you can help manage your grief.

Let me give you an example of how knowing my strengths helped me to be happier because it created congruence in my life. One of my strengths is spirituality. Engaging in a faith-based life makes my life satisfying. What might have happened if I had been so angry with God that I gave up my faith? Because spirituality is so important to me, I would have been incongruent. Incongruence would have created misery in me. So what I did was to try to come to grips with the death of my child without being angry at God. Of course, I was angry at God at first, but God has broad shoulders. God let me yell at him whenever I needed to. I always knew that even if I yelled, he would always love me. It took some searching, but I knew I would need to keep my faith in order to remain congruent. So what do you know about yourself, and how can you use that to remain congruent in the face of the adversity of losing someone you love?

Meaning

Third, create meaning in your life through your career, your relationships, and your volunteer activities. Let's look at how each of these can help you to heal. If you do not see the meaningfulness in your career, start reframing what you think about what you spend eight hours a day, five days a week doing. A man I worked with in therapy, whose career was in maintenance, could not figure out how his job could possibly be meaningful. He had been going through a divorce, which he did not want. He and his wife worked at the same place. He had described to me his feelings one day when his wife walked by when he was standing on a ladder replacing a light bulb in a rather dark hallway. Later, in therapy, when he was trying to figure out how to make his life more satisfying now that she was not in his life and we were working on the meaningfulness of his life, I used what he had told me about replacing the light bulb. I helped him see that when he was changing that light bulb, he was making the hallway safe for coworkers. Creating a safe work environment at his place of employment gave meaning to his job. How does your career create meaning in your life?

The second area of meaningfulness is the area of relationships. Creating a network of relationships will enhance your life. First, keeping up with close relationships even when you are sad may be difficult and you need to do it for you. Reaching out to make new friendships takes energy. So when your energy level starts to rise, take the opportunity to use some of it to create some new relationships. Look around in your community and think about where opportunity to make new friendships presents itself to you. Look in your civic groups, in your church membership, in the schools your children attend, in your neighborhood, and in your volunteer activities. Wherever you spend time and energy, look for the opportunity to create new friendships.

When the fog lifted from my world, I looked in my community to see where I could increase my network of friendships. I was very lucky to have a friend who invited me to join a service organization. From my involvement in this organization came, not only many new friends, but also opportunities for travel, great learning experiences, and enhancement of my leadership skills. Over the years, my life has been so much more satisfying than it would have been without this organization in my life. Another friend invited me to join a service sorority. It opened the pathway to engage in fun, fellowship, and service activities with fourteen other women on a monthly basis. I value each of these avenues that brought me more friendships and enhanced my life. My life is so much more satisfying because of these activities and the people whom I met because of my involvement. So I encourage you to get involved in activities that can present opportunities to meet new friends.

The third area of meaningfulness is volunteer work. There is nothing better than giving to others to decrease dwelling on your own problems. When you volunteer, you shift your focus from having yourself as the center of your universe. When you get out of the center of your universe, you can see life from a new perspective. I became very involved in my children's schools and their activities. Again, you will see that I used what was meaningful to me when I volunteered. I was the photographer for the mother's club at the high school my children attended. I was the photographer for the children's theatre group in which my children participated. A few friends and I made the marquees for the musicals. My world had meaning because I volunteered in an area that gave me joy. What volunteer activities would create meaning in your world?

Evaluate each of these areas to see what you can choose to do to increase your life satisfaction without your loved one in your life. So what else is left to think about in the area of surviving? One last thought to end this chapter: surviving takes courage. Courage takes being unafraid to face life without your loved one there to enjoy it with you. So choose to be courageous enough to be unafraid to live your life.

Choosing to Be Unafraid

When you love, you open yourself up to be vulnerable. When love is lost, the vulnerability permeates your being. It is only through courage that you can choose to continue to love others. Only courage will help you to conquer the vulnerability and allow you to open yourself up to the possibility of loving other people. Let's look at one way you can come out of the fog and see clearly again. One concept you can use is that of walking out of darkness into the light. Here is how.

Do you remember when you were young and used to play pin the tail on the donkey? You were blindfolded so you could see nothing and had to feel your way to the destination. Do you remember ever being in the total darkness when the electricity went out at night, and you had to talk to each other to find out where the other was? Have you ever gone into a dark room, not knowing where the light switch was, and had to feel around for it? Sometimes we are placed in situations in which the need arises for us to acknowledge we are in the dark, decide to do something about it, face the fear, and then make a plan about what to do. This is a time to embrace the darkness and set yourself free to find the light.

So how does this work? It's like a sunrise. The darkness of night gives way to the light of the dawn. This is what you do. First, you acknowledge you are in the dark. Second, you choose to do something about it. Third, you make a plan to get out of the darkness. Fourth, you observe yourself performing your plan. Fifth, you use the information you gather about yourself to make a plan for how to proceed. This is the process you use in the above situations.

For instance, when you enter a dark room and don't know where the light switch is, you realize you are in the dark, you decide to find the light switch, and you tell yourself that there is no need to be afraid. Then you gather the confidence you need to feel along the wall, gathering information as you go to rule out the space that does not have the switch. As you proceed, you make a plan about how to cover the territory until you find it. You go slowly until you find the switch which, when turned on, will put you in the light.

Here is an example of something in life in which you can choose to use this process. Let's say you are bored with your job yet you do not know what you would want to do if you quit. First, you realize you are bored and don't know what else you can do. Second, you make up your mind to do something about your situation. Third, you can generate the confidence in yourself to know that discovery is a growth process. You might even discover that after you gather data, you choose to stay in the same job. Fourth, you get curious about yourself and gather some information about your interests, your strengths, and your goals. This might take self-reflection, or it might take finding a helpful resource person such as a coach to guide you through the process. Then fifth, when you have the information, you make a plan about how to use the information to make a decision. This process takes you out of the darkness and puts you into the light. It's like waking up in the dark and then watching the sunrise. Light is shed on the process of self-discovery, which is inside you.

When you decide to walk out of the fog and be vulnerable to others, it is like coming out of the darkness into the light. When you lose a child, you can use this process. First, you would acknowledge that you lost one child and have other children who need you to be a parent to them. Second, you decide to stop being consumed with sadness. Third, you make a strategy to participate in all activities in which your children participate. Fourth, you risk going to their activities and being present to the moment. While there, you note what you are doing and how you are feeling. Fifth, you use what you observed about yourself and make a plan for how you want to proceed in the future. You step slowly out of the dark into the light of joy of watching your children. The fog clears, and you see clearly that you can choose to be an effective parent to your other children.

What if you lost a spouse? How would you use this process? First, you would acknowledge that you lost your partner, and at the same time desire to have love in your life. Second, you decide to risk interacting and networking with others. Third, you make a strategy to accept social invitations and to join some new groups. Fourth, you get curious about people and watch how you are responding to the interactions you have. Fifth, you watch for the opportunities to take casual relationships to new levels. You step out of the darkness into the light of new friendships. The fog clears, and you see clearly that you can choose to share new love with a new person. So whether you use this as an internal strategy to help you become self-aware or you use it to help you with your interactions with others, choose to embrace the darkness by using a process that takes you from darkness to light.

Review

In order to walk out of the fog so you can see clearly, the following suggestions might help. At first, hibernating helps you to move through the shock. Be patient with yourself. Then keep busy with a purpose. Choose something to do that has meaning to you. Next, keep busy with passions. Choose something so engaging to you that time passes, and you are not even aware that hours have gone by. When you are ready, start interacting with others. Have your succinct speech prepared. Consider using the wave imagery when alone to create a peaceful environment. Use all five senses to calm yourself. Be sure to base expectations on your own behavior and not the behavior of others. Look for the possibilities and the opportunities that come your way. Recreate your life dream without your loved one in it. Take charge of creating your own life satisfaction. Increase your pleasures, your congruence, and the meaning of your life. Lastly, choose to be unafraid. Walk out of the darkness into the light so you can get rid of the fog and see clearly.

Remember: you can choose to do these things or not. Each will move you one step closer to decreasing the misery and increasing the satisfaction in your life. The benefit of being satisfied with your life is that when you are satisfied, you are happier. When you are happier, you have the potential to mend your broken heart. Believe that you can survive. Believe in yourself. It's time to mend your broken heart.

So how do you get happier? Abraham Lincoln stated, "A man is about as happy as he makes up his mind to be." Essentially, what he was saying is that happiness is a choice. You can choose to increase your happiness by changing your attitude.

Choose to Be Happy

Most people think that they need to be unhappy in order to show that the person that is gone is missed. I would like for you to consider the idea that missing someone and being happy are not mutually exclusive. Mutually exclusive means you choose one or the other, but you cannot choose both. I would like to propose that you can miss someone and at the same time you can be happy. Missing someone does not mean that you cannot be happy too. Your present circumstance is not the criteria for your entire life satisfaction.

Being happy has to do with how you view life. Your overall happiness has very little to do with situational events. It has a great deal to do with how you view those events. You are in charge of your perception of events in your life, so you have control of how happy you are. A death can distort your view of life. What you think about a person's death frames the experience. From your frame, you then extract either positive or negative emotions. Even though an event is tragic, it does not have to spin you into total negative feelings about everything in your world. You have a choice. If your thoughts are negative, you can reframe them. The key is to notice your negative thoughts and then change the thoughts.

Perhaps you might be thinking something like, *My life will be awful without this person in it.* If you continue to think that, then yes, your life will be miserable. Perhaps you might consider this thought instead, *It is difficult to enjoy things without sharing them with this person, but at the same time, my life is filled with many people and activities and beauty and meaning that do create happiness in me.* Then, despite the fact that this person is no longer with you, you can be happy.

Your happiness is composed of many facets. Being connected to one person does not in and of itself create happiness in you. Notice I did not say "make you happy." No one person can make you happy. You choose to be happy by the way you think about your world. So if you think that you will never be happy because this person is no longer in your world, it will become a self-fulfilling prophecy. You will never be happy if you think that way.

Thinking has to do with perspective. Your perspective about a person in your life dying is extremely important to your overall well-being. I will discuss that in another chapter. However, in this chapter, I want to get you to examine just what creates satisfaction in your life and, therefore, your happiness. You can choose to think about and do things that create life satisfaction. Let's start with what makes choice so important.

Choice in Life

William Schutz, in the 1950s, indicated that "to control" is a basic emotional need of all human beings. Therefore, choice takes on a significant meaning in our lives. People balk at others telling them what to do. Just look at a typical two-year-old, a teenager, a disgruntled employee, a parent who can no longer live independently, or a spouse who has a picture of how an event should happen in his/her mind, and you have the exact opposite picture. Lack of choice obviously leads to conflict.

When we believe we cannot control our world, we usually respond with aggression, criticism, or oppositional behavior. In each of the above scenarios, if choice were a part of the process of decision making, conflict would be held to a minimum.

Likewise, when we have an internal conflict when trying to discern the course of our journey in life, choice is an important aspect. Choosing freely to follow a certain path makes the path easier to travel because with choice comes commitment. For instance, when a college freshman chooses a major based on Mom's or Dad's wishes, rather than on a discovery of a combination of aptitude and interest, it makes it harder to study and attain the degree.

So it is also with us when a person we love dies. We have no choice about the death. What we do have is a choice in how we respond to it. So even though it seems we do not have a choice in our happiness at a time of grief, we actually do.

Let's start with our language. The word *choose* means to pick, select, prefer, or decide. In each of these synonyms, it is clear that there is more than one option. So in the matter of "choice," alternatives become very important, particularly to happiness.

Generating alternatives can be difficult, unless we have an expectation that we are not stuck with only one. When we realize that we do have options, we feel freer. When we feel freer, we are more likely to be more satisfied and thus carry out our selection with a happier attitude.

So how does that apply to your life? Have you ever said to yourself, "I have no choice. I have to!" With almost everything, you do have a choice "to or not to" do something. The only thing that is not a choice is dying. However, sometimes people even take that into their own hands and choose to commit suicide, therefore making death a choice.

The struggle in believing that you have no choice is not that you "have to" do something, but that you are "choosing to" do something because you do not like the consequences if you do not do it. For instance, a teen may say, "I have to study for that test." No, the teen could choose not to study or only partially study, but the consequences might be that the teen would get an F on the test and that thought might propel the teen into choosing to study. You might say, "I have to pay my taxes." No, you do not have to, but if you do not, you might end up in jail, so you choose to pay your taxes because you do not like the consequences of not paying.

Sometimes it might be appropriate to choose to "do nothing." That is still a choice. If you believe an injustice has been done to you but do nothing about it, then you are making a choice. For example, if you buy a loaf of bread and it molds within a day, you may think you have been taken advantage of by the local grocery store. However, you may choose not to take it back because your time and the gas it would take to drive to the store is worth more than $2.89. You made a conscious choice to do nothing. If you continue to be disgruntled about the loaf of bread being moldy, even though you consciously made a choice not to take it back, you deplete your potential for happiness.

In all the instances above, a choice was made. The key is to reflect on the fact that you did make a choice and no one is forcing you into it. You choose freely from among alternatives. Some alternatives would bring you consequences you do not want, and even though you may not like the choice, you choose it. Because you choose it from among options, you can choose to be happy with your choice and therefore, let your anger go. Thus, you become a happier person.

Did you realize how powerful choice becomes in creating happiness in life? So from now on say, "I choose to" instead of "I have to" so that your life can be happier. Choosing has to do with seeing the alternatives. Sometimes we get stuck in ways of responding that are negative. Being able to create choices in your life will be important to your healing after the loss of a loved one.

Producing options coaxes you into being creative. When you are creative, you begin to view a situation from a different perspective. With this creative view, you have the potential to problem solve on a deeper, more intense level that becomes more fulfilling. You begin to make choices that create happiness instead of being stuck in your sadness.

Part of being stuck in life has to do with doing the same thing over and over again. With repetition comes boredom. When you are bored, you are unsatisfied. When you are unsatisfied, you start to criticize not only yourself but others too. When this inner dissatisfaction becomes manifested outwardly, those around you become annoyed and retaliate with negative expressions. When you get negative expressions sent back to you, you feel badly. Thus, you spiral downward into a negative attitude toward all of life.

So what you do to stop this downward spiral is to be creative. Creativity emerges when one brainstorms the potentials of life, not only with problem solving, but also with how you spend your time and energy. When you begin to look at all the possibilities, you open up your imagination to help stimulate your creative potential. It's like a domino effect. When you think of a new way to do something, it is challenging and you focus your attention more intensely. When your focus of attention is more intense, you get absorbed. When you are absorbed, you enjoy the experience more. When you enjoy the experience, you get this sense of happiness. When you are happier, you don't feel as stuck in life.

To obtain alternatives, you brainstorm. What is brainstorming all about? Well, you make a list of all the possible ways to do something or to handle a situation. Put in ones that you would never do and ones that are humorous to take the seriousness out of the mix. Just let your mind go. Dream. Visualize. Go beyond the ordinary. One "off the wall" thought might lead to another and another, and then something real might pop up because of all the different things you are thinking. Most usually, after the far-out thinking comes a really wonderful choice, that without the stretching of the mind would never have emerged. So try this idea when you feel stuck in life or when you are faced with a problem to be solved.

So how does this apply to a situation in which you have lost someone very special to you? Let me give you a few examples in which choosing by being creative and brainstorming might be helpful. The first example is what everyone faces when a family member dies. What do we do with the clothes? Do not let this situation spiral you into deep sadness and steal your happiness. Instead, think of all the possibilities. You could just box them up and keep them. You could give them to other family members. You could sell them at a garage sale. You could give them to Goodwill or The Salvation Army. You could do nothing with them. Those are the traditional responses. However, put your creative hat on. You could take the meaningful clothes and have a quilt made of them. You could have several stuffed animals made with the clothes and give them as Christmas presents. You could give the clothes to a community theatre or high school drama club. Get the idea of doing something interesting with the clothes. My mom had a lot of costume jewelry, and when she died, I made a brooch to put on my coat using her costume jewelry. Be creative. Do something with them that puts a smile on your face instead of a frown.

Another situation that could spiral you into sadness and steal your happiness is what to do with the space your loved one occupied in the house. If she had her own bedroom, you can be very creative. If you lost a spouse and occupied the same room, that takes a lot more creativity. Let's go with the idea that the person had her own room. How can you be creative? Let's brainstorm. You could make it the guest room. You could make it a memorial to that person. You could put all the toys and games in that room and create a playroom. You could put some comfy chairs in the room and make it the reading room. You could make it a theme room and wait for the next opportunity to have a foreign exchange student live with you and let the student stay in the theme room.

What I did with my son's room was a combination. I call it my angel room. It can be used as my study because it has my laptop with a docking station. It can be used as a guest room. It is my peaceful reading room with a big recliner. It is decorated with my son's pictures and angel pictures, since I consider him my favorite angel. Be creative. Make it into a happy room instead of a sad room.

Ways to Grow Happier Despite Your Loss

Now let's turn to ideas about what you can choose to do to create your own happiness every day, despite the fact that you have lost a very important person in your life. You can choose to make each day a happy day. Here's how.

Be Thankful

Being thankful has to do with gratitude. Gratitude makes life more satisfying. What is gratitude? Gratitude is thankful appreciation, that is, becoming aware of the benefits or enjoyment of something or someone in your life and acknowledging those benefits or that enjoyment. When people are grateful, life satisfaction is increased. In other words, when you are grateful, you can increase your happiness. I bet you want to know how to do that. Okay, let's look at how with a small amount of energy you can increase your happiness by being grateful.

First, be aware and notice every day the little things that make your day special. For instance, you walk into your office one morning, and your secretary has brought a few plants from her home and put them in your office to make the atmosphere more comfortable and inviting for your clients. You think to yourself that she went out of her way without anyone asking her in order to make your clients more relaxed. You appreciate her initiative and thank her gratefully. Inside, you feel special because she is working hard to increase your business by doing small things that make a difference, and you will reap the benefit from that.

Another example of noticing might be that at noon you go out for lunch and it is a beautiful fall day. The leaves are turning brilliant colors and falling from the trees. The breeze is crisp with a hint of chill in the air. The sun shines on the lake in the park where you choose to eat your lunch away from the hustle and bustle of the office. You watch the swans on the lake swim gracefully by. You take a deep breath after you eat your lunch, and you say to yourself, *Wow, what a beautiful day. Wes (your loved one) would have enjoyed this one.*

Still another idea about how to begin noticing is to think of something you take for granted on a daily basis. Spend a week appreciating whatever you have taken for granted. For instance, if you take for granted your hearing, appreciate all the sounds you hear this week. If you have taken for granted your ability to walk, appreciate it by walking more places this week instead of driving. If you have taken for granted your partner or spouse, tell that person how much you appreciate him or her at least once a day. The idea is to become more aware of what you take for granted, start feeling appreciation, and then begin expressing your thankfulness.

Second, after noticing, express gratitude for what you notice. How do you express your gratitude once you become cognitively aware that there are people and things in your life for which you are grateful? For example, when you go home and your spouse has your favorite meal waiting, thank him for taking the time because you know he also has been busy most of the day yet stopped to cook for the family because he knew you had to run the children to activities after school. You are grateful, so you give him a kiss and thank him profusely.

Another way of expressing gratitude is to send a note to someone who has done something for you, expressing your thanks and sincere appreciation. Be descriptive. Define what that person did for you and tell how it was helpful to you in your life. There are many chances to do this after a funeral. So many people do such kind gestures that you could probably write for days and not be done thanking everyone who showed a kind gesture to you.

You could even take the time to visit a person who has done something for you and bring her a small token of your appreciation. Laminate a bookmark with a favorite saying or poem on it that expresses your appreciation. Pick some wild flowers and put them in a vase, with a colorful ribbon tied around the vase. Get a rock and paint the word *thanks* on it in a vibrant color. Just give something little and not very costly. A small handmade gift will express the fact that you took a few minutes to think about the person you are appreciating.

Third, think of these examples of situations or people for which you are grateful as treasures. Do you remember as a child going on a treasure hunt? Visions of pirates with eye patches, maps with X marking the spot, chests of gold coins, and adventure at every corner were enough to make the day exciting. When was the last time you hunted for treasure in your life?

A treasure isn't necessarily something monetary. It can be seeing your baby sleep peacefully after having a cold. It can be a hug from an old friend not seen in years. It could be a good deed someone does for you. It could be getting up in the morning without as many aches and pains. It could be watching your son or daughter graduate. It could be listening to someone play your favorite song on a guitar. It could be watching the sun set over the ocean. It could be smelling the aroma of freshly brewed coffee in the morning. It could be tasting a delicious meal prepared by someone you love. It could be touching a soft kitten as it sleeps on your overstuffed couch. Your treasure can be any little thing or any big event that occurs on any day at any time. Becoming aware of your treasures can enrich your life.

Hold a family oriented treasure hunt. You could gather as a family each night, and share with each other the treasure that happened to each of you during the day. Or you could create a treasure book, where each of you could write down three things for which you are thankful. Sometime during the evening or at bedtime, these could be read aloud. If you cannot gather together, have the treasure book somewhere so that anyone can write in it or read it any time.

The point here is to hunt for your treasure on a daily basis. Share your treasure with your family. When you are grateful on a daily basis, you increase your overall life satisfaction. When you increase your life satisfaction, you are happier. So choose to hunt for your treasures of life every day.

If you are alone and do not have a family with which to share, when you climb into bed at night, just before you go to sleep, look back on the day and reflect on the treasures you discovered that day. You can choose to think, *I am so lucky to have a secretary who cares about my business. I enjoyed the beautiful fall day I experienced at lunch. I appreciate fast food when I am rushed and don't have time to cook.* The awareness of your treasures of the day and your reflection on those treasures just before you drift off to sleep will help you to be peaceful. When you are peaceful, you are much more likely to be a happy person.

Let Go

You are probably wondering, *Let go of what?* Let go of anger, not your memories. You can never let go of your history. Experiencing the death of your loved one is part of your history. However, you can let go of anger. When you hold on to anger, contempt, and resentment, you use energy in the present to keep alive the past. Of course, you can choose to do that. If, however, you want more energy to spend in the present moment, then holding on to the past will cost you a vast amount of the energy you could have available for today. One way to increase your energy is to let go of events that caused you adversity yesterday.

Okay, I hear you. What you are saying is, "Easier said than done." Yes, that may be true for the vast majority of people. At the same time, you know I would not be talking about this subject unless I had an idea about what to do instead. My mom always said that I could complain about anything as long as I had a better idea. If I did not have a better idea, then she said that she would not listen to my complaints. So, consistent with my upbringing, here is a better idea for you.

I would like for you to entertain this idea. It might be helpful to let go of the cloud so that you can see the sunshine. It's an old idea, and there was even a song written about it. It still holds true today. To let go of the past, look for the silver lining in every adversity. When I have clients do this to obtain more energy for focusing on and getting to their present goals, they are amazed. For example, one woman was stuck in her anger because she kept holding on to the fact that her husband had left her. When she let go of the anger and resentment, she used the energy she had been wasting on past resentments to go back to college to obtain a business degree and start her own business. Had her husband never divorced her, she would not be the successful business woman she is today. From the adversity of her divorce came the courage to achieve things she would have never dreamed of before the adversity.

Another way to say this same thing would be to look at the idea that when one road is closed to you look for the road that appears to you. That can make all the difference in your life. From adversity often comes a new pathway that would not have been open to you had you not gone through the difficult time. Start embracing your adversities, and use them to help you move forward in your life by noticing what happens to you as a result of the difficulties you encounter. For instance, one man indicated that when he let go of not getting a promotion, he then became energized to start his own business. If he had gotten the promotion, he would never have ventured out on his own to start the successful business he has today.

You can become much more mentally healthy by looking at your adversities in a positive light to discover the silver lining or the new pathway. It is your choice. You can choose to be in charge of your perceptions of adversity and use them to your benefit, or you can choose to let your adversities send you into despair and misery. Which will you choose? Will you choose to let go so you don't waste energy on the past? Will you choose to use your energy for the present moment so the future will be bright? Be good to yourself and choose to let go. Remember that letting go allows you to have more energy to be productive and have a satisfying life in the present.

So how does this idea apply to the death of a loved one? Dramatically so, but it is very hard to hear. Even though you would give anything to have that loved one back, there is still something that will happen to you as a result of not having that loved one around. Don't burn the book. Just think about it. Your life goes on even though the life of your loved one stopped. There are all sorts of good things that will appear for you if you notice them as such. Yes, no question, I know that you would give up ten thousand good things if you could only have that person back. The idea is to focus on the choices you have now.

Let me give you an example. Let's say that you are a woman who has always been eager to be involved in politics, but your husband was in a profession in which outspoken stands on political issues could be a detriment to his business, so he always asked you not to participate at the public level in politics. Your husband dies. You then run for city council and advocate for the construction of a boys and girls club that would help thousands of children each year. The center was your idea, and you advocated for it. In your position, you were able to gain information about grants that helped fund the center. The center would never have been built without you being a city council representative. You would never have taken the time away from your husband to do the project. You never would have been in a position to find grants or talk with people who made a difference in contributions if you were not on the city council. Perhaps you poured yourself into the project to run from your grief, and in the middle of it all, you discovered a passion that enhanced your life and created meaning for others. An amazing thing happened for the children of your city because you chose a positive outlet instead of dwelling on your grief.

Get Excited

Have you ever been somewhere on vacation and experienced the most beautiful orange sunset you have ever seen? I call a time like that a "tangerine moment." At the exact moment you see that awesome sight, you get excited about life, and enthusiasm becomes part of your experience. Let's talk about what makes getting excited and being enthusiastic in life so very important.

Enthusiasm increases life satisfaction. When you get excited, your experience is heightened. When your experience is heightened, you create added value to the event. When added value is experienced, you increase your life satisfaction. Let's say that you choose to attend your daughter's dance recital that lasts at least two hours. She only dances in two dances that take about three minutes each. You are thus captured for another one hour and fifty-four minutes, watching the recital. You have a choice here. You can be excited about seeing her perform and anticipate her appearance on stage as you enjoy the other dances, or you can be bored waiting for her to appear. If you choose the first, then you increase your own life satisfaction, even though you sit through the other dance numbers that do not include your daughter. As you enjoy the other dances, you have added value to your experience. You have succeeded in making your experience a "tangerine moment."

Here is another example. You volunteer to be the cashier at a bake sale for your church. You can think of ten other things you would rather be doing on a Saturday morning. Instead you get excited about giving the gift of your time to your church. You greet each person with a smile and thank each person for the contribution to your bake-sale efforts. You get positive feedback about how cheerful you are for such an early hour on a Saturday morning. You feel good that you have brightened the day for others. By being enthusiastic, you have added value to your experience. You have succeeded in making your experience a "tangerine moment."

In order to increase your enthusiasm, be present to the moment. Be enthusiastic no matter what you are doing. Whether you are scrubbing toilets, mowing the lawn, celebrating a birthday, shopping, or visiting with friends, get excited about what you are doing. Do not wish you were somewhere else, doing something different. When you do get excited and are present to the moment, you make your life more satisfying.

So start increasing your enthusiasm by doing these three steps. First, once you choose to participate in an event, get excited by anticipating it. Second, when the event arrives, be present to the moment during it. Third, when the event is over, reflect on how your experience was increased by your own attitude toward it.

You have control of how excited you get about anything. Your excitement can make any event even more enjoyable. So choose to have more "tangerine moments." You can take charge of your own life satisfaction by being enthusiastic about whatever you do.

How does that apply to the death of a loved one? Simple. Accept offers from others. Do not be reclusive. Yes, you need some time to mourn and be sad and cry and be angry at the world. After a time period of that, you need to get back in life. When someone invites you to dinner, go. Be present to the moment. Don't wish you were somewhere else, doing something different. Be grateful for being included. When someone asks you to go to a ballgame, go. Focus on the game and the fellowship you are enjoying. Be grateful for the friendship. When someone needs your help, give it. Take pleasure in giving the gift of your time. No matter what you do, just be present to the moment. When you do, you will start noticing that some times will stand out more than others. Those are the amazing "tangerine moments" of which I speak. "Tangerine moments" create more life satisfaction. When you are satisfied with life, then you are happier.

Ask Questions

Questioning involves being curious. Curiosity is an eager desire to learn or know. A curious person wants to have a new experience, find an answer, explore something, learn a new fact, or discover something. A curious person wants variety, novelty, and challenge. The behavior that identifies a curious person is someone who asks many questions.

There are many benefits to being curious. One benefit of curiosity is that it counteracts depression and anxiety. The opposite of curiosity is boredom, disinterest, and weariness. When you are bored, disinterested, and weary, you are more prone to depression and anxiety. Curious people naturally keep depression and anxiety at a distance.

Another benefit is that curiosity attracts others to the curious person. Curious people are like people magnets. It is hard to stay away from curious people because they pull you into their environment. You desire to attach to them. They are like this for two reasons. First, curious people are inquisitive not only about their environment but also about themselves and others. Because of these interests, curious people are usually considered good conversationalists and good listeners. Have you ever gone away from meeting someone, thinking he or she was a great conversationalist, only to discover that you hardly know anything about that person because the time was spent by the other person being curious and asking questions about you? When you feel listened to and validated, that creates life satisfaction.

Second, curious people are fun to be with because they bring novelty and variety into relationships. Have you ever found yourself looking forward to spending time with a friend because you know that when you are with that particular friend exciting things always come up or he has planned something extraordinary or fascinating due to his varied interests? When you anticipate doing something with or being with someone, that creates more life satisfaction.

Another benefit of curiosity is that it can be contagious, just like a yawn. Have you ever found yourself getting excited enough to ask some questions because the person you are with got excited and started asking questions, leading you to ask similar questions and to get interested? Then, the world seems more exciting to you just because you were in the same place as the curious person. Therefore, you like to be around curious people because their curiosity rubs off on you and you get excited. When you get excited, that creates more life satisfaction for you.

Fourth, curiosity creates an expansion of who you are. Because you experience new situations, new ideas, and new people, you grow and become enriched. Curiosity is like a fuel that fires the flames of knowledge and understanding, thus widening your perspective about others and about your world. Have you ever wanted to travel to a foreign country just to experience the culture, customs, food, and lifestyle? And when you did travel there, did it somehow change you? I remember traveling to Rome. I asked many questions of the tour guide. Seeing the buildings that were thousands of years old gave me a greater appreciation of beauty than before I went. I also remember traveling to Ireland. Experiencing the friendliness of the Irish people by interacting with them and asking many questions gave me a desire to be more amiable to others than before I went. Each of these experiences changed me in some way. When you are enriched and grow, that creates greater life satisfaction.

A fifth benefit is that curiosity reclaims your energy from anger when curiosity is substituted for the anger you are experiencing. When curiosity takes over where anger once stood, understanding can allow one to forgive. When you forgive because of understanding, then you do not waste your energy on things from the past, which cannot be changed. You are then free to use that energy you used to waste on resentment for the experience of today. This creates more life satisfaction in the present moment.

Curiosity can also be used during adversity to help you out of difficult situations. As stated above, instead of an angry response to a situation or a person, you can choose to use curiosity. Your curiosity will keep you in your head and out of your emotions. By doing this, you can tackle the adversity as a problem to be solved.

So you are probably wondering how to get more curious. Two things need to happen. First, you need to become aware of your desire to be curious. Second, you need to ask more questions.

A good way to start the process is to make a plan to ask three questions with each interaction you have with a person. Let's say you are introduced to a person by your best friend. You could ask these three questions: How do you know Sarah? What's your favorite story about Sarah? What makes Sarah a true friend to you? In other words, get curious about the relationship between Sarah and this new person to whom you have just been introduced.

Another plan is to ask a question each time you are puzzled about something. One day my computer kept running and running on a consistent basis. I wondered what made it do that because prior to my downloading something, it did not run like that. So I made an inquiry and found out that what I had downloaded brought with it many other items that were making my computer work much too hard. I ran my virus protector and spyware, and before long, it stopped running constantly. It was back to normal. If I had not been puzzled, then who knows what could have gotten into my computer? Ask questions when you are puzzled.

Curious questions need to be powerful. Let's talk about what makes a question powerful. Powerful questions stimulate exploration, not merely finding facts. Powerful questions are open-ended ones.

That means that you cannot answer yes or no to it. You need to elaborate. So powerful questions open up the mind to consider other options, understand new viewpoints, and discover ideas not available before asking the question. This leads to enhanced creativity and valuable insights.

A trick to asking powerful questions, especially when you are asking them of another person, is to ask what, where, when, how, and who questions. Yes, I left out the dreaded why questions for a reason. Why questions often make others defensive. Every why question can be restated as a what question. For example, the question "Why is the sky blue?" can be restated by asking, "What makes the sky blue?" Here is another one. You could see a friend crying, and instead of saying, "Why are you crying?" you could say instead, "What caused the tears?"

Now let's look at some powerful questions. Remember, powerful questions are open ended and stimulate exploration. I will give you some questions that anticipate certain outcomes. For example, when you want to inquire about what a person is anticipating, you might ask, "What might happen?" If you want some clarification, you might ask, "What do you mean?" If you want to explore a subject more, you might ask, "What is another possibility?" If you do not understand and want an example of something, you might ask, "What's an example of that?" If you wonder what another person expects, you might inquire, "What are you expecting?" If you wonder what the other person is planning, ask, "What do you plan to do about it?" These are just a few powerful questions to help you get the idea and get started.

So how can you get curious when you are sad and full of grief? It's easy to get curious about others and harder to get curious about yourself. I was always curious about what made people avoid me. I noticed that people who used to talk to me avoided speaking with me in public. What I learned is that some people have a difficult time knowing what to say to people who have lost a loved one. They feel trapped between wanting to inquire to show caring and not wanting to inquire because they might upset you. I always found myself taking care of others when they spoke with me about my son's death. I tried to be as honest as possible about how I was doing and how I felt, without going on and on. What most people want to hear is merely that you are doing fine.

In getting curious about myself, I often asked the question "What is healthy about crying?" The answer I gave myself was that when my body needs to shed tears, it will. I then have the choice as to how long the faucet stays open. So I gave myself a rule when I went back to work after taking off several months. When I am staying home for the day and I feel like crying, I cry. When I am going to work for the day, after I turn the shower off in the morning, the tears also stop. Getting curious about self and others helps make life happier.

Think Positive

Do you have a tendency to be hopeful? Do you take a cheerful view of the future? Do you expect that what you want will happen? Do you believe in yourself? If so, you think from a positive frame of reference, and you are considered an optimist.

Optimism has to do with perspective. Perspective is how we think about our world and about ourselves in our world. You have heard a dozen examples comparing optimism to pessimism. For example, the most quoted example is: Do you see the glass half full or half empty? The quote from Harry Truman states, "A pessimist is one who makes difficulties of his opportunities, and an optimist is one who makes opportunities of his difficulties." My all-time favorite is a quote by Kahlil Gibran: "The optimist sees the rose and not its thorns; the pessimist stares at the thorns, oblivious of the rose." Which are you? Do you see the glass half full? Do you see opportunity in your difficulty? Do you see the rose? If so, you are an optimist. If not, keep reading, because we need to do some work on that attitude of yours.

If you have a tendency to be negative instead of positive about how you view your world, your circumstances, and yourself, you can choose to change that right now. The first step is to catch yourself being negative. Listen to yourself. Do you complain? Do you use negative language? Do you point out the bad points of people or things? Do you believe what you want will not happen? Better yet, get some feedback from a friend. Be sure it is a friend who won't sugarcoat what is said to you. Pick someone who is blatantly honest. Ask your friend the question, do I use negative language when I talk with you? Then listen very carefully to what is said. If you get the idea that your friend is answering the question with a resounding *yes*, then commit to yourself that you will change that immediately.

So how do you change once you are clued into the knowledge that you are a pessimist and not an optimist? Here are four steps to changing that attitude. First, train your brain to work for you by stating positive affirmations. Second, change your language to use only positive words. Third, set goals. Fourth, believe in yourself. Let's look at each step in detail.

First, train your brain to think positive thoughts. In order to do this, when you arise each morning before your feet hit the floor, say to yourself, "I am an optimist. I think and speak positively." Say this seven times. Then start your day with a smile as you say these words to yourself. When you go to bed at night, as your head hits the pillow, again say to yourself, "I am an optimist. I think and speak positively." Say this seven times. Then sleep on it. After doing these two things for twenty-one days, you will notice a difference. If you don't, then you don't believe in yourself. I will explain more about that later.

Here is an example of how to use this idea when you have lost a loved one. When you catch yourself saying things like, "I don't think I can make it without him," catch yourself and restate to something like, "Although it is really hard living without him, I know I can be happy."

Second, change your language to use only positive words. When you are faced with a task, say to yourself, "I *can* do this." Start taking all the negative words such as *can't*, *won't*, *maybe*, *try*, *hard*, *wrong*, *bad* (and on and on) out of your language choice. Yes, you have a choice in your language. You are in charge of choosing the words you use. My favorite language change is to take the dichotomous words *right/wrong* and *good/bad* and just change them to *effective/not effective*. For instance, instead of saying to yourself, "That behavior was wrong or bad," say instead, "That behavior was not effective at getting me to my goal." Change negative words to positive words. You will be surprised at how changing the words will change your thinking.

Here is an example of changing your language when you lose a loved one. When you look at those clothes hanging in the closet, and you have decided to take them to the quilt maker to make a quilt, say to yourself, "I can do this." Even more powerful, you could say, "I choose to do this."

The third step to becoming optimistic is to set goals. When you set a goal for the future, you are better able to make decisions in the present based on where you want to go in the future. When you set goals, you are also more likely to set yourself up to succeed in accomplishing your dreams. When you accomplish even a small goal, you then begin to think that if you achieved that small goal, you can accomplish a larger goal. When you make effective decisions and succeed, you feel confident in yourself. When you gain confidence in yourself, you also develop hope. Hope is important to have when you lose a loved one. You hope that someday the pain will not be so great. When you have confidence and hope, you have a positive perspective of life without your loved one. So set goals for yourself.

The goals you set at first after losing a loved one are small. It might be that you set a goal to just get through the day. Then it might be to be productive around the house. Then it could proceed to being able to get out of the house. Then you might choose to go back to work. Then you might choose to be social. You begin to put your life back together in small, successive steps to the goal of enjoying life.

Fourth, believe in yourself. My very last section in this chapter has to do with developing the skill of believing in you. Right now, what I want you to think about until you read the last section is that you can choose to believe in your ability to think in a positive way. If you think you can, you can. So just say to yourself, "I believe I can think positive."

Revise Love

What do you do when your heart is so full of love to give to a person but that person is no longer with you? That's a big question, and the answer can help you move forward. Widening your perspective of what love is about can help you quiet your aching heart. I call this the lilac love concept. Let me explain.

Love is a strong affection for or attachment to someone or something. Let's broaden that to think about love being like a lilac. A lilac is composed of many facets. When you look at a lilac, it has many little flowers that make one large lilac. Likewise, love has many facets. We have many kinds of love, just as a lilac has many little flowers that compose one flower. We have love for our significant other, whether that is a spouse or a boyfriend or a girlfriend, love for our children, love for our friends, love for our parents, or even love for the way of life to which we have become accustomed. All these loves are very different in nature. The love I have for my children is not the same as the love I have for a friend. The love I have for a friend is not the love I have for my spouse. All love does have one thing in common, and that is to care about another person or thing.

Caring brings with it a certain vulnerability that for many people seems very frightening. So love can be scary, although I believe it is the best scary feeling in the world. It brings with it pain (like the pain I had when my son died), worry (like the worry I have about the safety of my children), sorrow (as when a relationship ends by death or by choice), hurt (as when someone you love says mean things in anger), disappointment (as when someone you love does not live up to your expectations), but it also brings with it joy (like sharing the moment when someone you love accomplishes a goal), anticipation (like looking forward to having an experience with someone you care about), excitement (like laughing and smiling when you are with someone you love), ecstasy (like holding and touching a special someone), and happiness (like being content in front of a fire, watching the misty day meet the night sky). So to love, you choose to risk having many feelings.

So love brings with it both joys and sorrows. When you lose a loved one, you are missing the joys. You only feel the sorrow. It is very effective at first to dwell in your sorrow. Feeling sorrow means that the person that is gone was an extremely important part of your life, and it validates that person's life. Extended sorrow only blocks your happiness though. So how do you revise your love and retrain your heart?

Love is one of the three basic emotional needs that we as humans have. A person becomes stingy with love after the death of a loved one. Being able to revise how you express love to that person becomes significant. I could no longer hold Wes or cook for him or celebrate his successes, but I could continue to buy gifts to give in his memory and think about him and celebrate his memory on his special day. When you can still be expressive in a new way toward the person who died, you are free to then express love to others. A person gets stuck into thinking, *I can no longer love that person who died.* That just is not true. You can love that person. Your expression of love is just different. So you revise how you love that person. That opens your heart up to the possibility of loving others in a similar way or in new ways of sharing your love.

Let me give you some examples. If you lost a child, you might want to share your love by donating time to other children who need your help. Perhaps you go to a foreign country and help vaccinate children. Perhaps you volunteer at a local health agency. Getting passionate about causes that help others provides a venue to express that need to care about others, which is the crux of loving.

If you lose a spouse, you might want to try something a little different. First you could choose to conceptualize your loss, as if that person has a portion of your heart, but not all of your heart. The memory can be preserved with the love, and you also have enough love in your heart to give love to another person at the appropriate time that seems right to you. Don't be stingy with your love. Many people are looking for love, so why hoard the love you have when others are looking for a chance to connect and make life more enhanced? Look around and see the opportunities that surround you to be connected with others. Perhaps one of those connections will develop into a significant love interest.

What I am suggesting is that you retrain your heart to keep the love you have for a person who has died and at the same time look for other opportunities that can help you spread your love. You are revising the way you think about love and retraining your heart how to express love for that person so that you are free to express your love when another chance appears.

I needed to do this with my love for Wes because I had two other children who needed my expression of love. I could not focus on the lost child and neglect my other two living children. I chose to put my love for Wes in a special part of my heart. I am a visual person, so I thought of putting my love in a little treasure box in my heart. It was there, and I could open it with a key anytime I wanted to, but it was locked so that no one else saw it. Not that I forgot him or did not mention him, for I did, but it was just not a prevalent expression on a daily basis.

I remember when I made that choice. It was the morning of the funeral. In the funeral home, as we gathered to say our last good-byes, I looked at his little body, lying so quietly in the coffin, and I just let him know in silence that I would always love him. I kissed him, and then as I turned to look at my other two children, I said to myself, "I will never let my love for Wes interfere with the love that I will give to my other two children. I promise myself that." I made a conscious choice that day. If you ask my children, I believe they would tell you that I indeed have succeeded in loving them to my potential, despite the fact that Wes died.

We have so much love in our hearts that a death does not have to prevent us from giving our love to others, whether it be another child or another spouse. Don't be stingy with your love. Open your heart. You will find that there are so many benefits to you for sharing your love. You deserve love in your life. Don't deny yourself a precious gift. There are others that want to love you. Drop the shield and let others love you. You will be more satisfied with your life if you do.

Believe in Yourself

Believing in yourself takes self-confidence. Most people do not think they are confident. So here is what you do to teach yourself you are more confident in yourself than you think you are. Get a piece of paper and write down self-estimates. For instance, write down "cook." Then give yourself a plus or minus depending on whether you think you are effective at cooking or not effective. If you think you are a little of both, put a plus and a minus. Write down "friend." Give yourself a plus or a minus. Write down "honesty." Give yourself a plus or a minus. Write down all the roles of your life (parent, daughter, teacher, volunteer). Write down all the functions of your life (driving, loving, housekeeping). Write down all the qualities in you (honesty, responsibility, cleanliness). Give yourself a plus or minus or both for each area. Then count the pluses and the minuses. Most of the time, you will find that you have more pluses than minuses. If you don't, then either start thinking of yourself in a more positive way or seek therapy for that negative self-perception. Your self-concept or self-esteem is made up of self-estimates. How do you estimate yourself? If you estimate yourself in a positive way, then you will have a better chance of believing in yourself. If you estimate yourself in a negative way, then you will not believe in yourself.

It is vastly important to believe in yourself if you want to recover from the loss of a loved one. If you believe in your own self-worth, then you will begin to set goals. You will believe you can be happy without your loved one. You will choose to socialize again. You will make your life meaningful. All of these are necessary to your own life satisfaction. Finally, when you believe in yourself, you can then start to like yourself for the way you are behaving in life, and that makes you happy.

Love Yourself

Love of life has to do with how you feel about you in the world. When you love yourself, you feel satisfied. When you lose a loved one, you feel sorrowful and then may do things that you would not necessarily do otherwise. You might start doing things that you do not necessarily consider to be appropriate. You always hear about the little phrase "drowning your sorrows." That could mean drinking alcohol to excess, trying drugs, doing risky behaviors such as driving fast or having unprotected sex, overeating, not eating enough to stay healthy, isolating yourself from social contact, being irritable to others, overdosing, manipulating, or other behaviors that could lead you to not like yourself very much.

So what do you do if you have gotten into this downward spiral? You can choose to take a look at your behaviors and ask yourself, "Is this behavior getting me to the goal of being happy without my loved one in my life?" If the answer is no, then stop that behavior and substitute a behavior that will get you to your goal. Instead of drinking to excess, get involved in a community service project, which might get you involved with others, which might put you into a situation in which you meet new friends. Instead of overeating, get a part-time job teaching aerobics and generate more income to go on more vacations and enjoy life. Involvement leads to new experiences. New experiences give you the opportunity to be who you want to be. When you are who you want to be, you like yourself. You are congruent.

Congruence means that how you see yourself in your mind matches how you are behaving. If you were a loving mother, and a death sent you on a path to be someone you did not like, you can change that. If you change your behavior to match who you believe you are, then you are congruent. When you are congruent, you are more satisfied with your life. When you are satisfied with your life, you are happy.

Review

Remember that missing someone and being happy are not mutually exclusive. You can do both at the same time. So despite the fact that you lost a loved one, you can choose to be happy. Choosing the following things in your life will help. Choose to be thankful, to let go, to get excited, to ask questions, to think positive, to revise love, to believe in yourself, and to love yourself. When you do these things, you will create your own life satisfaction. Your satisfaction does not depend on who is with you in life; it depends on how you think about life and what you are doing in life. Believe you can be happy despite the loss of a loved one. Believe in yourself. It's time to mend your broken heart.

In the next chapter, we will discuss how to manage your emotions so that when negative emotions sweep over you, you will be prepared to handle them. Negative emotions can wash over you like a tidal wave. You are rarely prepared for the force with which they hit you. Denying your negative emotions just leads to stuffing them inside. When they are stuffed inside you, they tend to come out in your body in the form of aches and pains. They can also emerge as anger. So instead of denying them, you can learn to manage them.

Manage Emotions

One of the most difficult tasks during any loss is what to do with the feelings that keep rushing over you. It is as if you are stretched out on a sandy beach and feelings like waves keep washing over you. They may not be as steady as the waves are but are sometimes as often and as forceful. So what do you do with feelings once they begin to wash over you and you feel out of control?

A lot of research and writing has been done in the field of emotional intelligence. Emotional intelligence has to do with the regulation of emotion. It concerns what you do with the emotions once you get them. I am going to teach you the way I have dealt with my emotions for thirty years. It may not be the most current way, yet it is a way that has worked for me. I would like to share that with you as one way among many to handle those emotions that sweep over you like a wave.

Learning to manage your emotions has to do with getting both your body and your mind under control. First, you need to be able to stop the tense feeling in your body when you become emotional. Second, you need to choose to run the feeling through your cognitive filter before deciding upon a response.

Let's start first with understanding what happens when you get emotional. When you become emotional, this uneasy, anxious, uncomfortable feeling starts to sweep over your body, making your mind start to race. When this state grabs you, you use energy that you could use for performing tasks, solving problems, or being creative. Emotionality steals your energy and leaves you drained and tired. So when your emotions rise, you can choose to learn to do something to make them manageable. I am going to teach you two ways to do that. First, I will teach you a physical way, using your breathing to handle your emotions. Then I will teach you a cognitive way, using your mind to handle your emotions. In combination when applied, these two techniques will help you to manage your emotions when they rise within you.

Let's understand what happens when you feel emotional, no matter what emotion that happens to be. When you feel uneasy or anxious or uncomfortable, your mind begins to race, that is, sometimes you get confused, and other times you have so many thoughts at once you feel overwhelmed. When you are confused and overwhelmed, it is harder to take action. It is as if you are on pause. It is not clear what you need to do at that particular moment.

Let me give you a common example of this. You need to choose a headstone for the grave site. You visit the merchant and are shown all the choices and prices. You get so confused and overwhelmed that you are unable to decide. So you go home with your brain feeling as if it is a jet speeding across the sky. You cannot focus on anything else. Your mind seems out of control. You know you need to make the decision soon. You become gripped with fear.

Your mind is racing with all the what ifs. What if I choose something that doesn't represent my loved one? What if I forget to put something on it that is important? What if the merchant asks a question I cannot answer? What if others in the family do not like what I choose? Your heart starts to beat faster. You have a nauseous feeling in the pit of your stomach. You pace the floor. Your body is tense. Your muscles ache. So what can you do so the fear does not steal your energy that you need to make the best decision?

First, the most important thing to do is to get control of the physical aspects of your emotion; in this case, it is fear. When you are emotional, your body is tense. What you can choose to do is to create an opposite response. That is, you can choose to make your body relax. When your body is relaxed, it cannot be tense. Tension and relaxation are what we call mutually exclusive body functions. You choose one or the other because the body cannot do them both at the same time. When you choose to make your body relax, then the tension cannot stay. You have willed away the tension by helping your body to relax. When your body is relaxed, your mind slows down, and you can think clearer. When you can think clearer, then you can make some wise choices. So let's look at the first step of a two-step process to learn to manage your emotions.

Physiological

The question is, how do you take your body from tenseness to relaxation? What you want to do is create a relaxation response to your tenseness. I want to teach you a deep-breathing technique, which I call "creating relaxation," that will help you get your body to relax. Listen carefully and do this technique. First, sit down in a comfortable easy chair or lie on your couch or your bed. Pick anywhere you will not be distracted for the next three minutes. I am going to take you through a series of eighteen deep breaths. We will go through six steps, and at each step, you will take three deep breaths.

So first, just take three huge, deep breaths. Make your diaphragm expand with each deep breath. As you take in the deep breath, let the air go all the way to your diaphragm. Hold it in your diaphragm for the count of three. Then expel the air by blowing it out with your mouth open. Breathe in. Hold one, two, three. Expel. Breathe in. Hold one, two, three. Do it one more time. Breathe in. Hold one, two, three. Expel. Okay, do you have the idea of deep breathing?

That's just the first step of six steps I will teach you. The first set of three deep breaths I call "just breathe." When you sense your body feeling tense, you stop and just start taking three deep breaths. This allows you to start taking control of your body.

The second step is to take your focus of awareness to the diaphragm and feel the diaphragm moving in and out. Take three more deep breaths. So as you breathe three more times, let your mind wander to your diaphragm as you feel it going in and out. Be sure to take three deep breaths and hold them for the count of three.

The third step is very important because it engages your right brain, where pictures and metaphors exist. With the next set of three deep breaths, keep your focus of attention at the diaphragm area and begin to create a tranquil, peaceful scene using all five senses. It can be a place at which you have felt peaceful in the past, or it can be an imaginary place you dream up in your mind of your ultimate peaceful spot. Either will work. The important thing to remember is to create this peaceful place using all five senses of sight, sound, smell, touch, and taste.

Let me give you an example of the one I use. I was in Colorado one year in August. I woke up one morning about six. I grabbed a cup of coffee and went outside to sit by the small stream that ran next to the cabin at which I was staying. As I walked out, the sun was just coming up. I could see the sparkles the sun created on the stream. I could hear the water rushing over the rocks in the stream. I could smell the campfires from other cabins and the aroma of my coffee. I could feel the gentle breeze on my face. I sat down next to the stream. I touched the cold water in the stream. I tasted my cinnamon coffee. Then I took a deep breath and thought how wonderful it was to be at such a peaceful, tranquil place. So that's the peaceful scene using all five senses that I use when I need to will away tension and bring relaxation back to my body.

Here is another example using all five senses. Think of walking on a beach. See the colorful sailboats on the water. Hear the ocean waves lapping up on the sand. Smell the fresh salt water. Feel the heat of the sand beneath your feet. Take a cool sip of your lemonade as you kick at the water covering your feet as the waves roll gently upon the shore. So either remember or dream up a peaceful place. After you get the image, then take three deep breaths as you create this peaceful place using your five senses of sight, sound, smell, touch, and taste. Be sure to feel that peaceful feeling the scene creates for you.

With the fourth set of three deep breaths, you will move the peaceful feeling to the heart area. So as you take the next three deep breaths, move your peaceful feeling to the heart. The heart area is synonymous with feelings. So you want to move the peaceful feeling to the heart area, where that other feeling is causing you to be emotional. You want to override the tense feeling with the peaceful feeling.

Once you feel the peacefulness around the heart area, then you take the fifth set of three deep breaths while you move the peaceful feeling throughout your body. Move the peaceful feeling to your torso, especially to the shoulder area, where tension loves to reside. Move the peaceful feeling to your legs, to your arms, and to your head. Feel the peaceful feeling moving throughout your body.

For the sixth set of three deep breaths, you do what I call "bask in the glow of the peacefulness." You just breathe with this feeling of renewed confidence in yourself and your ability to handle anything that life presents to you.

Let's review. First, just breathe. Second, take your focus of attention to the diaphragm. Third, create a peaceful scene using all five senses and feel the peacefulness. Fourth, move the peaceful feeling to the heart area to replace the current emotional response. Fifth, spread the peacefulness throughout your body. Sixth, bask in the glow of the peacefulness.

What I recommend that you do is to do this deep-breathing technique twice a day for five weeks to really be able to get the best relaxation response you can, so that when you become emotional, you can call up the relaxation response any time in just seconds. The first week, keep your eyes closed when you do the technique. During the second week, open your eyes and focus on an object when you do the technique. The third week, begin to reduce the number of breaths at each step by one. That is, do only two deep breaths at each of the six steps with eyes opened, focused on an object. During the fourth week, take only one deep breath at each step, with eyes open, focused on an object. The fifth week, just take three deep breaths without focusing on anything. I have created the following chart for quick reference.

Have this chart beside you to read for the first few times you try it.

Creating Relaxation

You will be taking eighteen deep breaths in a series of three, at six spots on your body. Sit in a comfortable chair with legs and arms uncrossed. Close your eyes. Follow this sequence, taking three deep breaths at each spot.

1. Just breathe
2. Take your focus of attention to the diaphragm area. Feel the diaphragm going in and out.

3. Create a peaceful scene using all five senses of sight, sound, smell, touch, and taste. (For example: see yourself walking on a sandy beach, hear the waves rolling onto the shore, smell the hotdogs at the vender's booths along the beach, feel the sun on your face, and taste your fresh lemonade.) Then feel the sense of peacefulness you have created.

4. Move the peacefulness to the heart area and feel the peacefulness there.

5. Spread the peacefulness throughout your body, especially to your legs and arms and head.

6. Bask in the glow of the peacefulness.

Here is the strategy to use to make this work quicker for you. Do each step twice a day for one week.

1. Do the eighteen deep breaths with your eyes closed twice a day.

2. Do the eighteen deep breaths with your eyes open and focused on an object twice a day.

3. Reduce the number of deep breaths by one at each spot, so you are doing only two deep breaths at each of the six spots on your body with eyes open and focused on an object twice a day.

4. Reduce the number of deep breaths by two at each spot, so you are doing only one deep breath at each of the six spots on your body

with eyes open and focused on an object twice a day.

5. Just take three very long deep breaths anywhere, twice a day.

So now you have learned what to do to help your body become relaxed and to help your mind slow down. Next, your task is to begin to manage your thoughts so that you can develop an action plan. You can choose to decide what to do about that emotion that captured you and held you hostage. Step two is to use cognitive processing.

Cognitive

I believe to know what to do with an emotion once it comes upon you, you need a technique to take what you feel and lead it to an action as a result of a thought. What this means is that the heart feels, then you take that feeling and run it through your brain so that you can problem solve about the feeling, and then you develop an action as a result of problem solving. Here is how it works. I have developed five questions to ask yourself once a feeling has taken command of you. I call this the process of de-escalating emotionality.

First, ask yourself, "What just happened, or what was I thinking?" Let's say as an action you just picked up a picture of your son who is dead and tears came to your eyes and you experienced this overwhelming feeling of sadness. So what happened was I picked up his picture and I started to cry because I had a feeling. Let's look at what you could have been thinking that might create a feeling. Say you were thinking that next Wednesday is his birthday. So what you were thinking was *I remembered it would soon be his birthday, and I started to cry because I had a feeling.* The important thing here is to verbalize your experience. Give words to it. That way it gets outside of you and you do not harbor it inside to come out as somatic complaints later.

Second, ask yourself, "What am I feeling?" I will take you through this using the example above about thinking that next Wednesday is his birthday. Label the feeling. Perhaps you were feeling "disappointed" because you loved giving him presents and watching his face light up when you had picked out just the right gift for him. Next Wednesday, you will "not" be able to experience that joy. So you are disappointed. You may be having other feelings too, like sadness that he is no longer with you. However, at this moment in time, deep down, you are really reacting to the disappointment. So label the deep-down feeling. Don't settle for labeling yourself as sad. Get to know the other feelings that an experience or a thought can create in you. Be a "feelings expert." Discern exactly what feeling you are dealing with at the time. Do not move to the next step until you give the feeling a name.

Third, ask yourself, "What does this mean to me?" Perhaps the meaning it has for you, besides not having your wonderful loved one to take care of and to share life with, is that you miss doing something special for someone that is important to you on that person's special day. So, in essence, you miss the joyfulness of giving. The important thing here is to know the meaning the feeling has created for you. This step takes the feeling to the mind. Once in the mind, the fourth step can be confronted. Never leave this question unanswered because it is paramount to the next step.

Fourth, ask yourself, "What can I do or think about this?" In essence, you problem solve. You solve the problem in the context of the meaning it holds for you and not necessarily what is happening. You could solve the problem of what is happening by putting the picture down and making yourself busy with other things. That might not get to the heart of the problem, and you will still be dealing with that feeling. So solve the problem in the context of the meaning. Remember the meaning is that you miss doing something for someone special to you and miss the joy of giving, so you are feeling disappointed.

You can solve a problem in two ways. You can solve it by doing something or by thinking something different. So here are some examples of what you can do. On his special day, I can give a monetary gift to his favorite charity. So you give a gift to some charity in his name. For instance, on my son's birthday each year, I would give two films that had just come out to the film library at the hospital that took care of my son during his eight years of treatment.

On his special day, I can send a random gift to another person that I love or appreciate, such as one of his special friends. I did not do this on his birthday, but I did send a present to my son's best friend at Christmastime. On his special day, I can take flowers to his grave. I change his flowers every season, so on his special day, I bring a happy birthday balloon to his grave and tie it on the flower holder. On his special day, I can write him a letter and put it in a special box, and every year on his special day, I can add to the collection. I have never written him letters, but I do think this is a good idea for people who love to journal.

So now, let me give you some examples of what you could think in order to solve the problem. I can think that his special day will be a joy-filled day because I am going to have the attitude that I am so thankful that he was born and I got to share these few wonderful years with him. For example, we found my son's first brain tumor when he was three. He had three major brain surgeries over eight years until his death. I had him for eight more years than I could have had him. I am thankful for those additional years, although I always wish there had been more.

I can think that his special day will be joyful, because I am going to celebrate it by taking off work and spending it with a friend doing something I really love doing. For example, once I took off work on his birthday and spent the day photographing scenery, because I love photography. Another one of his birthdays, I took off work and spent the day writing an article to put on my Web site, because I love to share my ideas with people. Just do something that you absolutely love doing. In essence, you are equating his birthday with your pleasure. So when you think of his birthday, you think of fun.

So let's say you choose to give a gift to a charity and take off work to take some photographs because you enjoy photography. Do not stop with deciding what to do or what to think. Take the next step. Often, when a person comes up with a solution, the solution never gets implemented. Why? The answer is because no plan is made to carry out the solution.

Fifth, ask yourself, "What is my plan?" You develop a strategy for making your solution happen. So you say to yourself, "Tomorrow at work, I am going to ask for Wednesday off this coming week. On Saturday, I will look up on the Internet all the charities that do special things for terminally ill children. Sunday, I will choose one of those charities. When I awake on Wednesday, I will send a check to the charity I chose. Sometime Wednesday morning, I will take my camera and head to the nearest zoo and take photos of the animals. I will use my digital camera and spend the afternoon printing off some photos to have framed. I will take the photos to the framer or frame them myself. When the photos are framed, I will put them up in the house as a special reminder of how alive I am, even though my son is no longer with me."

So you develop a plan for that day to create some joyfulness in you. What is important here is that you make a plan based on expectations of yourself and not on others. That way, you are empowered to do something about your feelings, so that you don't feel so out of control. You use the feeling to create an action or a different way of thinking (a new perspective). In essence, you are actually using the feeling to your benefit, not letting it overpower you.

Now you have no excuse not to be capable of handling those emotions that wash over you like a wave. However, with all things that you learn, "practice makes perfect." You won't be able to do this the first dozen times you try to manage your emotions. It's just like learning to play the piano. If you have never played before, you start out learning just a few notes, and as you get better with practice, you can play a song.

De-escalating Emotionality

Ask yourself the following questions when your emotions overtake you and you need to manage them.

> What just happened, or what was I thinking?
> What am I feeling?
> What does this mean to me?
> What can I do or think about this?
> What is my plan?

So, you can handle the emotions that come to you by asking yourself some questions that help you de-escalate your emotionality and help you to think at a rational level. This method takes some time and thought. At times, though, we need ideas that we can implement quickly. Following, I have described some techniques to use when time does not permit pondering.

Brief Techniques to Manage Emotions

Sometimes, we just need some brief ways to immediately handle our emotions as we are working on the ways that take more practice, such as the two above. Here is a list of the easier ways to handle emotions in the moment. Remember that the ones above are much better to use in the long run.

Places and Situational Reminders

Sometimes you experience either places or situations that remind you of your dead loved one. When this happens, a wave of feeling rushes over you. What do you do with that feeling if it is a negative one? First, prepare yourself for these. You know what places and what situations give rise to those feelings. Sometimes, you can design a response that helps you to manage the emotions that come along with the place or situation. Sometimes, you just need to avoid those places or situations. Let me give you some examples.

I knew that seeing the sunbeams flowing out of a cloud reminded me of Wes being in heaven. So every time I would be driving and saw the sunbeams, I would have an emotion sweep over me. Sometimes it was so strong it would take my breath away. For the longest time, I would become tearful. Eventually, I decided I needed to prepare for this and could choose my response. I could not tell the sun to stop creating that amazing sight in the sky, but I could do something about my response to it. I decided that when I saw the sunbeams flowing out of a cloud, instead of responding with sadness, I would think that beautiful picture was an affirmation that Wes was happy in heaven. It was like thinking that the sunbeams were his smile. Each time I see the sunbeams flowing from a cloud now, I smile because Wes is smiling.

On the other hand, I never have been able to comfortably sit in nine o'clock mass without being emotional. That was the time that we went to mass with Wes on a regular basis. I can go to five thirty mass, seven o'clock mass, or eleven o'clock mass just fine, but the nine o'clock mass just creates too many memories that flood my mind, so I avoid it. I have choices. I can go to the same church, but I just avoid the time that does not work for me. If there were only one time, then I would work on changing my thinking, but since I have other choices, then I do not invest emotional energy in being able to handle this situation. Remember, you always have choices.

So, see how you can take a negative and change it into a positive? Or if you have other choices, you can choose not to waste emotional energy on it. You are in control of what you think. So when it is negative, change it into a positive if you choose to spend time doing that.

Not Mutually Exclusive

Most people maintain the fallacy that joy and sorrow are mutually exclusive. That means that if you feel sorrow, then you absolutely cannot feel joy. Wrong. Joy and sorrow walk hand in hand. In fact, to know sorrow helps to enhance your joy.

Sometimes, a person gets caught up in the belief that if joy is felt that negates missing the person. One thinks that if one truly misses the dead person that one cannot possibly experience joy. Have you ever caught yourself thinking the following ideas? To be joyful would take away from my memory of that person. To be joyful would show I don't really miss that person. To be joyful would be self-ish. How can I be joyful when I am so miserable? What would others think if I came to a party when I am supposed to be grieving? This thinking only prevents the grieving process from progressing and stops resolution from happening. Let me walk you through the idea that you can be joyful and sorrowful at the same time.

Let's say that joy and sorrow are on opposite ends of the spectrum. If you are full of sorrow, you are sad, you grieve, you feel a sense of loss, you are disappointed, you suffer, you mourn, and you cry. On the opposite end, if you are full of joy, you are glad, you are happy, you are delighted, you feel great pleasure, you are pleased, and you smile. Let's say that you are extremely sad because your son died. At the same time, your daughter gets an award at school, and you are so proud of her that you experience joy. You can have both feelings at the same time. One does not diminish the other. You can be as filled with sorrow as you are filled with joy, and it goes on inside you simultaneously.

I will give you an example of this from my own life. I remember the day that my son Tony won the high school senior boy award for loyalty, service, and character during graduation awards day. I was so proud of him. When I walked out of the high school gym that day, the first thought in my mind was that I must call my mother and let her know. She always was so joyful at learning about honors that the children received. I immediately became sad because eight months earlier my mom had died. So all at once, I experienced joy and sorrow at the same time: joy that my son won the award and sorrow that I no longer had my mom to share that joyful experience with me.

Now let me talk about the idea that when you have known great sorrow, you can experience great joy. This is presented so that you can choose to have a thought that leads you to greater joy in your life because you have suffered great sorrow. So here is how you can use your sorrow to give you even greater joy. What a great way to use your sorrow!

Let's think of this like looking at a ruler. Put great sorrow on the zero end of the ruler and great joy at twelve inches. Most people live life between four and eight on the ruler of life. They don't experience deep sadness or great joy. Once a person experiences a two in sadness, he/she is better able to experience a ten in joy. Why? The answer is that because there is a new comparison level. When you feel the great sorrow, you then have a comparison from which to feel greater joy too. I would imagine the opposite is true also. When you have had the great joy of success, failure seems much greater than if you had never experienced great success before. Get the idea?

Here is the example from my life. Since my son died at age eleven, I did not get to witness his excitement over his first date, his graduation from high school, his wedding day nor any of the other milestones of life. So when my other children experienced these milestones, it was as if the joy in my heart was tenfold. I am sure they often wondered why I was so excited and invested in their enthusiasm about their milestones of life. I was so thankful that they were able to experience them and that I was there to witness their joy. Since I knew the experience of a broken heart from the death of my child, I was able to know the joy of a heart that was expanding with joy for the experiences of my other children.

So the bottom line here is to choose to believe that your sorrow enhances your joy. You can do that because you have control of what you think and what you do. You can change your thinking or your behavior anytime you want to, so if you are thinking that you cannot be joyful because you are sorrowful, throw that thought out. It is not getting you to the goal of living a satisfying life even though you have had a loss in your life.

Shortcut

I am going to give you an idea for a shortcut too. Sometimes, you just don't feel like going through the steps to de-escalate and just want to solve the problem to the situation and not the meaning. So if that is what you desire, here is a quick fix.

If a negative emotion hits you and you want to do something immediately, do this. First, say to yourself, "I feel (state a feeling) because (state a reason)." Second, do something about the reason. For example, you might say, "I feel scared because I won't be able to stop crying when I write the thank-you notes for the funeral flowers." Brainstorm what you can do about not being able to stop crying when you write thank-you notes. You could have a friend or friends write them for you. You could write a dozen each day and expect to cry during that time. You could take one day and do nothing but write thank-you notes and cry until you get them done. There are many things you can do to deal with your scared feeling and get rid of it.

Let me tell you about one with which I dealt. I cried a lot at first after Wes died. At one point, I said to myself, "I am frustrated with myself because I cannot control the crying." Crying was getting in the way of my being productive. I don't feel good unless I am productive. I did not want to go on medication to help control the crying. So after brainstorming a lot of alternatives, I finally decided that I would limit my crying. I would allow myself to cry until after I took a shower in the morning. As soon as the shower was turned off, then so were the tears. Then I gave myself three major things to accomplish each day. When those three things were done, then if I so chose, I could cry again because I had been productive. I got rid of the feeling of frustration because I could now control the crying in order to be more productive.

Use a shortcut for managing the emotion. Identify your feeling. Find the reason for the feeling. Then do something about the reason. Just say to yourself, "I feel (state the feeling) because (state the reason)." Then proceed to do something about the reason.

Keeping on Track

You only have control of two things in your life. You have control of your own behavior and not the behavior of others, and you have control of what you think, which is your perspective of life. You do not have control over events that happen or who is or is not in your world. To keep on track, ask yourself this little question to manage the emotions that roll over you like a wave. I call this the monitoring question. Ask yourself, "Is what I am doing now or thinking now getting me to my goal?" In this case, the goal is mending my broken heart. Let me explain.

Let's do an example of a behavior. When you refuse an invitation to have dinner with friends because you believe you are too sad and would not be good company, ask yourself this question, "Is denying myself spending time with friends who really care about me getting me to the goal of mending my broken heart?" If they are friends who are always negative or uninteresting, then perhaps the answer to the question would be yes. If they are friends who lift you up by just being around them because they are positive people, then the answer to your question is no. If the answer is no, then change what you are doing. In this case, you would accept your friends' invitation and know that you will have fun.

Let's take another example. This time, we will do a thinking example. You keep thinking that you will always be unable to face the milestones that your son would experience had he lived. So ask yourself, "Is my thinking I will be unable to manage my emotions getting me to the goal of mending my broken heart?" No, it isn't. So instead, say to yourself, "I will think, instead, that the year that my son should have graduated from high school will be difficult, and I know that I will be able to handle my emotions." Your thoughts become a self-fulfilling prophecy. I remember the year that my son would have graduated. I purposely planned a vacation at that time so that I would be out of town having fun.

To keep on track, ask yourself , "Is what I am doing now or thinking now getting me to my goal?" If the answer is no, change what you are doing or thinking. If the answer is yes, then keep doing that behavior or keep thinking that thought, because it is getting you to your goal.

Command Technique

When all else fails to help with that wave of emotion, here is one quick technique that helps. When the wave hits you and your thoughts start racing, say to

yourself, "Stop, (insert your name)! Don't go there."
So you command yourself to stop your thought.
Then you tell yourself not to think that way. Then
you make yourself think about something else.

I used this method at first when I would see sunbeams projected from clouds. I would begin thinking of Wes and start to cry. It's hard to drive when
I am crying, so I knew I needed to take control
of that emotion. I just said, "Stop, Rita! Don't go
there." Then I thought about what I needed to cook
for supper or what I needed to buy at the grocery
store. Later, I implemented a more productive technique that changed my perception, but at first, I just
needed to make the feeling go away quickly.

This works in the short term when you need to
focus on other things, but it does not help in the
long run. Use it when you need to stay focused and
don't have time for the longer versions of managing
your emotions.

Review

Let's review the ideas in this chapter. The first
step is to get your body relaxed and stop the racing
thoughts. The second step is to define an action
plan for what to do with your feelings. Here is a
review of each step.

To begin with, it is important to get your body to
stop being tense and get relaxed instead. To accomplish this, choose to learn the relaxation response. Yes,
it will take you about a month to really learn it well;
however, it is well worth the time spent. It is just like
riding a bike. Once you learn it, it is in your memory,
and you can choose to use it anytime you desire.

Let's go through the steps once more. First, just breathe. Second, take your focus of attention to the diaphragm. Third, create a peaceful scene using all your senses, and feel the peacefulness. Fourth, move the peaceful feeling to the heart area to replace the current emotional response. Fifth, spread the peacefulness throughout your body. Sixth, bask in the glow of the peacefulness.

Next, once your body is relaxed, it is important to get your mind to stop racing so you can think clearly in order to take effective action. To accomplish this, choose to understand your emotions and then make an action plan to help you be effective. Let's review how to filter your emotions through your mind.

First, you can choose to de-escalate your emotions by asking yourself five questions for developing a plan to get rid of the negative feeling, so you feel more in charge of the negative emotions. Those questions are:

What just happened, or what was I thinking?
What am I feeling?
What does this mean to me?
What can I do or think about this?
What is my plan?

Second, you can choose to either prepare yourself for situations, or choose alternatives and not waste emotional energy.

Third, you can choose to believe that joy and sorrow walk hand in hand. You do not need to exclude joy from your life just because you are sorrowful.

Fourth, you can choose to take a short cut to get rid of a feeling so it does not render you helpless.

State the following sentence: I feel (state a feeling) because (state a reason). Then do something about the reason.

Fifth, you can choose to use the monitoring question that monitors the two things you control in your life, that is, your behavior and your thoughts. Ask, "Is what I am doing now or thinking now getting me to my goal?" If the answer is no, change what you are doing or thinking. If the answer is yes, then keep doing that behavior or keep thinking that thought because it is getting you to your goal.

Sixth, you can choose to use the command technique when you need to stay focused. Say to yourself, "Stop!" State your name. Then add, "Don't go there." Next, either do or think something different to get back on track.

I know you have the potential to handle your emotions in a way that is effective in your life. You can choose to be powerful in dealing with any emotional wave that sweeps over you. So, relax on the beach of life and know that when the wave comes in you are prepared to deal with it. Believe you can manage your emotions. Believe in yourself. It's time to mend your broken heart.

How you think about what is happening to you has a lot to do with your response. Maintaining a positive perspective is paramount to mending your broken heart. Your positive perspective can create a pro-action versus a reaction to events in your life. To begin, you can learn to change your negative perceptions.

Change Perceptions

"People are not disturbed by things, but by the view they take of them" (Epictetus, AD 55–135). Epictetus was speaking of perspective. The way we view our world either creates misery or allows us to flourish. Do you want the death of someone you love to create misery in your life? Or do you want to flourish, despite the death of your loved one? It is your choice. Perspective can help you with that choice.

What do I mean by perspective? Perspective is an evaluation with proportional importance given to the component parts. That means that all of us take in information. Then we process it in some way. Next, we come up with a conclusion about how to use the information for ways of behaving or thinking. Being able to see the big picture is what makes perspective an effective strength to have.

What are some of the perceptions that a person has when experiencing grief? One perception is that the crying will never end. Another is that the pain will never go away. These are both fear perceptions. When you get stuck in your fear of never being able to control your emotions, then you feel helpless and hopeless. Those two feelings lead to the state of depression. Taking a healthy perspective of the death of a loved one will aid in decreasing depression and increasing life satisfaction. So let's look at a few ways to gain greater perspective

Reframing

One technique you can choose to use concerning the death of a loved one is to reframe your thoughts about the event. To reframe, a person chooses to look at something in another way. Imagine this example: if you take a picture you have painted and make six prints of it, then ask six different framers to be creative and frame the print, you will have six very different looks to the same print. Some of the frames will appeal to you, and you would hang them in your home. Some you might not believe fit your style, and you would not hang them in your home.

Let me give you an ordinary example of a reframe. I live in the country. I have a private bridge on the private lane from the county road that allows me to get to my home. Because of drainage over the years from some new subdivisions, my bridge took a beating and the concrete gave way, so the bridge had to be condemned and a new one constructed. During the months of waiting before the bridge could be built, I had to drive through the neighbor's pasture for about a mile to get access to the county road. Now, I could have been upset on a daily basis, complaining about the inconvenience it caused me, the extra time, the bumping around on all the holes and mounds, the wear and tear on the car, and getting out in the rain to open gates to pastures. Or, I could look at it from the perspective that each and every day I get to see wild turkey, deer, coyotes, a myriad of birds, beautiful, fall wildflowers, very old oak and birch trees, and much more that brings beauty and joy to my world. You can do the same thing with an incident that happens to you, like the death of a loved one.

Reframing is just taking something negative and turning it into a positive. This choice is up to you in your daily living. So how does this apply to the death of a loved one? Although you may believe that you can never make the death of a loved one a positive idea, that may not be entirely true for every death. When a loved one is suffering, you can reframe the death to peacefulness for that person. If you have a strong Christian belief, you may think that heaven is a better place for your loved one or that God is calling your loved one to heaven for some unknown reason. These reframes focus on the loved one who died.

However, I want you to think of a reframe in terms of yourself and not in terms of your loved one. Let's look at those fear perceptions one at a time and reframe each. To reframe, state the reality in a positive way and then predict a positive outcome. The perception of "the crying will never end" can be reframed to the idea that the tears show how much I care and eventually the tears will give way to happy memories. The perception of "the pain will never go away" can be framed to the idea that the pain shows the depth of my love and eventually the pain will turn to gratitude that I was fortunate enough to spend part of my journey in life with my loved one. In each of these examples, I took a negative thought and changed it into a positive perspective with a positive outcome.

Let's move to another helpful way of dealing with perspective. This one has to do with being totally consumed with centering your thoughts only on you. This is good for a time when your heart is aching, but harmful to you if you continue to stay stuck in that spot.

Center of the Universe Thinking

I often talk to my clients about "center of the universe thinking," in which one focuses so much on the self that the big picture is lost and poor choices follow. Let me give you a picture of this. Let's say you are in the center of a circle. In order to see the entire environment around you, you would have to turn around 360 degrees. If you do that enough times to really get to know your environment, you would eventually get dizzy and fall down. However, if you walk to the periphery or the outer edge of the circle and turn and face inward, you are able to stand in one place and see the environment of the entire circle. When you stepped from the center to the periphery, you took a new perspective.

Here is another way to get the big picture. Let's say there is a mountain just on the border of the circle. If you climb up the mountain and look down upon the circle of your environment, then you get an even different view than from the periphery. This is the so-called "bird's eye" view. It is also called the "meta" view, meaning "higher" view. The idea is that it gives you a different way of seeing life, which, in turn, widens your perspective.

For example, one peripheral thought that might help widen your perspective is thinking of all traits as if they are on a continuum. Let me give you an illustration of this perceptual framework. Let's take the continuum of being rigid to being flexible. Seeing yourself as well as others as exhibiting traits that are mobile so that you can move up and down the continuum without feeling fake or phony is important to perspective. Take the example of deciding what to do socially with friends. Perhaps you are very flexible when it comes to what you do, such as see a movie, or have dinner, or go bowling with your friends. However, you may be rigid about how much money you spend on an evening out. You have, thus, in the same context (social) moved from one end of the continuum (flexible) to the other (rigid) while still being you.

In the case of death, what continuum do you use? In our lives, we have the continuum of holding on and letting go. We use it with our emotions. For instance, we hold on to resentment, contempt, and anger when we have been hurt. We use it with thoughts. For instance, we hold on to thinking that we cannot paint a picture when we have never tried, so we really don't know if we could paint or not. We use it with possessions. For instance, we hold on to old clothes that we know we will never wear again just in case we might need them. Letting go is difficult in many areas of our lives.

When it comes to death, we do not want to

let go because we fear we will forget the person. However, letting go and forgetting do not go hand in hand. We can let go and still have all the amazing memories we shared with that person. Yes, time dims some memories. In fact, time embellishes some memories too. At times, we idealize the dead loved one. We remember the good things and tend to forget the difficult times. That is normal. Remembering only the good things makes us peaceful. However, if we idealize the person, then it is more difficult to let go. Just know that letting go does not mean you will forget that person.

Many times, letting go has to do with what we find to fill the void left by our loved one. What are you doing with your time and energy that used to be filled with your loved one? I struggled with that at first. I finally filled my time with activities in which I was really interested. For instance, I enjoyed helping with the musicals my children were involved with in the local children's theatre. Pouring my energy into my other two children created happiness in my life. Yes, there was always that little part of me that wished Wes was in those musicals too, as he used to be. Wishing that did not stop me from being present to the moment and from feeling the happiness that was in my life. I stepped out of the center of the universe and to the periphery. I then saw that my life was filled with many opportunities to experience joy. I had a choice to put joy back in my life, or be stuck in the misery of missing Wes. Choosing to let go of the dream of having him there with me was my first step to reclaiming my happiness.

Getting out of the center of the universe will help you to widen your perspective. When you widen your perspective, you can let go easier. When you let go, you choose to reclaim your happiness. Let's look now at another way to gain perspective. This way has to do with being congruent.

Congruence versus Disharmony

The way we see our world can help us to move through our grief or be stuck in it. So what is your picture of the world? Do you have some rules that the world must abide by? If so, then it is time to take a look at that picture. Your perception just might be skewed compared to your reality. Making your reality closely match your picture of the world can add peace and tranquility where sorrow and pain exists. When your world gets peaceful and tranquil, then you are on your way to mending your broken heart. So how do you go through this integration process? First, what do I mean by your perception matching your reality? Let me explain.

Perception means what you are thinking in your head. Reality is what is really happening in your world. So if what is in your head is the same thing happening in your life, then you are what we call congruent. When perception and reality do not match, disharmony and incongruence result.

Let me give you some examples of disharmony. You think your daughter should get an award because she has done so many outstanding things in school and for her community, but someone else gets the award. Or, you worked really hard with your son in elementary school and middle school to teach him basketball. You even put him on many competitive teams and think he should be chosen for the high school basketball team, but he does not get chosen. Here's another. You think your wife does a lot of extra work for her employer, but when she asked for a raise, she does not get one. People around you are losing their jobs because the company is downsizing, and you think you are a valuable enough asset to keep, but you are let go. The picture in your mind does not match your reality.

Now let's look at perceptions about death. Let's say that your picture of the world is that a parent should never live longer than a child, but your child dies before you do. Here's another one: your picture of the world is that a couple should live happily into old age, but your wife dies young. All these are instances of how you think the world should be, but the picture does not really match your reality. This brings about disharmony in your life. This disharmony is especially prominent when someone dies.

The trick is to help your picture and your reality match more closely when they are far apart. When you get your picture and your reality to match, you are congruent. That means that all parts are coinciding exactly. You are then in harmony with yourself and you are peaceful. Being congruent creates tranquility in your life.

So what do you do if your reality and your perceptions are far apart? Several things are helpful. First, I want you to understand that your perceptions are one thing you can choose to change any time you want to. They are totally under your control. If you don't like the way you are thinking and it is not getting you to your goals, you can change your thoughts any time you desire to change them. Thinking can be controlled.

Say for instance that you are sad as I was because my son died. I can choose to think about it as positive or negative. The positive will lead to congruence and the negative will lead to disharmony. If I think that nothing will be the same and it is awful and I will continue to be sad and have no energy to be productive, then that is what will happen. If I think that nothing will be the same and although I am sad I will make my life productive, then that is what will happen. As I think, so it becomes.

Being present to your reality is very important to mending your broken heart. What perspective do you have of balance in your life? Your life has gotten out of balance. You need to get your life back in balance without your loved one in it. So first assess where you presently are concerning balance in your life. Remember in chapter four when we discussed creating life satisfaction? Let's now assess those areas of your life to see if you need balance. I am adding two more areas that need to be balanced. They are quiet time and fun time.

Get a poster board. Draw a big circle. Divide the circle into eight parts. Label the parts as follows: physical pleasures, mental pleasures, strengths, relationships, career, volunteerism, quiet time, and fun time. Give yourself a present moment rating between zero and ten on each.

Let's say that you rate physical pleasures a two. You are a slug when it comes to physical pleasures. You like hot showers, but you don't take time to exercise, get a massage, or relax on a park bench. Maybe you give yourself a zero on mental pleasures. You have nothing in your life that stirs you.

You have nothing that gets you so absorbed that time passes and you don't even realize it has passed. You have no hobbies that engage you totally. Maybe you rate your relationships as five. You have a few good friends, but lately since the death of your loved one, you have not engaged in activities with them. Maybe you give yourself an eight on career. You are doing pretty well, and although the death of your loved one can overpower you at home, you seem to do better when your career gives your mind something to focus on besides your grief. Perhaps you give yourself a three on volunteerism. You used to give your time but have not had the energy to give since the death of your loved one. Maybe you give yourself a four on quiet time. Even when you relax and try to enjoy just being quiet and peaceful, your mind drifts to your sadness. Maybe you give yourself a zero on fun time. You just do not feel like being joyful, no matter how much you used to enjoy activities in the past.

After you assess your present circumstances, ask yourself the following four questions:

Do I need more balance?
What areas need to change?
What can I add to or subtract from my life?
What are some strategies to get me to the goal of balance?

If your assessment is between eight and ten for all areas, you are in balance, and you are probably pretty happy. If several areas are low, then you need to change some things. Let's say your physical pleasures area is at a two. You can choose to add an exercise class or a massage. So your strategy is to sign up at your local exercise center to take a class once a week and call a massage therapist and get a massage scheduled for the first Wednesday of each month. Even if you do not have the luxury of spending money on classes or a massage, you could do this instead: You decide to walk with a friend during your lunch break on Tuesdays and Thursdays and ask your spouse to trade foot massages once a month. Remember that increasing those areas of your life that you rate as low will help you balance your life. When you have all areas of life satisfaction in balance, then you are more likely to be happy.

Next, I would like to share a perspective I learned from my son, Wes. He was a master at it. I believe this perspective allowed him to live a happy life, despite the fact that he had cancer.

Be Present to the Moment

Wes was always present to the moment. The past did not intrude on his happiness. The future never was a cause for worry. He truly lived in the moment. When he needed to take a bath, he enjoyed playing with the tub toys. When he needed to eat, he enjoyed making sandwiches. When he was tired, he rested. When he had energy, he played. He embraced all aspects of life.

How do you develop the skill of being present? To focus on the moment, you first need to notice what is going on around you. Second, experience something about what you see. Third, mentally note something about the experience. Fourth, take an action as a result of your thought. Let's look at each step.

First, you need to notice what is going on around you. Do you notice the sunset? Do you watch the clouds make figures in the sky? Do you see the daisies blooming along the road? Do you put music on so you can hear the relaxing, soothing sound? Do you hear the birds singing? Are you amazed at how the Internet works? Do you catch the excited expression on a child's face? Do you delight when a friend does an unexpected gesture for you? Do you marvel at a dancer gliding across the stage? Do you know what sculpture is in the park in which you walk? Do you realize what style architecture the homes around you are? Do you recognize what thrilled you about the last movie you watched? If you do, then you notice.

Many of us do not notice the little things in life, let alone the big things. Remember that saying about stopping to smell the roses? When you look out the window, what do you see? When you walk for exercise or take the dog for a walk, what do you see? When you are sitting in your easy chair, what do you see? When you are in the grocery store, what do you see? When you are on the subway or are taking a drive, what do you see? When you are at your job or sitting at your desk, what do you see? When you are cooking dinner, what do you see? So first, just notice what is around you, no matter where you are or what you are doing.

The second step is to experience something about what you see. The best way to do that is to actually have a feeling about it and label the feeling you are experiencing. When you catch the excited expression on a child's face, what do you feel? Happy? When you notice the sunset, what do you feel? Exuberant? When a friend does an unexpected gesture for you, what do you feel? Delighted? When you wonder how the Internet works, what do you feel? Curious? Each time you notice something, label the feeling it creates in you.

The third step is to take your experience to the brain and mentally note something about the experience. When you put music on to listen to the relaxing, soothing sound and feel peaceful, put the idea in your mind that when you need to feel peaceful, that Bach and not Mozart is more relaxing to you. When you hear the birds singing and you get curious as to what the bird looks like, note that you need to stop by the library and get a book on birds. When you wonder what sculpture is in the park in which you walk and feel curious to find out, make a note in your mind that you need to explore that question. When the last movie you watched was outstanding because you felt like crying and laughing all at the same time, note that you need to share information about this amazing film.

Fourth, because of your thought, take an action. Put Bach on instead of Mozart when you need to relax. Go to the library to get a book on birds. Stop and read the words on the sculpture in the park or call city hall to ask the history of the sculpture. Call a friend who enjoys movies and tell your friend about the great movie you watched.

Thus, one way to be present to the moment is to notice. You can choose to realize what you have noticed, claim what you felt about what you noticed, think about what you noticed, and do something with what you have noticed. The amazing thing about this is that you did it all yourself.

You choose to increase your awareness of the present. When you stay focused on the present, you will not lapse into past memories, which might pull you into sadness.

A second way to be present to the moment is to stop wishing you were somewhere else doing something different. When your focus of attention shifts from where you are to where you want to be, the comparison makes you miserable. If you choose to go to your son's baseball game, let your mind be there at the game. Do not wish you were home baking cookies for the bake sale. When you choose to take your daughter to the park, let your mind be there at the park. Do not wish you were shopping. Likewise, when you choose to help at the PTA fundraiser, do not let your mind drift to thinking that you would have had more fundraisers to attend if only your loved one was alive. Do you understand how wishing for something instead of being present to what you are doing can create misery in you?

All of this has to do with the way you think about your world. The way you think about your world has to do with perspective. Your perspective is under your control because perspective has to do with thinking. What you think is your choice. So if you are thinking something that is making you miserable, you can choose to change it. If the dream in your mind is one that has your loved one as a star player, then your thinking will make you miserable. So let's revise your dream.

Revise the Dream

What is your picture of the world without your loved one in it? Let's do some work on painting a new picture of your world. The old one is no longer effective. You can choose to create a new picture without your loved one in it. The choice is yours.

A large part of healing is to let go of the life you dreamed of having that included the person who died. When you hold on to the dream, you are never satisfied with your life. Holding on to the dream causes you misery. You, in essence, create your own misery by wishing that your loved one was still in your life. You cannot control that, so your wish will never come true, and you will continue to be dissatisfied. You are not only dissatisfied; you become irritable and unpleasant to be around because you see only the negative side of life.

What you can choose to do is to make up a new dream that does not include the person who died. Yes, I know that is not what you want to do. I know you wish with your whole heart that your loved one was with you again. I know it is difficult. I also know that your loved one would be really upset with you if he knew that you were miserable because you are thinking and longing for him. So recreate your dream in honor of your loved one. Do it because it will help you heal. If your loved one was a loving person, he would want you to mend your broken heart.

Just listen to an idea about how to do this before you negate it. First, get a dry erase board or a chalkboard. Get colored markers or colored chalk. Get a timer. Get some relaxing music and something to play it on. Go to a quiet spot in your house. Turn on the music. Set your timer for thirty minutes. Relax in a chair or on a couch or on the floor. Close your eyes. Take in big deep breaths for about three minutes. Then ask yourself the question: What will make my life satisfying without (name of your loved one who died)? Ponder that, keeping your eyes closed for another few minutes. Then open your eyes and look at the blank board. Pick up the marker or chalk and let your hand do the work. Work on the picture for the remainder of the thirty minutes. When the timer goes off, quit where you are. If you do not have any more ideas about what to draw and still have time, just keep looking at what you have drawn until something occurs to you or the timer goes off. Do not erase it. Keep it somewhere safe so other family members do not erase it.

Let a few days go by, and then do the process over again. Put your music on. This time set your timer for twenty minutes. Relax and breathe deeply. Ponder this question: what do I need to add to my picture so that my life will be satisfying without (name of your loved one who died)? Look at the picture and add whatever comes to your mind. Keep drawing or just looking at the picture until the timer goes off.

Do this a third time a few days later. Set your timer for ten minutes. Relax and breathe deeply. Ponder a third question: What would add value and happiness to my picture of life without (name of your loved one)? Look at the picture and draw what occurs to you.

Perhaps you will draw a picture. Perhaps your picture will have stick people or buildings or lines or swirls or words. Whatever comes to your mind, draw or write it. During another time, go to your quiet spot and this time just look at your picture and think about what message the picture has for you. For example, your picture might be a whole bunch of people in a circle. What would that mean in your life? It might mean that to make your life more satisfying, thus increasing happiness, you might need to join a group.

Another example might be that you drew a dollar sign. What would that mean to your life? Perhaps it means that you need to look for more meaningful work that brings different financial benefits to you. What if your picture was full of words: sun, fun, water, sky, fish, green, blue, and ships? What would that mean to your life? It could mean you need a tropical vacation. It could mean you need to move to a place that would create more fun, relaxing times in your life.

The whole point is to let your mind help you to create a picture of your life without your loved one in it. Redirecting your life by creating a new dream will help you stay positively focused on your life. When your focus is positive, your life will be more satisfying.

So, what if you have reframed your thoughts, gotten out of the center of the universe, begun to operate in a congruent manner, started to be present to the moment, revised the dream, and still you are consistently unhappy? Here is one last thought about time that might help.

Time and Letting Go

What is your perspective of time? Most people ask the following questions: When will the pain go away? When will I quit crying so much? When will I have clarity in my head? Here are some answers that might help. The pain and sadness will last on and off intensely for about two years. Then happier days begin to outweigh the sadder days. It is a slow process. That is normal.

You will grieve in your own way and in your own time. What is important is that you grieve without destroying yourself in the process. Destroying yourself comes in many forms. You might isolate and destroy your social networking, which is important to happiness. You might not eat properly and destroy your health by either losing or gaining too much weight. You might not take care of yourself and decrease the immune system, thus jeopardizing your health. Don't let your grief take control of you.

Thus, your perspective on time plays an important role in predicting your future. Give yourself approximately two years to revive from the fog, the pain, the tears, and the sadness. If after that you still feel miserable more days than not and you have not already done so, seek professional help. A therapist can help you increase the intensity with which you can apply the techniques in this book.

I remember that it was two years after my son's death that I felt strong enough to start my own private practice. We often do symbolic things to help us get out of the fog. I knew I was not happy in the job that I had. I knew that I needed to be in control of my own potential to increase my income. My family went skiing at Easter that year. Everyone wanted to sleep in on Easter morning, but I was determined to go to the sunrise service at the top of the mountain. In the dark with snowflakes encircling me, I made my way to the gondola that took me to the top of the mountain. Just as the sun began to rise over the mountain and the minister was preaching a sermon, from somewhere in my mind, I knew that I needed to quit my job.

The following week, a few things happened that gave me a sign that I was indeed done with that job. I gave my notice. Through a series of circumstances, I was led to open my private practice. I opened it on my son's birthday and took his initials and gave my practice a name. His initials were CWE, Charles Wesley Esterly. I named my practice "Choosing Wellness Eagerly, Inc." I had given birth, not to a baby, but to a new life without Wes. Memorializing his memory by symbolically representing him in the naming of my practice helped me to let go and still remember. It is as if he is always with me as I go to my job and help people. Within two years, I had let go by revising the dream.

It is the perception that you give yourself to consider that makes all the difference in how you process what happens in your world. When circumstances are out of your control, it is the response you make to those circumstances that either renders you helpless or gives you power. It is your choice, because your perspective is up to you. So take a perspective that helps you hold your precious memories at the same time that you move forward. Balance your memories and your new path of life.

Review

The way you think about the death of your loved one has a great deal to do with how you live your life. Your thoughts can propel you into deep depression, or they can help you create a satisfying life. The choice is yours.

Some techniques that will help you with effective thinking are to reframe your thoughts, step out of center of the universe thinking, operate in a congruent manner so what you think about yourself matches your behavior, keep your thoughts on whatever you are doing in the present moment, revise your life dream, and realize that letting go takes time, so be patient with yourself.

Remember that it takes about two years to really begin to do these techniques on a consistent basis. You then are operating out of a new behavior pattern that is automatic, so you don't have to remind yourself to get out of the center of the universe or to be present to the moment. You just automatically do them. You can choose to take a perspective that will help you mend your broken heart. It will take time, so just believe you can do it. Believe in yourself. It's time to mend your broken heart.

We all have our strong points. We usually refer to them as our strengths. I consider myself to be a persistent person. However, about ten years after my son's death, I found out that persistence was not my greatest strength. Persistence was high, but not as high as my other strengths. I learned what the true strengths were that I used to weather this adversity in my life.

You have the advantage that I did not have. You can learn what your strengths are and how to use them to cope with any adversity in life. First, I will teach you how to access your strengths. Then, I will explain how to use these strengths to weather your adversity.

Use Your Strengths

Benjamin Franklin stated, "While we may not be able to control all that happens to us, we can control what happens inside us." What strengths do we have within us to help us in our time of greatest sorrow?

I wish I had known this information to help me through my adversity, but unfortunately this information has only come into our literature through recent research. However, you are lucky. You can obtain this information and use it to your benefit to manage your grief. Read carefully and choose to learn all about how to use your strengths during adversity.

As was stated in chapter six, Marty Seligman and Chris Peterson, in their book *Strengths and Virtues: A Classification and Handbook*, suggest people have, in varying degrees, twenty-four signature strengths. The research by these two men suggests that when you are utilizing your top five signature strengths on a daily basis you are a happier person. So by choosing to learn more about how to use your strengths to weather adversity, you can manage your grief and create more life satisfaction. If you would like to find out about your signature strengths, go to www.authentichappiness.org and take the Values in Action Signature Strengths Survey.

I learned about these strengths long after my child died, but I have reflected on which ones of my top five I actually used during my time of adversity. If I had known this concept, it might have helped me to weather my sorrow in a different manner. Let me reveal my strengths and then take you through how I used mine to help me. My top five signature strengths are: (1) appreciation of beauty and excellence; (2) zest, enthusiasm, and energy; (3) spirituality, sense of purpose, and faith; (4) gratitude; and (5) honesty, authenticity, and genuineness. Let me explain how each of my strengths provided a way for me to cope with the illness and death of my son.

My Strengths

Appreciation of beauty and excellence has to do with noticing the beauty around you and the excellence you see, especially within that beauty. Do you notice the orange, blue, and mauve of the sunset? Do you notice that the lilac is composed of many small flowers banded together to make a larger flower? Do you hear the call of the whippoorwill? Do you catch the excited glee of a child sitting on Santa's lap? Do you feel appreciation when a friend does a kind deed for you? Do you recognize what makes you enjoy your favorite television program? If you do, then you are someone who appreciates beauty and excellence just as I do.

I used this strength to help me cope by immersing myself in a creative project. This was the process of being "in flow." Flow, according to Mihaly Csikszentmihalyi, is the process of total involvement with life. When a person is "in flow," time can pass without the person noticing. I have a passion for photography. Capturing beauty, whether it is a flower or the expression on a child's face, excites me. Give me a camera, and I can occupy my time for hours. I took thousands of pictures of my children. They each have a photograph album for each year of their lives through their high school days. During those eight years when I went to doctor's offices, stayed in hospitals, or stayed home with my son, I took photographs of him, of scenery, of hospital personnel helping my son, or whatever would occupy my attention so that I was happy and not so focused on the negative process of his disease. When Wes and I would stay in the hospital for his treatments, I would bring my photographs and make albums for my children. I filled my time with something happy rather than being unsettled that I was spending time in a hospital. I was using my signature strength of appreciation of beauty and excellence to help me cope with my situation.

Zest, enthusiasm, and energy have to do with approaching whatever you do with excitement and eagerness. Do you do things with gusto? Do you have intense feelings? Do you have zeal? Do you experience keen enjoyment? Do you get as excited about washing dishes as you do about opening presents? If you do, then you are someone who has zest, enthusiasm, and energy just as I do.

The way I used this strength to help me cope was to be outwardly excited about whatever my son and I needed to do. The night before he had a radiation treatment, I would tell him to get excited because we would go to the park after seeing the nurse. When we were going to the hospital for his autologous bone marrow transplant, I talked to him about how much fun we would have going to Washington, D.C. to see the Space Museum and all the monuments before heading to the hospital. Even though inside I was fearful, anxious, and unsure, I also knew that these treatments might help him live and that was exciting. So I ignored the negative feelings and let my strength help me cope. I got excited and focused on something positive, no matter what we were going to do concerning his treatments.

The amazing thing about this strength is that in order to accomplish it, you really need to be present to the moment. As I described in a previous chapter, Wes taught me how to be present to each moment. That is what I tried to do. I did not think about the future, and I tried desperately to dismiss the past. I lived in each moment, whether it was snuggling with Wes, watching him get chemotherapy, seeing him smile on the amazing vacation that the Dream Factory sent us on to Disney World, or kissing his tiny hand as he entered the MRI. I was there. All of me was present. Being present to the moment helped me cope. I was actually using my signature strength of zest, enthusiasm, and energy to help me cope with my situation.

Spirituality, sense of purpose, and faith have to

do with the comfort that comes when your beliefs shape your actions. It usually has to do with your strong belief that there exists a higher purpose and meaning in the universe. It also implies that you have a sense of how you fit in the larger scheme of life. A person who is spiritual spends time discerning what meaning is created by his life. Do you have a plan for your life? Are you determined to accomplish whatever you are on Earth to do? Do you deliberately direct the goals of your life toward a higher purpose? Do you experience courage when you need it most? Does your life have real meaning? If so then, you are someone who is spiritual, has a sense of purpose, and experiences faith just as I do.

The way I used this strength to help me cope was to know totally that there had to be a sense of purpose for this experience, even though I had no idea what that purpose was. When you are spiritual, it is much easier to be enthusiastic because you have purposefulness. I trusted that each day, each hour, each minute created a growth experience for me. I had faith that whatever I was going through would allow me to understand and be more empathetic with others, given the fact that I was studying to be a psychologist at that time.

I even imagined that Wes was given to my husband and me because we were the perfect parents to help him through whatever he must go through in life. Why us, I was not sure, but holding that thought in mind gave me comfort. Being a first child in my own family of origin, I do things as perfectly as I can. So my spirit of excellence made me the best parent a little boy with cancer could ever wish for. My husband gave him fun and humor. I gave him order and structure. We both gave him security and love. What more could a little boy want? I had a sense of purpose being his mother. Not that I liked it, but I could understand it in a way that made sense to me and that I accepted as a compliment. Yes, we certainly skew things when we need some justification for something that seems so horrendous that we can hardly believe it is happening to us. We dream up these off-the-wall reasons for justifying what life throws our way. I had a purpose. I was actually using my signature strength of spirituality, sense of purpose, and faith to help me cope with my situation.

My great sense of faith had a lot to do with how I coped. As stated in chapter two, my first visit when I found out about Wes's situation was to my priest for prayer. He faithfully prayed with me during each recurrence and in the end gave a reflection of Wes at his funeral. People often questioned me about how I could have such great faith when Wes was experiencing such difficulties. My answer was always that my faith was what gave me the strength to cope and to be the mother that I needed to be to Wes. Ever since I was a little girl, I have prayed twice daily. I considered God to be my best friend so I spoke to him every day. The power of speaking with God sustained me during those years of struggle.

Gratitude has to do with appreciating and being thankful to someone who does something for you. Are you thankful? Do you appreciate the favors you receive from the gifts of time and energy others give to you? Do you count your blessings? Do you express your thanks to others? Do you show your appreciation? If you do, then you are someone who has gratitude just as I do.

The way I used this strength to help me cope was to show my appreciation to anyone who helped my son or me. There were so many people to whom I am so grateful and to whom I still feel warmly toward even if I will never see them again. There were many nurses, doctors, friends, relatives, and even strangers who made life easier by their generous gestures of kindness. Although I can never repay these people for what they have done for me, I keep their memory preciously alive in my heart. No gift, no expression of gratitude, no return gesture could compare to what they have meant to me. I will merely mention a few for purposes of example.

The greatest appreciation goes to the doctor who was the neurosurgeon who extracted three brain tumors and still kept Wes functioning cognitively on a high level. One tumor was in the cerebellar area. The doctor operated, and Wes was still able to walk. One tumor was wrapped around Wes's optic nerve. The same doctor operated, and Wes still had his sight. One tumor was in Wes's frontal lobes. This same doctor operated, and Wes was still able to manage his emotions. Do you see why I appreciate this doctor? I am thankful to him for all he did for Wes.

I cannot tell you how much appreciation I have for Wes's best friend in elementary school. Chris always included Wes whenever he could. Even if Wes could not run as fast, think as quickly, or attend school or other activities as consistently as his other friends, Chris never forgot his friendship with Wes. In a sophomore English class on

Thursday, December 17, 1998, five years after Wes's death, Chris wrote the following poem. I appreciate the fact that Chris has given me his permission to include it in this book.

Some Advice: Friend

By: Chris Rozier

December 17, 1998

A friend is someone who is mostly taken for granted, so I've learned:

Don't let them slip away like a leaf blowing in the wind.

Don't let your ignorance for their differences stand in the way of your relationship towards them. Understand him as he understands you.

The disease, like a silent annoyance; the pain only he knows, don't be afraid, for he's not.

The outside is only a cover of choice plastered to hide the true beauty of oneself.

I'm sorry I couldn't show what was really important.

Thank you for the times that you showed me, and you let me show you.

Friend, you were everything that I needed.

Now you can look after me, with all your heart and soul.

Welcome.

I cannot ever read this poem without tears streaming down my face. Can you see the love this young man had for his friend? Whether that friend was Wes or not, I was not sure. When I asked permission to include this writing, Chris shared with me the following: "I must tell you that this poem was about Wes, as well as inspired by him. I had Wes in mind the entire time I wrote this poem … Wes taught me what a good friend is. Even at our young age, I could tell that Wes was a truly selfless person and a true joy and inspiration to everyone he encountered."

When Wes died, Chris wrote the following in a card to me: "Wes meant so much to me. We were good friends. I miss him very much. Wes was a wonderful person. I could always depend on him. If I had a favor, he would do it to the best of his ability, and I would do the same for him. I am glad I could be a friend of Wes's. I can always remember his warm smile … I can remember when we were together. We were always happy."

This young man, who was a small boy when he was Wes's friend, truly acted like a friend to Wes, and I appreciate that. I am thankful to Chris for his friendship with my son.

My dear friend Peggy took care of getting my daughter, Ali, to all her extracurricular activities when I was either taking Wes to doctor's appointments or staying in the hospital with Wes. If it were not for Peggy, my daughter would not be the talented, outgoing, well-adjusted young woman she is today. I appreciate the time and energy that my friend gave to Ali when I could not be there for my daughter. I am thankful that Peggy was a surrogate mother to my daughter when she needed a mother by her side.

When Wes died, my friend Cindi was there for me. She was by my side, gently guiding me through the fog of the days that followed his death. She just appeared. She had an uncanny sense of when to materialize, just at the moment she was needed the most. Without her generous gift of time and energy, I would have been unable to make decisions or generate the energy to move through those days. I am thankful to Cindi for holding me up when I felt like falling.

These are just a few of the people to whom I am thankful. My heart is full of gratitude toward them. I do my best to remember them in small ways. Nothing can ever pay back their kind gestures. In a way, they filled my heart with gratitude so my broken heart could mend. I was actually using my signature strength of gratitude to help me cope with my situation.

Honesty has to do with being frank and open. When one is honest, one speaks what one really thinks and feels. *Authenticity and genuineness* both have to do with someone being what a person seems to be without pretending. When one is authentic and genuine, one behaves out of a desire to be honest. All three lead to the idea of being congruent. That means what you believe about yourself inside of you matches how you behave and who you present to the world outside of you. This leads to you being trusted by others. So if you are honest, authentic, and genuine, you are trustworthy. Being congruent takes bravery! When you have an opinion that is the exact opposite of others in a group, do you speak your opinion? If your boss asks you to do something and you know what is being asked of you would cause difficulty in the organization, do you speak up? If a friend asks you for your true opinion and you know that what you want to say would lead to hard feelings, do you find a way to be honest with your friend without offending? If you speak up, then you are a person who is honest just like me.

I used this strength to help me cope by being honest with my children, as well as myself. My husband and I believed that honesty was the best policy. We never kept our other children in the dark about what was happening concerning Wes, even when they were very young. We informed them when Wes had a tumor and was going to the hospital for surgery. Again, as you read in the chapter on siblings, we told them when Wes was going to die. Secrets cause anxiety. Fear of the unknown is the greatest fear. I never wanted my children to be fearful because they did not know.

I also was honest with myself. I did not like what was happening to my family. I was honest with myself about that. I also knew there was nothing I could do about what was happening. I knew the only thing I had control of was my response to what was happening. So I told myself that I would try to be honest with the doctors, nurses, friends, and relatives, especially about my feelings, without being obnoxious. Whether or not I succeeded does not really matter. When I believed I was being honest, I was coping. I was actually using my signature strength of honesty, authenticity, and genuineness to help me cope with my situation.

So that is how I used my signature strengths, even though at the time I did not know I was using them. I will go over just a few other examples to give you some more ideas about how each strength may be used to weather the grieving process.

Another signature strength is *perseverance,*

industry, and diligence. When we think of perseverance, images of endurance and persistence, such
as running a marathon, come to mind. When we
think of diligence, images of being careful and producing steady effort, such as a doctor doing surgery,
come to mind. When we think of industry, images
of working hard to get results, such as starting a
business, come to mind. So what do these all have
in common? The answer is working until the job
is done, no matter how long it takes. Finishing the
race, putting the last stitch in the incision after the
surgery has been performed, and working until a
profit is obtained from the business are all examples of working until the job is done. Perseverance
focuses on persisting until the job is done and never,
ever giving up.

Let's look at the signature strength of *judgment,
critical thinking, and open-mindedness.* We have
opinions on many things. Once we get on one side
of the fence, we tend to stay there even if appealing
evidence emerges that would make us change our
minds. An open-minded person, however, would
absorb the new evidence presented and then make
a more informed choice. Sometimes the open-
minded person would stay put. At other times, the
open-minded person would choose to switch sides.
Are you an open-minded person, or once you have
a belief, do you become resistant to counter-evi-
dence? The benefits of open-mindedness are many.
People who are open-minded tend to be swayed
less by singular events and use multiple events to
base opinions. Open-mindedness allows people
to be more resistant to suggestion and manipula-
tion by others. Open-minded individuals are more
capable of predicting how others will behave.

Open-minded people have better relationships. In combination, all these benefits add up to a person who is independent about opinions and does not get pulled into the drama created by the opinions of others.

What about the signature strength of *citizenship, teamwork, and loyalty*? What these words have in common is the aspect of being a member of a group and the commitment that being a member involves. You function as a group member every day. For example, you are part of a family, whether it is your family of origin or a family you create with a spouse. Another context in which you function as a group member may be your worksite. You may work with others to produce a product or get a project done. In your community, you may be a member of an organization, a church, or a volunteer group. For leisure, you may be a member of a sports team. In all aspect of your life, you function as a member of a group. Do you excel at being an effective team player in all the groups of your life? Do you work collaboratively? Do you do your share of the work? Do you exhibit loyalty to other team members? Do you value group outcomes over individual success? If so, you have the signature strength of citizenship, teamwork, and loyalty.

If you choose to take the survey and learn about your strengths, you can help weather adversity by purposefully using the strengths. Look at your top five strengths. Determine which ones you are already using. Begin to use them more on a daily basis to weather your adversity. Then make a strategy for using the ones from the top five you are not using. You will find that you are a happier person when you are using your strengths to help you weather any adversity.

If you find it difficult to design a strategy, then consult a strengths coach. Be sure you choose a coach trained in how to assess and work with your strengths, because if you don't, the coach may not know what kind of specific help you require. I took the vanguard training class that Marty Seligman taught about happiness and using your strengths. Then I took another class by Chris Peterson about how to use strengths in coaching. This training, plus my personal experience, makes me a strengths coach who can help people effectively weather adversity. You can check out my Web site at www. yesyoucanchoose.com. You don't have to live in the same town that your coach does because coaching is usually done over the phone, so the coach you choose can live anywhere. It would probably take six sessions to develop a workable plan of action to help you understand and use your strengths so that you can more effectively weather your adversity.

My Reflection on Strengths

I would like to share with you something that I wrote in 2003 after learning about signature strengths in my Authentic Happiness Vanguard Class. My words from 2003 are in italics, and my comments are in regular print.

I wonder often how I even got through the day, let alone eight years of watching my son suffer. I think God was with him every step, because although the cancer was there and he had to undergo chemotherapy, he was very rarely sick. Okay, he threw up sometimes at the hospital and rarely ate, but he was always happy.

One Christmas season, I was making a Christmas stocking for a nephew who had been born over the past year. As a tradition (my great aunt had made my siblings and I stockings, so when she died, I continued the tradition for my siblings' children), *I made a felt stocking for all the nieces and nephews to have at my mother's home. On the stocking were the words* Buon Natale *which meant "Merry Christmas" in Italian* (my great aunt was Italian). *I brought the material to the hospital to keep me occupied. In order to see as I sewed the name on with sequins, I went out in the hallway just outside Wes's hospital room as he was already asleep, and I was not quite tired enough to sleep. As I sat there, groans and cries came from the room across the hall. I heard the parent who was staying with that child cry out in agony.*

I just sat quietly and said a thankful prayer that although this was a horrible situation for Wes, it could be so much worse. I was thankful that Wes never had to come back to the hospital between treatments because his blood counts were too low. I was thankful that he was not sick and throwing up constantly between treatments. I was thankful his blood counts were adequate and he did not have to constantly have platelets. It is so paradoxical that I felt very lucky sitting there in the hallway in that hospital that Christmas season.

In that situation, I found out years later, I was using two of my top signature strengths to cope, gratitude and spirituality. In using them, I was able to face my adversity and be able to function in a way that allowed me to be the person I wanted to be.

I used my signature strength of spirituality when we first knew that Wes had a brain tumor at age three.

As we sat in the cafeteria after they had taken him to the operating room to remove his first brain tumor, Chuck and I lifted him up to God. We gave him to God, and God gave him back to us for eight wonderful years beyond that day. We put faith in God. We prayed for the surgeon so that his hands would be directed to resect the entire tumor and not hurt anything else in the brain. During the second of three operations, we were told the tumor was wrapped around the optic nerve. We were scared that he would lose his eyesight, but he didn't. God guided the surgeon's hands to allow Wes to continue to see the beauty of each new day.

I also used my signature strength of honesty, authenticity, and genuineness when I asked for information from the doctors, especially when I did not understand, for I needed to know in order to cope. Of course, I was probably a burden to them with all my questions and fears, yet that's who I am, and I needed to be authentic. I hated to be dismissed with perfunctory statements that did not explain what would give me a picture of what was happening, or what we planned to do for Wes's treatments.

Most of all, though, I used my signature strengths of zest, enthusiasm, and energy to interact when I was with Wes and when I spoke with others about the situation. I seemed almost joyful telling people that although the situation was awful, we were very, very lucky. I am sure some people could not really understand what I meant, but at least it stopped them from feeling sorry for my family.

I also wondered how my other children coped, and when I had them discover their strengths, both of them had as their top signature strength, playfulness and humor. They used this to cope. Until I discovered this, I thought they were not being serious or had not pro-

cessed the death of their brother. I came to realize that their top signature strength of playfulness and humor allowed both of them to live with a brother who had a terminal illness in a way that was healthy for all. I am thankful that they both have that signature strength.

Ali also has gratitude and spirituality as signature strengths, just as I do. These two, along with her playfulness and humor, probably helped her to cope. She also has the incredible capacity to love and be loved by others. This is another of her signature strengths that helped her to cope. She would play with Wes in such a loving way. Although he was two years older, people often mistook them for twins. They both had beautiful, blonde hair, and since Wes had radiation at such a young age, he was somewhat shorter than normal.

Tony, I imagine, used in addition to humor and playfulness, his signature strengths of bravery and social intelligence to help him to cope and stand up for his brother when needed. Wes was rarely teased about having no hair. His teachers at school were very good about explaining in the classroom that Wes was just a regular guy, only without any hair.

Tony also has the signature strength of perspective and wisdom. He could see Wes's situation in a rather mature outlook. He also shares my honesty strength. He needed to know what was going on with Wes just like I did in order to cope.

That's exactly why I needed to let my children be informed of whatever was happening to Wes. We talked about it as a family. We were always open with them each time he had an operation. When we knew he was going to die, we were honest about that too.

I think back now on how I managed those two days of telling the schools and telling Wes and the children, and I cannot believe I could have done all that without totally breaking down and being a limp rag. *Where did that bravery come from? Where did the energy come from? I guess the energy came from my signature strengths, but the bravery? That's not one of them.*

Bravery is, however, one of Chuck's signature strengths. He was always brave when it came to Wes. Chuck and I share gratitude as one of our signature strengths, so he, too, was grateful for having Wes another eight years when he could have been taken from us at three. Chuck also has judgment, critical thinking, and open mindedness as one of his signature strengths. That helped when we needed to make decisions on what to do about treatments. His top strength is industry, diligence, and perseverance, so it was not hard for him to balance work, see Wes at the hospital, and take care of the other two children. As I think back on it, his persistence kept him functioning at a high pace while being at home when Wes was in the hospital, and my zest and energy helped me function at the hospital while I was with Wes.

It was not an easy time for any of us, let alone for the little life that was going through the illness. Because we had these wonderful strengths and used them, we survived and live productive lives now: the children with their great capacity to use humor and playfulness, Chuck with his perseverance, gratitude, and bravery, and me with my zest and energy, gratitude and spirituality. God gives us each a way to cope with our adversity. It is our job to discover how to use what God gives us.

When Strengths Get in the Way of Healing

Even though our signature strengths are helpful during adversity, they can also prevent our healing. Our greatest strengths are also our greatest weaknesses. They bring us struggles. Let me explain how sometimes our strengths get in the way of our healing.

I believe the signature strength of *fairness, equity, and justice* is perhaps the one that most stands in the way of healing. Justice has to do with giving a sound reason or giving a reward or penalty as deserved. If a person has this strength, the person may get stuck in two ways. First, the person may get stuck asking, "Why?" as I often did. For what reason is this happening to our family? To me? Knowing a reason helps people who have the strength of fairness, equity, and justice to cope. So if a reason is not found, difficulty coping with the situation results. A second way a person may get stuck is thinking that the situation has to do with a penalty she deserves for not living a righteous life. At one point, I was stuck in this thinking. I kept asking myself, "What did I do to deserve this?" If a person gets stuck in this thinking, misery results.

A person's idea of fairness comes from comparison to other individuals or situations. When a person compares his situation to another's situation, misery can result. If I compare my situation of losing a child to my friend's situation in which she has her three children living wonderful, productive lives, I could get stuck in misery. So I taught myself to think of this quote to help me stay unstuck from this irrational idea: "Comparison is the basis of all misery." I tried very hard with extreme diligence to live this statement every day. Using this quote can help prevent your wonderful strength of *fairness, equity, and justice* from prohibiting you from mending your broken heart.

Another signature strength that might get in the way of healing is *self-control and self-regulation*. These strengths have to do with being disciplined and regulating your emotions and desires. Lack of this strength lets your emotions and impulses hold you hostage. However, when this is one of your strengths, you may swing the opposite way and never deal with your emotions. Let's say that you are in the stage of anger and need to deal with the anger of a loved one dying. If your strength of self-control and self-regulation does not allow you to work through the anger and let it go, then you may be stuck in the anger phase of grief and not be able to reach resolution.

A helpful way to tackle this problem if you get stuck in your self-control and self-regulation is to use a monitoring question. You have control of only two things in your life: your own behavior (not the behavior of others) and your perception of things (the way you think about the situation). This question helps keep you on track by releasing your emotions held hostage by your strength so that you can process them in an effective way. Ask yourself, "Is what I am doing now or thinking now getting me to my goal?" If your goal is to deal with your anger, is holding the anger in going to get you to that goal? If the answer to the question is no, then stop and do a behavior that will get you to your goal. If your goal is to deal with your anger, is thinking: *I will never get over my loss*, going to get you to your goal? If not, then change your thinking to something like: *Although this is very difficult, I need to get beyond the anger and come to resolution.* So asking yourself the monitoring question and checking to see if your behavior or your thinking is effective in getting you to your goal will help you to alleviate this wonderful strength of self-control and self-regulation from thwarting your journey to mending your broken heart.

Let's look at the signature strength called the *capacity to love and be loved.* Sounds like a wonderful strength; however, it can get in your way in two ways. First, it can prevent you from giving love to others because you are holding on to your love for the person who died. Let's say that your love for one child who dies is so strong that you negate the love that your other children deserve from you. I was extremely aware of this when Wes died. I told myself that I would never neglect my other children, no matter how much love I had for Wes. So don't let this strength stand in your way. Just believe that you have an abundant capacity to give love and give lots of it away. So give your love to the other children while still holding on to your love for the one who died.

Second, you deserve to be loved too. Let's say that your wife dies. This amazing strength gives you the capacity to accept love, but because you loved her so much, you negate other love interests in your life. You deny yourself the pleasure of being loved. You allow your love for the person who died to stand in the way of accepting the love others have to give you. It is a gift to be loved. Accept the gift. This amazing strength of the capacity to love and be loved can hinder you by creating many very lonely years, instead of allowing you to enjoy the loving companionship of another person. Choose to accept the gift of others' love.

So even though your strengths can help you through adversity, they can also cause you difficulty and struggles. When you overuse or use one of your strengths inappropriately, it leads to struggles. Monitor those strengths, and when one is getting in your way, change your behavior or your thinking to help you make the strengths work for you instead of against you.

Review

Ralph Waldo Emerson stated, "What lies behind you and what lies before you are tiny matters compared to what lies within you." What strength within you can help you as you seek to mend your broken heart? Discover the strengths that can help you to weather your adversity. What can you choose to do or to think that can help you live a more productive, happier life without your loved one? Your strengths can help or hinder. If they are hindering you, change your behavior or your thinking so that your strengths help you to weather your adversity. What lies within you? It is up to you to discover your strengths so that you can mend your broken heart. Believe in yourself. It's time to mend your broken heart.

The strength of *creativity* can help you heal by using fantasy. Some people fear fantasy because they believe it is an escape from reality. However, fantasy gave me the freedom to create an alternative reality in which I could rejuvenate. It gave me the power to survive in a powerless reality. I used fantasy to help me cope as I watched my child suffer. When Wes died, I again used fantasy to help me mend my broken heart. You, too, can use your strength of creativity to heal.

Draw On Fantasy

When I was young, I loved short stories. One of my favorites was *The Secret Life of Walter Mitty* by James Thurber. I understand now why that story stuck in my mind into adulthood. It was a gift in my life. It was the foundation for the fantasy that helped me to meet the challenge of my child's illness and cope with his death.

Some people may misinterpret what I mean by that. Fantasy is not a place I run to in order to escape. It is a place I pleasantly go to for a refreshing descent into the warmth of control. It is similar to taking a hot shower or relaxing in a hammock. Fantasy is a place where I go to make the world exactly how I want it to be. Fantasy allows me the freedom to create an alternate reality. In that alternate reality, I can rejuvenate myself. I can gain the power that I need to survive in my powerless reality. That's what James Thurber taught me that I could do when I read *The Secret Life of Walter Mitty*. I am so grateful for that short story. It empowered me to use my creativity to make my life more satisfying, especially in the grips of grief.

So how did I use fantasy? I used it when all seemed hopeless and I was totally helpless to control a situation. I could go to my fantasy place and feel powerful. Reveling in the power from my fantasy, I could then approach the real world with enthusiasm and energy. I would come back to reality with the much needed power to cope with whatever life was throwing at me.

Let me give you two examples of how I used fantasy to cope. The first one I used when coping while Wes was still alive. The second one I used after his death.

Before His Death

Wes was eight years old when he and I went to a hospital for him to get an autologous bone marrow transplant. I used my fantasy coping mechanism in the recovery room while I was waiting for him to wake up. Helping him through his autologous bone marrow transplant created stress for which I was unprepared.

Internally, I was struggling with my anger versus my gratitude. On the one hand, I kept asking the following perpetual questions. Why did this have to happen to Wes? Why did this happen to our family? Why do we have to spend money on hospitals instead of on vacations having fun with our children? Why do we have to be apart for so long? Why does Wes have to endure a life-threatening illness? Why couldn't we have a normal life? On the other hand, I kept stating the following perpetual statements: I am grateful for doctors who can help Wes. I am grateful for nurses that treat us with sensitivity and kindness. I am grateful that there is medicine that can help him. I am grateful that there are hospitals that are doing research to improve the methods of treatment for children like Wes. I am grateful for insurance companies that will approve a tremendously expensive procedure for Wes. It was always that same internal struggle.

As I sat by his side in the recovery room, waiting for him to wake up, I felt weak and fragile and tearful and helpless. Once I felt that, I went to my fantasy spot. I imagined that I was this powerful magician who could wave her wand and change things into other things or make anything disappear. I saw myself standing on a mountain. I was dressed in a long green dress with a heavy purple cape with a hood on it (green and purple are my favorite colors). I had a silver wand in my right hand. A bright yellow light encircled me. I looked up into the sky. It was dark, with treacherous bolts of lightning striking the earth and starting fires. I waved my magic wand, and the sun came out, chasing the clouds away, filling the land with warmth. I looked over the land. I saw ugliness throughout. I waved my wand, and the earth became green and lush. I saw monsters doing harm to children. I waved my wand, and the monsters disappeared. I saw people being mean to other people. I waved my wand, and people were kind. I smiled because the world was now more pleasant. I took three, big, deep breaths and felt the power and the energy and the enthusiasm returning to my body and mind. I felt rejuvenated. I could then return to the present moment in a more powerful state. As Wes awoke, I was then able to talk to him and read a story to him with enthusiasm.

As you see, this was not an escape. It was a powerful tool that I used to help me cope with the unbearable sorrow of seeing my child suffer. I could be in the present moment with him without my anger, without my questions, without my sorrow. My fantasy gave me the freedom to be that strong individual that I knew deep down that I always was, despite what was happening in my world.

How to Use Fantasy to Go to a Powerful Spot

I encourage you to dream up a powerful fantasy when you feel helpless. It does not have to last long or be in detail. It can be short and succinct. It can fill you with energy and power in minutes, or even seconds, when needed. Here are some suggestions to get you started.

Perhaps you are a person who loves gardening. In your mind, go to a spot where you are a master gardener. You grow these incredible flowers that everyone stops to see. You get e-mails telling you what an amazing "green thumb" you have. People come to you for advice about gardening. You help people plan their garden plots. Your neighborhood wins the most beautiful street award given by the city.

Make up something that allows you to feel powerful. You can even choose something you have never done before but want to be powerful at. Let's say you have never run for a political office but you have always wanted to. Go to a fantasy spot where people seek you out to run for office. See yourself giving speeches. See yourself getting elected. See yourself doing good work for the people.

You can also create a make-believe place as I did. Think of some of the children's movies you have watched. They always have some fantasy scenes in them that you can conjure up in your mind to get you started. Let's say you watch *The Sword in the Stone* and picture when Arthur pulls the sword out of that stone. Perhaps you watch *Aladdin* and picture when the genie pops out of the lamp.

If you are really creative, you can make up your own fantasy place. Go to a spot where you think power exists. Stand by a river. Watch a plane take off. Look at a mountain. Ponder a tree. Then, create a fantasy around that powerful image.

Remember, in this activity, short is best. Catch an image, and let the image be powerful and let the image represent you. Be the river. Be the plane. Be the mountain. Be the tree. Use the powerful image to rejuvenate yourself. Feel the power flowing into your body, into your mind, into your spirit, and into your broken heart.

Use your fantasy to give you freedom to create an alternate reality in which you can rejuvenate. In fantasy, you can repair your energy and enthusiasm. You can restore your hopefulness. You can gain the power that you need to survive in your powerless reality. Fantasy gives you the freedom to always be the person you want to be, no matter how difficult your reality is.

After His Death

After Wes died, I used fantasy to cope with my grief. I wrote many short stories. I even collaborated with a fantasy artist, Gary Delamatre, who worked on illustrating the story that follows. He has given me permission to use the amazing illustration he drew. I gladly share my story with my readers. You will obviously see the symbolism and the story of my struggle after Wes's death.

I needed to be rescued from the grief I felt when Wes died. I created this story to help me realize that I could come back from the fog that I walked through during my grief. I could survive. I could mend. In the story, the boy's help and his touch healed the fairy, as did the help and touch I received from people in my reality. Writing this story helped me understand how I could mend my broken heart.

The High Stone Wall

The boy lived in a wonderful home with a high stone wall surrounding his world. He often played in the yard with his mighty tin soldiers or designed huge sandcastles in the sandbox. He swung on his tire swing that hung from the strong, sturdy oak. He played hopscotch on the sidewalk with a smooth stone he had found in the creek that bordered the back wall of the property. He had spent hours reading under the strong, sturdy oak tree on hot summer days and loved it even more when he could sit on a pile of autumn leaves as he read. As he read, he would often look up in the sky and watch the clouds change from dragons to teddy bears. He loved to play king of the hill. He would climb on the small mound of dirt he had carried from the creek and address his tin soldiers, often delivering moving monologues. There was a garden in the yard with an assortment of beautiful flowers that bloomed for every season. In the autumn, a tutor would appear to teach him his lessons in the mornings, but he knew that the afternoons were for his own creative play. His life had a pattern, and it was perfectly comfortable with much beauty and lots to keep him busy.

One day, he discovered the hole in the wall, and all he could see as he peered through it was what he thought was a beautiful yellow flower. It caught his eye like no other flower in his own garden had. He would play for a time and then return to the wall to peer through the hole. The brilliance of the yellow beckoned to him. He sighed and went off to play again. Several days later, he returned to the hole and peered through. The flower, he guessed, must be magical, because that day it was red. The radiance of the color and the brilliance of the light that surrounded it entranced him. As he played that afternoon, he kept returning to the wall, time after time, to glance at the flower. Again, some time passed because he always kept himself very busy. One afternoon, as he peered through, the magic flower had turned to purple. He smiled with delight. The flower had captured his imagination. As he went through his morning ritual of studies, his mind kept drifting to the flower. He knew he needed to concentrate, so he put the flower out of his mind so he could focus on his studies. But as soon as he was done, he ran straight to the hole in the wall and peered through. This time, the flower was blue.

Being very curious, the boy wanted to be able to examine the magical flower better, so one day he brought along his binoculars to see the intricacies of each petal. What he discovered when he saw it close up was that it wasn't a flower at all, but instead, it was a beautiful fairy with iridescent wings. A brilliant light surrounded her as she sat on the flower. The light created beautiful, changing colors. He noticed she was spinning thread and marveled at how she could make the magical thread from almost nothing. As he watched, the fairy spread her magical wings and flew away from the flower, out of his sight. He was awed by the delicacy of the fairy as she spread her wings to take flight. He was also worried because he wondered if she would come back, or if he would no longer see the magic of her changing wings to color his days. He went back to play in the yard, but his mind was never far from wondering if she had returned.

She was a delicate creature with an ever-changing nature. She spent her days on the flower, spinning delicate, magical thread. Birds would come to her flower to obtain a strand of her thread to take to their nests to help make their nests strong and sturdy. Each day, she gave away her magical thread to as many birds as she could. She loved to help the birds. Her heart was happy each time she gave away her thread. She always hoped the birds would use the thread and not drop the thread before they returned to their nests.

In the late evening, she would leave the flower to fly to the rock garden where she would teach other fairies to spin the delicate, magical thread, so more birds would have stronger nests. She knew she could not help every bird, so in teaching the other fairies, she knew more birds would be helped. Some days, she would fly to various flowers in the garden to be sure they were getting enough nutrients to thrive. She liked helping those flowers that needed some assistance to continue to exist. She also liked the freedom to roam the yard and see what was happening in the tiny corners she could not see from her own flower. She was content to sit on her flower, spinning and helping the birds. She was content to fly to the rock garden to be with the other fairies. She was content to help supply nutrients to the weary flowers. Her life had a pattern, and it was comfortable.

However, as she sat on her flower, she often wondered what was beyond the big yard in which she lived. She would look at the high, stone wall that surrounded her world and dream of what it must be like beyond the wall. She never thought to venture over the wall because her life was simple and comfortable, and she did not want to risk the dangers of the unknown. So she sat comfortably, but curiously, upon her beautiful flower.

One day, something happened to change her comfortable world. In the late afternoon, she was returning to her flower when she was attacked by a swarm of bees. First, one assaulted her, stinging her with its poison, then another put its stinger into her delicate body, and another and another. One bee in particular stung her with such horrible poison that she felt as if she would die. She fell to the ground, her strong wings collapsing under the relentless assaults. The bees buzzed around her, diving at her occasionally to see if they had killed their prey. She lay on the ground weak, barely alive. She could see the ugliness of the bees swarming around her body. Her thoughts were slowing, and her *mind was almost blank. Her brilliant light began to fade and her colors grew dim.*

He had come to the wall that day to secretly watch the fairy spin her magical thread. Smiling, he watched as she was returning to her flower. Suddenly without warning, the sky darkened; the horrible buzz of bees filled his ears. He stood, unable to move as he saw the bees attack the fairy. The boy's heart began to pound in his chest. His breathing became rapid. He looked around, trying to find something with which to scare the bees away. He ran to the garden hose, grabbed it, turned the knob on the faucet, and climbed the ivy vine trellis to the top of the wall. He leaned over the wall as far as he could and pointed the hose in the direction of the swarm of bees. He turned the hose on to a gentle spray so he would not hurt the fairy. He hoped the water would make the bees fly away. He watched as the bees began to disappear.

For some reason, the bees left. In her dim view of the world, she remembered a gentle rain falling upon her, and then the bees were gone. She looked in the direction from which the gentle rain had come and she spied the boy for the first time. He was like an angel who had saved her. She lay lifeless for what seemed to be hours, not knowing whether to let her colors fade and her light disappear, or to try to repair the damage that had been done to her. Her thoughts began to come back to her as she lay there. Eventually, her spirit revived enough so that she could make herself get up and climb the stalk of her flower to the gentle petals where she stretched out and fell asleep. She slept and slept and slept.

The boy watched her for hours. Would she ever move? He felt helpless there behind his wall. Eventually, he noticed that she moved, and slowly but surely, he watched her climb the stalk of her flower. She stretched out on the petals and closed her eyes to go to sleep. He had done what he could to help, and she seemed to be back safely where she needed to be. He climbed down the ivy vine trellis back into his yard and ran off to play with his tin soldiers.

Each day, the boy would come to the hole in the wall and peer through. Each day, he saw that the fairy was still asleep. Her brilliant colors began to fade even more until she became a soft grey color. The boy was sad for her, but he knew nothing to do that would be of any help. He came again and again to the wall, and again and again he saw her light grow dimmer and dimmer. He wondered how he could help the fairy. He knew he could not leave his comfortable place where he knew what to do and how to do it. He was torn between helping the fairy and not leaving his safe space. He pondered this dilemma as he often did with other things about which he debated. Finally, he slowly and methodically designed a plan.

Late one night, at the height of the full moon, he dressed all in black and crept to the wall when everyone else was asleep. He had made these plans for days until he knew exactly what he would do. He climbed the ivy vine trellis and sat on the top of the wall surveying the other side of the wall. The trellis on the other side of the wall was not as sturdy as the one on his side had been. He worried that if he risked climbing down into the yard beyond the wall, he might be unable to climb back up and get back to his own yard. He weighed the risks, and eventually decided to risk having to find another way home. He climbed gently down the trellis on her side of the wall. He crept carefully over to the flower upon which she lay. In the silver of the moonlight, she looked so delicate and so beautiful. As he approached her, she looked breathtaking to him. He wasn't quite sure what to do, so he stood beside the flower, looking at her.

She had been healing herself for a long time, but something was missing. She gently opened her eyes and could dimly see a shadow in the silvery brilliance of the moonlight. She was afraid at first, not knowing if the shadow would hurt her. As she saw more clearly with the moon's ever-glowing light, she became aware that it was the same boy who had helped her when she was attacked by the bees. She smiled and looked at him with a loving, thankful smile. Her eyes began to sparkle.

As the boy stood there, he noticed that she moved ever so slightly. He saw her slowly open her eyes. They sparkled at him. He saw a glowing smile on her lips, and faintly at first, the brilliance of her light began to return. He could not resist touching her delicate wings and the softness of her face. As he touched her, the grey began to change and her colors began to return. The light that had faded began to grow more brilliant. The boy backed away. He was at first frightened, but then knew that he had helped to return her to life. He ran back to the wall and carefully climbed up the ivy vine trellis, hoping that it would hold him and get him safely back to his own yard. It did, and he was happy that he was safe again. He was also happy that he had risked helping the fairy.

The Healing Touch
Illustration by the fantasy artist Gary Delamatre

She felt his touch ever so gently on her wings and on her face. As he touched her, a radiant energy ran through her body. His gentleness, as compared to the brutal attack she had experienced, created hopefulness in her. Her colors began to come back. Her light began to glow brighter. She knew she was growing stronger because of his healing touch. She saw him back away from her, and with a smile on his face, he ran to the stone wall. She watched as he climbed the ivy vine trellis. He disappeared into the night. She lay upon her petals, touched and moved. She would never be the same again.

As the days passed, she grew stronger. She let the energy of his touch heal her. First, she was able to awaken her mind. It became stronger and stronger each day. Then, her body awakened. Her whole being was changed and somehow enhanced. She felt brighter and lighter. Her colors glowed with enriched hues. Her light beamed brighter than ever. She felt more alive than she *had in her comfortable little space on the petals of her flower. The poison of the one bee, though, kept recurring in her body, sapping the energy she would generate. As she healed, she kept watching the wall to see if she could glimpse the boy again.*

The boy came to the wall every day to see how the fairy was doing. He smiled as he began to see her colors glow and her light become brighter. He felt reassured that she would again be able to resume her work with the birds. He continued to play in his yard with his tin soldiers and read under the sturdy oak tree, but every so often, his mind would wander to the fairy on her flower.

The fairy resumed her work, spinning thread for the birds, teaching the other fairies to spin thread, and seeing that the bewildered flowers were nourished. Occasionally, her mind would dart to the wall, and she wondered what the boy's world was like. She thought for many days about the boy and how his touch had affected her. Finally, one day, after careful consideration, she decided to risk the flight to the wall to peer into his world. She straightened her wings and flew to the top of the wall. She hovered just above the wall and glimpsed him reading a book. She saw him look her way out of the corner of his eye. She became frightened and darted back to the safety of her own yard.

The boy was reading under the sturdy oak, and out of the corner of his eye, he thought he saw a bright glow just above the wall. As he turned to look, he saw the fairy dart away quickly. He became curious about what made her seek out his presence. He put his book down and went to the hole in the wall. He saw her going from flower to flower, nurturing them as she went. He went back to reading, but the idea of her approaching his world made him wonder what it would be like to have her come to his yard. One day, he decided to risk seeing if she would come to him, so he climbed the ivy vine trellis and peered over at her. He motioned for her to fly to him.

The fairy, although working hard, continued to wonder about the boy. Very unexpectedly one day, she saw the boy at the top of the wall. Their eyes met and held for a moment. She saw the sparkle in his eyes and the laughter on his face as he motioned for her to fly to the wall. At first, she hesitated and wondered. As he looked longingly at her with his slate blue eyes, she saw gentleness and peacefulness. She put down the thread she had been spinning and straightened her wings. She flew delicately to the wall and hovered by him. He put out his hand, and she lit on it without fear. It seemed like the natural thing for her to do.

The boy had wondered whether or not she would respond to his gesture. He caught her eye. He looked into her bright green eyes and saw mystery and magic. He knew at that moment that he wanted her in his world. He got up as much courage as he could and beckoned for her to come to the wall. He held his breath until she finally flew to him. He gently put out his hand for her to land upon. Then he climbed slowly down the ivy vine trellis with her in his hand. When he got securely on the ground, he cupped both hands and let her sit in them securely.

She wasn't sure what made her trust him. All she knew was that she felt safe and protected in his cupped hands. As she was in his hands, she began to feel the poison of the one bee that had stung her so hard. She fell backwards in the boy's hands. She felt him gently stroke her delicate wings. She immediately felt his understanding nature. The energy he gave her by his touch helped to give her the strength to fight off the poison in her body and mind. She soon revived through the gentleness of his touch. She knew he would help her recover totally. She knew it by how he looked at her and by his gentle touch.

He tried to be ever so gentle with her, being certain she had enough space, and his hands were not too tight around her. As he carried her to the sturdy tree to read to her, he felt her fall backwards in his hands. He carefully stroked her delicate wings as if to reassure her that everything would be fine, as it takes time to recover from what she had experienced.

The boy sat under the tree and put the fairy on his lap as he opened his great book and began to read to her. He liked having her there to listen to him read. He felt comfortable in her presence. She seemed to bring peacefulness to his world. They spent hours together that day, enjoying the time they had. He watched as she turned colors for him. It made him smile. For him it was a magical moment in his otherwise busy existence.

She loved to hear him read and to be part of his world. She glowed brightly and changed colors as her creativity was stimulated by his presence. Her light became brighter as she saw his response to her magic. She felt alive with him and creative. As a result, her magic blossomed.

Alas, it was time for him to go back into the house, so he took her to the wall and put her in his left hand as he climbed the ivy vine trellis with his right hand. At the top of the wall, he opened his cupped hand. He gave her a smile. He watched her pause slightly returning his smile by turning several different colors. Then he reluctantly watched her fly back to her flower in the yard next door.

She did not want to leave the safety and protection of his hand as he climbed the ivy vine trellis. She looked up at him and watched a smile appear on his face. She lingered in his hand just for a moment as he opened it for her to fly back to her flower. She took a deep breath, straightened her wings, changed colors several times to return his smile, and then flew back to her flower. She kept wondering if she would ever feel this way again.

He would come to the wall on occasion to beckon for her to come with him. He always had a creative plan for them when they shared time. He showed her his mound of dirt from which he gave his moving monologues. He showed her his garden. He was careful to keep her away from his tin soldiers. He thought they would not understand why he wanted the fairy in his world. They played by the creek, in the lush grass, and climbed the sturdy oak tree. He even put her in his pocket as he swung on the tire swing. He enjoyed being with her. His time with her was limited by the activities and duties he had in his world. His life had a pattern, and it was comfortable.

She loved being with him. His courage had opened the door to friendship between them. She would fly to the wall when he chose to beckon for her to join him. Excitedly, she would put on her most brilliant colors to entertain him. He would make the day seem especially exciting. She loved to listen to his stories and loved to be shown his world. She wondered what made him keep her away from the tin soldiers, but she hesitated to ask. She was often afraid to go to the wall without him beckoning because she never wanted to interrupt his world. Although she longed to be with him, she knew the boundaries by his unspoken actions. That was different for her because she was so used to things being very clear, like her colors. With him, though, things were not clear. This often created confusion for her as she longingly looked at the wall from her flower. She wondered if he would ever again break free of his wall as he had done once to save her. Yet she knew that they both were comfortable. She also knew that comfort does not bring change. It is only in crisis that one moves beyond the boundaries of comfort to experience growth. So the fairy decided to just enjoy her time with the boy whenever she could. She was thankful that once he had been willing to risk his comfort to help her.

How to Use Fantasy to Write Your Own Story

Write stories to express yourself symbolically. Allow yourself to go to a spot where your imagination takes you away to a land in which the mind can repair itself. Write any story that pops into your head. Or try the following techniques.

Use dreams to stimulate your writing. Sometimes you can get pieces of dreams that you can remember. Take that piece of your dream and let your imagination run with it.

Get a book of fables. Read them. Then write your own fable. Let's say you pick *Aesop's Fables* and you read *The Wind and the Sun*. Write a similar story about *The Moon and the Snow*.

Get a book of short stories. Read them. Then write your own short story. Let's say you choose *Arabian Nights*. You read *The Tale of the Three Apples*. Write a similar story about *The Tale of the Four Strawberries*.

Just write. It is for you. It is not for others. No

one cares if you follow a pattern of something you have read. Just get whatever is inside of you out onto paper in a symbolic way.

Another idea is to go somewhere you have never been. Pick an object and write about it. Let's say you have never been to a trout farm. Go to a trout farm and watch the trout. Bring pen and paper. Write down words that occur to you as you watch the trout. Sit down on a bench or bring a blanket and sit on the ground. Lie on your blanket and look up at the sky. Then close your eyes and remember the trout. What story comes to your mind?

This technique is very different from journaling. When you journal, you work with reality. You put facts, thoughts, and feelings in your writing. You saw in chapter two concerning my own story how I made journal entries. Journaling helps to reduce the emotional high by expressing your thoughts and feelings in words. Once your thoughts and feelings are given words, you are better able to cope. With story writing, you experience a different benefit. You open up a whole new way of discovering symbolically what is inside of you.

Unlike the powerful spot fantasy which you can do in minutes or seconds, writing a story requires time. It won't be accomplished in a day, or a month, or perhaps even a year, although it can come that quickly. Sometimes the story just comes out of you as fast as you can write it down. One of the short stories I wrote just flowed out. It was done in a matter of hours. I awoke with it in my head, and it just came pouring out. Give yourself time to complete your writing. You might even choose to schedule writing. Let's say you choose to give yourself one hour on Saturday morning to devote to healing through story writing. However you assimilate this idea into your life is up to you. Try it. It might work or it may not for you. If it does, you are taking one step forward to mend your broken heart. If it does not, then you have not lost any ground. You are just stuck, and perhaps something else in this book may be more effective for you in mending your broken heart.

Review

Fantasy is definitely not a place I run to in order to escape. Fantasy gives me the freedom to create an alternate reality in which I can rejuvenate. In fantasy, I can repair my energy and enthusiasm. I can gain the power that I need to survive in my powerless reality. It gives me the freedom to always be the person I want to be. It is like a tune-up on a car. The car runs roughly. With a tune-up, it runs smoothly. I desire to run smoothly. With fantasy, I have that choice. Fantasy empowered me to use my creativity to make my life more satisfying, especially in the grips of grief. I encourage you to use fantasy as I did to help you cope with the chronic illness, terminal illness, or the death of someone you love.

Additionally, I encourage you to write stories. When you express yourself in symbolic ways, you can use the symbolism to understand yourself. When you understand the deeper meaning inside of you, then you have the potential to heal. Believe in yourself. It's time to mend your broken heart.

Another powerful and creative way to help maintain strength in a helpless reality is to use music. If you want to be resilient and help your child to be vibrant even in the midst of struggles, use music.

Listen to Music

Courage is needed when a person is struggling with the eminent death of a loved one. It is also needed after the loved one dies. Courage is the quality of being fearless or brave. What gives us courage? We get courage from many things. I built my courage through music.

My Song

There was a Broadway play in 1965 called *Man of La Mancha* starring Richard Kiley. It was made into a movie in 1972 and starred Peter O'Toole. In the play within the play, Miguel de Cervantes reenacts the story of Don Quixote. Miguel sings a song called "The Impossible Dream." The words to this song sustained me in my darkest moments. They gave me the courage I needed to fear nothing, to persevere, and to believe that there was always hope.

I knew from the start the first day that the doctor talked to us that there was only a 20 percent chance that my son would survive. This song said it all for me about how I would face life with my son. Let me explain what I mean through the lyrics of the song.

The Impossible Dream
Music by: Mitch Leigh
Lyrics by: Joe Darion
Andrew Scott Music 1965

To dream the impossible dream
To fight the unbeatable foe
To bear with unbearable sorrow
To run where the brave dare not go

To right the unrightable wrong
To love pure and chaste from afar
To try when your arms are too weary
To reach the unreachable star

This is my quest
To follow that star
No matter how hopeless
No matter how far

To fight for the right
Without question or pause
To be willing to march into Hell
For a heavenly cause

And I know if I'll only be true
To this glorious quest
That my heart will lie peaceful and calm
When I'm laid to my rest

And the world will be better for this
That one man, scorned and covered with scars
Still strove with his last ounce of courage
To reach the unreachable star

To dream the impossible dream was to believe that my son would conquer this cancer that consumed his brain. I believed without a shadow of a doubt that my son would survive. I saw him projected into the future as a sensitive, caring, thriving adult. Even though I was scared and anxious every time he had an MRI, my mind was always filled with thoughts of his being in our family for a very long time.

To fight the unbeatable foe obviously was the cancer. Even though he would have three major brain operations, an autologous bone marrow transplant, radiation, and chemotherapy repeated times, I would fight for my son's life in whatever way I could.

To bear the unbearable sorrow goes without explanation. The sorrow that filled my heart when I saw him suffer was so overwhelming that at times I was surprised at myself. How could I be so calm in such horrid circumstances? How could I last another moment when he was crying? How could I comfort him? How could I reassure him? I could only do that by telling him that God was his best friend. God had been my best friend when I was a child. I wanted to pass that on to my son. The only way that I could bear the unbearable sorrow was through God's strength. God gave me the courage I needed when I needed it. Always. Without fail. Multiple times.

To run where the brave dare not go again was just being with a child when he was suffering. Even a brave-hearted person melts when a child is in pain. To be right by his side every moment was certainly brave. When he had surgeries, we were there. When he was in the hospital, we were there. When he had outpatient treatments, we were there. When he had to have blood drawn weekly, we were there. When we had to give him shots, we did. When he was at home with a tutor instead of at school, we were there. At the same time, we were brave enough to let him be a child. We let him play basketball, be in cub scouts, play soccer, act in plays, sleep over with peers, play baseball, swim, and take dance lessons. We did not confine him to a bubble. We were brave enough to let him live like a normal child. That took courage.

To right the unrightable wrong speaks to the fact that it is just plain wrong for children to have to suffer and die before parents. The only way to right the wrong was to fight for his life. I fought the battle because it was the right thing to do.

To love pure and chaste from afar went without saying. I loved him deeply, but did not smother him. He knew he was loved. As I have stated already, when I would tuck him in bed at night, I would say to him, "Who loves you most?" He would say, "God." And then I would say, "Who loves you second?" He would say, "Mommy." I would say, "Special boy." He would say, "Special girl." Then I would say, "I love you." Then we would do butterfly kisses on our cheeks, and I would kiss him gently on his forehead, tuck the covers around him, turn on his soft, relaxing music, turn on his nightlight, and quietly close his bedroom door. He knew he was loved. I knew that because he always felt safe. When a person is loved, one feels safe.

To try when your arms are too weary occurred many, many, many times. There were times when I was exhausted from his frequent awakenings at night. I was exhausted from the trips to the hospital, where it was impossible to get sleep. I was exhausted from working on my doctorate degree. I was exhausted from raising three children and taking them to all their activities. I was exhausted from the extra time it takes to do everything that a chronically ill child needs in place to survive. I was weary, but that made no difference. I would persevere, no matter what I had to do to help my child have a wonderful life, no matter how long that might be.

To reach the unreachable star was the hope that my son would beat the cancer and have a long, healthy life, even though the odds were against that happening.

This is my quest, to follow that star meant that no matter what the odds were, I would set my mind on the ultimate star of him living into adulthood. I would pursue that goal.

No matter how hopeless meant even though I knew from a realistic perspective that chances were very slim that he would survive, I would believe that he would.

No matter how far represented all the journeys I took with him. The longest journey we took was to a hospital in the eastern part of the United States. The other journeys were closer to home, such as to the hospital, which was about a forty-five-minute drive. During those drives, I would play music that kept both of us entertained and uplifted. The main music that made a difference in my son's life is described later in this chapter.

To fight for the right without question or pause had a deep meaning. It was the idea that my son had a right to life. This tragic incident of having a tumor did not have to stop his life. He had a right to a full and happy life. I advocated for him to be able to learn in school when he could be there. I advocated that he play sports when it was safe for him to do so. I advocated for him to participate in activities when his blood counts were high enough that he was not at risk. I advocated for him to have friends who cared about him and were involved in his life. There was no question that he should have these rights.

I remember at one point I asked his teacher to cease from giving him grades and instead give him a progress report defining what he was doing well and where he needed improvement. His sister and brother were very good students, and it frustrated him that his grades were not comparable. So why lower his self-confidence by comparison? It was fine with him not to have grades and to get a review instead. So that's what we did.

To be willing to march into hell for a heavenly cause defined the extent of my courage. During this time, I had little energy to reframe my thoughts; so many times, it would seem that I was marching into hell to keep his little life going. I spent what seemed to be endless days in the hospital. One of my pet peeves is wasting time. Playing in the hospital playroom, watching movies with him, or playing games in his hospital room in comparison to doing my studies was so difficult for me. My heart wanted to be present to what he was experiencing and to take his mind off being at the hospital. My mind also wanted to be learning. So I had a constant war going on within me. Yes, I wanted to be with my son, and yes, I also wanted to be reading my textbooks to learn about the courses I was studying in my doctoral program. I tried my best to balance both. When he was awake, I played with him. When he was asleep, I studied. It was a challenge and always an internal struggle.

This next part of the song was a philosophy that my husband and I held from the moment we found out about our son's tumor until the day of his funeral. *And I know if I'll only be true to this glorious quest that my heart will be peaceful and calm when I'm laid to my rest* meant that no matter what the odds were that he would live, he was one person, and as far as we were concerned, he had 100 percent chance or none. We chose to believe that he would have 100 percent chance of survival. We would pursue this quest of his survival and do all we could to make it happen. If the most unfortunate thing happened and he did not survive, we would be peaceful knowing that we had done everything we could within reason to make that happen.

We also tried to give him the happiest life he could have by treating him as we did our other children. Yes, we had to pay more attention to him because he had unique circumstances, but he was treated just the same as the other children. We gave him as normal a childhood as a child with cancer can have. At his funeral, my husband and I affirmed and validated the fact that we had been true to our quest and we were peaceful that we had given him the best life a little boy could have had.

The last thought is also a philosophy that applies to my life. *And the world will be better for this, that one man* (in my case, woman) *scorned and covered with scars* (mostly of the heart) *still strove with his* (her) *last ounce of courage, to reach the unreachable star* is what I help people do every day in my private practice. I help people have better lives by changing their behaviors or thoughts so they can reach their goals. Because of my experience with my son, I bring to the therapy relationship a wealth of understanding. It is through that understanding that I do not let people dwell in their own misery. I am a taskmaster in the therapy that I do with people. I do not let people dwell in self-pity. I take their scars and make them symbols of their badge of courage so that they can also reach their unreachable star.

This song painted my reality and gave me strength. I challenge you to find a song that fits for you and listen to it over and over and over and over again. Whether you are struggling now with a loved one who has a terminal illness, or whether you have already lost a loved one, find a song that fits for you. The words create a groove in your brain, as a wagon wheel does over the soft ground, until it is a permanent mark that lasts.

Your mind is marvelous, because when you hear something enough, you begin to think in terms of what you hear. I do that with my clients when I am teaching them to change their language from powerless language such as "should, have to, ought to" to the powerful language of choice with words such as "choose to, desire to, want to." The words to "The Impossible Dream" gave me courage when I needed it most. In fact, I still use that song when I am striving to meet a difficult goal.

Find your song. Find what fits for how you want to live your life during a struggle or during your grief process. Play the song again and again and again until you live the song.

Wes's Songs

I also used music to help Wes through his struggles. I was so fortunate to purchase at a Christian bookstore a cassette tape called *The Kid's Praise! Album*. I filled Wes with this amazing music. Ernie Rettino and Debby Kerner Rettino created songs that taught children about how God plays a part in their lives. Wes and I would listen to these songs as we traveled to his appointments, to the hospitals, and when we were sitting around at home. I truly believe that these songs gave Wes courage and contentment. Let me give some examples of how I believe this music affected Wes's life.

In *The Kid's Praise! Album*, the song "Heaven is a Wonderful Place" by O. A. Lambert creates a warm picture of what heaven is like. I believe because Wes listened to this song that all his imaginings of heaven were positive. One line in the song states, "Heaven is a wonderful place." The song goes on to tell what makes heaven such a wonderful place. However, I believe that just that concept of heaven being a wonderful place filled Wes's mind with positive images of heaven.

After I told Wes that God was calling him to heaven, we often spoke of what heaven would be like. He told me that he believed heaven is like a big, big castle with a huge playground and rooms and rooms full of Legos. For Wes, a huge place filled with rooms of Legos was a wonderful place. I believe this song allowed Wes to create the idea in his mind that when he got to heaven, it would be wonderful. The anticipation of going to heaven caused him little anxiety. He was so calm and peaceful, and my guess is that it had everything to do with this song in his mind. To him, heaven would be wonderful.

Another song, "Beautiful" by Dennis Cleveland from *Kid's Praise! 4 Singsational Servant* helped him to be content with his life. When he had to go to the hospital, he did. When he had to stay home from school and be tutored, he did. When he could participate in activities, he did. He was always content and never complained. "Beautiful" and the dialogue surrounding the song created the picture in his mind that his life was beautiful.

The dialogue went like this:

Psalty: *When you are his servant and you have given your talents to him, God will make something beautiful of your life.* (Song) *Now look at this daffodil bulb. It's kind of plain; nothing special about it, but if I plant it in the ground, water it, and wait, Jesus will make it into a beautiful flower.*

Little girl: *If God can do that with a daffodil bulb, think what he can do with me.*

The most powerful words of the song were "Jesus makes beautiful things of my life." I believe that Wes believed that no matter where he was or what he was doing that God would create something beautiful of his life. He was content in that thought, so his life was always peaceful even in the midst of chaos.

From *Kid's Praise! 5 Psalty's Camping Adventure*, two songs, gave Wes great courage. "One Step at a Time" taught him to be present to the moment and break problems down into manageable pieces. "All Through the Day" allowed him to experience contentment.

One Step at a Time
Words and music by: Ernie Rettino & Debby
Kerner Rettino
1985 Rettino/Kerner Publishing

When something seems too hard to handle
Too big to conquer
Too far away to touch.

When all your dreams begin to shatter,
And deep inside you
You're hurtin' oh, so much
That's when it's time to say …

Chorus:
I'm climbing my mountain … step by step
I'm climbing my mountain … day by day
I'm climbing my mountain … all the way
I'm climbing my mountain
I'm gonna make it

One step at a time
One step at a time
One step at a time
With Jesus by my side.

One step at a time
One step at a time
I'm climbing my mountain
One step at a time.

Even though you might grow weary
Don't be discouraged
In our weakness, God is strong.

Remember this, He'll never leave you
He won't forsake you
He's your strength and He's your song
So sing and start to say …

(Chorus repeated two times)

This song I tended to play over and over again for Wes and actually for me too. I cannot tell you how many times in the midst of struggle that I sang this song to myself. I believe this song sustained Wes through all his struggles with radiation, with chemotherapy, with operations, with needles, with shots, and with a lifestyle that no child should ever have to experience.

"All Through the Day" by Tom Howard, a second song from *Kid's Praise! 5 Psalty's Camping Adventure*, gave Wes contentment because he knew that he was always in God's hands. These words, "All through the day and night we're in His hand" reassured Wes that no matter what happened, God was there with him.

I believe this next song helped Wes glow with light. Wes was never surrounded with a cloud. There was no darkness enveloping him. Even though I felt the darkness, his little light would shine on me. Merely being around Wes created happiness in me. Every time I think of Wes, I think of the song "This Little Light of Mine" based on Matthew 5:16, NIV: "In the same way, let your light shine before men, that they may see your good deeds and praise your Father in the heavens." He was a poster boy for that song. This song was sung at his funeral. Remember the words from that African American spiritual.

> This little light of mine
> I'm gonna let it shine
> Let it shine, Let it shine, Let it shine.

Kid's Praise! 8 Play Ball had a song called "Put Jesus in Your Everyday Life" by Ernie Rettino and Debby Kerner Rettino. This song helped Wes realize that Jesus was his very best friend, always answering "Jesus" when I asked him who loved him most. I always knew that Jesus was continually there by his side, watching over him, protecting him, and keeping him safe. Wes was reassured of this each time he listened to the song as it stated, "Put Jesus in your everyday life. He wants to be your very best friend."

Wes believed that Jesus was his best friend. He took Jesus everywhere with him. I always told him that Jesus was right beside him holding his hand, even when I was not there with him. I believe this brought Wes comfort and helped him make every day a happy day, regardless of his struggles.

The song "God Has a Plan for My Life" by Ernie Rettino and Debby Kerner Rettino that helped Wes guard against hopelessness was from *Kid's Praise! 10 Salvation Celebration*. Wes wanted to be a lifeguard when he grew up. After he died, I imagined him doing just that, as an angel guarding his brother and sister's lives as they grew. The stanza of that song that helped Wes weather his hopelessness went like this:

> It won't all be easy
> But God will understand
> Through all the hard times
> He'll be there to hold my hand
> He knows just how special
> I'll turn out to be
> Yes, God has a plan for little ol' me

Perhaps it was not a big plan. Perhaps it was not an amazing plan. Perhaps the plan didn't have very many years to it. Perhaps it was not a carefree plan. Perhaps it was not an ordinary little boy plan. Whatever plan it was, it was God's plan, and that seemed to be just fine with Wes. He knew he was in God's hands. And that heaven was a wonderful place. That's all he needed to know, and he was content with that.

There is just one last song, "I'm Gonna Fight a Giant" by Ernie Rettino and Debby Kerner Rettino that was paramount to Wes's courage to live his life in a meaningful way. I used this song with Wes when we were on our journey to get his autologous bone marrow transplant. It came from *Kid's Praise! Psalty's Bible Stories, Parables & Songs* and was about the Bible story of David and Goliath.

> I'm gonna fight a giant
> Gonna fight a giant
> Gonna fight a giant
> I'll swing my sling shot round and round
> And knock that giant to the ground
> I'm gonna fight a giant
> Gonna fight a giant
> Gonna fight a giant

From this song I wrote some dialogue about Wes and what was going to happen to him during his autologous bone marrow transplant. Then I used the chorus to this song to challenge him to have the courage he needed.

Wes, the Giant Fighter

This is the story of Wes, the giant fighter. When we last left Wes, he was fighting dragons and spraying for dragon eggs. This summer, Wes continues his adventure. Just like David, Wes challenged a giant.

(chorus: "I'm Gonna Fight a Giant")

One day, Wes said good-bye to his brother, Tony, his sister, Ali, and his dad, and left with his mom and Lola on his quest to fight a giant. To fight the giant, Wes traveled to a city where he meets with a team of giant fighters. The team leader is Dr. Joe. Just as Dr. John led the team to fight the dragon, Dr. Joe helps Wes fight the giant.

(chorus: "I'm Gonna Fight a Giant")

To fight the giant, Wes takes his slingshot and the invisible armor of God. First, the giant fighters take pictures of Wes's body. Next, they take blood samples to see how prepared Wes's body is to fight the giant. Again, the battle against the giant will be within Wes's body.

(chorus: "I'm Gonna Fight a Giant")

What a surprise the team found. When the giant fighting team saw Wes's blood cells, they were excited and shouted, "Hooray!" They saw small cells, yet each one was filled with power, like mini super cells. These cells had the incredible power to fight infection and to keep Wes healthy after he fights the giant. These mini super cells are part of the invisible armor of God that he has given to Wes to help him fight the giant.

(chorus: "I'm Gonna Fight a Giant")

Dr. Joe began the fight one early morning. He, along with his team, put Wes into a deep sleep. While Wes was asleep, they took out the machine that makes Wes's blood cells in order to protect the mini super cells from being hit by the liquid pebbles from the slingshot which the giant fighting team attached to Wes's body to help him fight the giant. The slingshot sent many liquid pebbles into Wes's body for six days, to wage a war against the giant. Each pebble pelted against the mighty giant, and slowly with great persistence, the giant was worn down until he could no longer fight.

(chorus: "I'm Gonna Fight a Giant")

Wes was weak from the struggle, yet he knew that after the fight, his mini super cells would help him grow strong again. Dr. Joe and his team of giant fighters put back into Wes's body the machine that would produce Wes's mini super cells to help Wes regain his strength and fight infection. Each day, Wes grew stronger and stronger. His energy increased, and he was soon filled with mini super cells. These cells overpowered the giant so that Wes continues to grow strong and healthy.

(chorus: "I'm Gonna Fight a Giant")

I believe these songs gave Wes courage and created contentment in him. Even when he was scared, he also had this amazing courage, this undaunted contentment that went beyond his years.

Thoughts on My Efforts

At one point in my life after his death, I wondered, *With all the efforts with the psychological techniques I knew, how could I have failed him?* I felt like a failure. With time and with reflection, I realized that I did not fail him. All that I did with him had a purpose. The music had a purpose. The stories had a purpose. That purpose was not to create longevity for his life, but instead to give him a wonderful life while he was on Earth. I began to realize that basing expectations on anyone besides myself led to misery.

My expectations about what I was doing with music and stories were based on him living. I now know that when I base my expectations on others that I am often disappointed. I was disappointed because he died, and his death meant that I was a failure. This thinking made me miserable. I finally realized I was in control of what I thought, so I changed my thinking.

What I changed my thinking to was that my expectations were totally inappropriate. I rethought my expectations by basing them on my own behavior. I changed my thinking to what I could control. I could not control whether or not he died. What I could control is what I could do to make his life amazing while he was with me on Earth. I changed what I had expected of myself. I expected myself to help my son through his struggles. I did that with music, with stories, with positive statements, and with my love. That was all that I could expect of myself. I believe I did that. I believe that I succeeded at being his mother.

Being able to see myself in hindsight as a success helped me mend my broken heart. I began to think positive thoughts about myself and was less miserable. All my efforts with music and with stories were worth the time and energy. These efforts gave Wes a life of courage, contentment, joy, and love. My heart is quieted in that thought.

Review

In order to have courage to face your child's illness or death, choose a song that you can play over and over again so that it can lead you to thoughts of strength. Make it your song. Make your song work for you. Your song can give you strength. Your song can help you be resilient, even in the face of your struggles. Your song can give you courage when you need it most. Believe in yourself. It's time to mend your broken heart.

Even though you do believe you have successfully mended your broken heart, you will have setbacks. I call these setbacks "spiral times." Spiral times usually happen without warning. They come out of nowhere and attack you. Be prepared for them so they do not overwhelm you and cause regression.

Handle Spiral Times

As we progress through our grief process, we notice that some days, events, places, objects, words, smells, or feelings can send us spiraling back to our sorrow. Out of the blue, we might be irritable, and we wonder why. Many times, it has to do with our unconscious processing of what was and what can never be. Let's take a look at the concept of spiraling.

First, let's look at reoccurring days that send us spiraling back to feelings of sorrow. The biggest spiral days occur on the anniversary of days relating to our child. For instance, a huge spiral time is the anniversary of the day our child died. Another spiral time is the birthday of our dead child. I know that each year on the anniversary of my child's death that I have an anticipatory anxiety that stays at a low level for a few weeks before and after the event. Becoming aware of your own process during those anniversary times is important to coping. At first, his birthday brought great sorrow for me, but over the years, that has abated.

Second, events cause spiraling. I am referring to those times when an event is about to occur that would have been something special that only applies to our child, or that would have included our child. With almost every event that occurs, there is a low-level sorrow that pervades. An example of that is the day our child would have graduated from high school. I remember when my child would have progressed to the middle school; his elementary school dedicated their yearbook in his honor. It was a bittersweet day for me to attend that event. I was joyful because his class was honoring him and sorrowful because he was not there to be with them at this milestone.

Other significant spiral times concerning events may occur when our friend's children, who are the same age as our dead child, go through milestones. Examples of these times are when our friend's child graduates from high school or college, gets married, or has a first child. Although we are happy for our friend, it also brings such pains of sorrow for us that inside we may feel very conflicted. We want to be happy for our friend, and at the same time, we feel a void because we will never experience that event with our child. I remember talking joyfully with a friend who has a child the same age as Wes when her child was graduating from high school. I was so happy for her. She was beaming at his accomplishments and told me all about his wonderful college plans. I went home and cried for an hour. It was nothing she said. It was only the realization that my child would never get to experience those events.

Another friend's child who was Wes's age got married. Again, it was a bittersweet experience. I was so happy for her and her wonderful son. I participated in the events surrounding the wedding, and still, in my heart, there was a low-level sorrow. I accepted the wedding as a joyful event for my friend. I was happy to be present to my friend because it was not her burden to bear my grief. People will not share or invite you if they think it makes you sad. For me, being left out of the joyfulness of the events of others is even worse than bearing the pain of wishing that my child would have had a similarly long life.

In a like manner, if we have other children, milestones for them are bittersweet for us. On the day another of our children graduates or gets married, we may experience both great joy and great sorrow. We are extremely happy for our child, and at the same time, we feel sad that our dead child cannot be present to enjoy the special time. We also feel sad because we will never be able to experience this same special occasion with our dead child. I remember my son Tony's wedding. I was so very happy for him, yet through the whole experience, this quiet sadness in me pervaded.

Seasonal events can also spiral us back. Christmas is a good example. When one family member is not present, it makes the holiday less complete and joy filled, unless new traditions are adapted. Another seasonal event for me with Wes was kite flying in spring. Wes and I always flew kites in the spring together. So each year in March or April, I either drag out one of the old kites or buy a new one to fly. I dedicate my kite flying experience to the memory of Wes.

Third, visiting places that pertain to your child may create a spiral time. Driving my daughter to school at the same elementary school that Wes attended was difficult for me to do at first. Visiting the hospital where your loved one was treated can create anxiety and spiral you back to your sorrow. I rarely had an opportunity to visit the same hospital he was in off and on for eight years, but when I did, I felt my breathing getting shallow and my mind returning in flashing sequences to all the struggles he had with his cancer. Attending a church service at the same time that we most usually attended with our dead child can create a spiral time experience. I cannot attend a nine o'clock service at my church without it causing me anxiety because I just see pictures of my son with his mask on that he wore when he had to be around other people when his blood counts were low. The spiraling totally takes my focus of attention away from the present moment.

Fourth, objects may create a spiral time. When we see those items that were important to our dead child, it creates a spiral time. For a few minutes, we might be whisked back to the times when our child was with us. I remember when I would see Legos, whether it was in my home or in the store, it would spin me back to a visual image of him playing with the Legos. Another example occurs when I use Band-Aids. Wes always had to have a Band-Aid on for any part of his body that hurt, whether or not it was bleeding.

Fifth, words, even everyday words, may cause spiral times. A word that our child struggled with, a word that meant something to him or some combinations of words that he often said could cause a spiral time in us. For instance, the word *feather* reminds me of calling Wes feather head.

Sixth, smells that remind us of our dead child can bring on a spiral time. Perhaps we smell our child's favorite food and cannot take another bite. For example, when I smell kiwi, I am reminded of Wes because kiwi was his favorite fruit. We might smell lotion we used to put on our child and may just stare off into space for a few moments. If we detect the smell of antiseptic from the hospital if our child was hospitalized, we might experience a spiral time.

Seventh, we might have a feeling that spirals us back. When we are proud of one of our other children, it might remind us of how proud we were of our dead child for struggling through his illness. When we feel love for another child, we may also experience the sadness that we have such love to give to our dead child and he is not here with us to receive it. For example, Tony won an award his senior year of school for loyalty, service, and character. My proud feeling jolted me back to how proud I was of Wes when he had to endure brain surgery, an autologous bone marrow transplant, and many treatments of chemotherapy. Through all of this, he was always a happy child. I was very proud of his attitude toward his life. So when Tony received an award for character, in my heart, I knew that I had another son who also had great character.

All of this is bittersweet. We are joyful for the present, yet we are sorrowful because of what could have been for our dead child. So many things spiral us back to our sorrow that it seems impossible to move forward. However, it is not. We can choose to move forward. Let me suggest a few ways to handle the spiral times that definitely will come.

Handling Spiral Times

So what do you do with these spiral times? I planned for the spiral times. However, if a spiral time catches you off guard, then try this process. First, realize that they are spiral times. Second, acknowledge them as such. Third, grasp the experience for that moment in time. Fourth, take a deep breath. Fifth, spend some time, if you need to, just reflecting. Sixth, gently bring yourself back to the present moment. The trick here is not to spend an inordinate amount of time dwelling on the day, event, place, object, word, smell, or feeling from the past. Let it wash over you like a wave, and then let it go back out to sea.

Let me give you some examples of how I planned in each area. You will have your own healthy way of responding. My way is only what works for me. From my examples, begin to try some things that may help you. I had to try several things in some cases to be able to move past the intensity of a spiral time.

Let's start with days. On the anniversary of Wes's death, I take off of work. I spend the majority of the day devoted to his memory. One year, I looked at all the photo albums that I had made of him. Another year, I watched the home videos of him. Another year, I watched the Star Wars trilogy that Wes and I would watch when we spent time in the hospital. Each year, I devote the day to all my memories of him. I go to the grave site and spend a few moments talking to him in my thoughts. If I need to cry on that day, I do. For me, devoting this one day exclusively to him allows me to easily let go of all those other spiral times. In my mind, I honor him by devoting a day to him. Likewise, I honor myself. When I honor his memory on that one special day each year, then I am free to be present to any moment instead of being sucked back into my memories.

The first few years his birthday gave me great sorrow. I realized that he would not want me to be so sad on his birthday. After all, he was always happy, no matter what he had to do, so why should I be sad on his special day? Now, on his birthday, I get a happy birthday balloon and attach it to the flower vase on the side of his gravestone. I think of what he might have looked like now and what he might have chosen to do with his life. I rejoice in the fact that I had him in my life for eleven wonderful years and that he taught me so much about life in those short years. I rejoice in the wonder of his life.

Now let's look at events. When my son's class graduated from high school, I planned a vacation that week. While my son's class had their wonderful experience, I would be somewhere else having a wonderful experience. The week before the graduation, I could tell that a low-level anxiety was beginning to permeate me. I was really happy that I had anticipated this event and taken a preventative action. The vacation rejuvenated me and created joy. Therefore, by this preventative action, I constructed an environment for myself that week that would not allow for the sadness. I do not consider that running away from it. I consider it my choice to spend a difficult time having fun, instead of spending the time in sorrow. If being away from the event in a place that allows a fun time helps to dispel the sad situation, then I can choose to do that. And I did. And it worked.

When friends' children go through the milestones at the same time your child would have, you again have a choice. To what extent concerning that particular event do you choose to participate? For example, when my friend's son, who was the same age as my son, got married, I participated in the events surrounding the wedding, but since the wedding was many miles away, I chose not to go.

When my other son announced he was going to ask his girlfriend to marry him, I was so happy for him. He had found someone with whom he wanted to share the rest of his life. I knew I would have difficulty during the wedding because Wes would not be there to celebrate Tony's joy with him. Again, I thought ahead and asked Tony if I could create a special candle arrangement to remember all the relatives who could not be with us during this joyful event. He honored my wish. I asked my brother to help me with this project. My brother is wonderful at making a few simple candles, garland, and ribbon into a beautiful expression of joy and light. He decorated the table that was at the side of the altar on which the arrangement silently but visibly glowed. To me, Wes was present in the light of those candles. I almost felt as if by creating this table of light, I was bringing his spirit to the celebration of Tony's wedding. It was a peaceful feeling. My thoughts were present focused once the candles were lit. What I did was to create a symbolic representation that helped me let go of the sadness and welcome the joy of the moment.

Seasonal events such as Christmas or Easter or Halloween or whatever you celebrate can be particularly sad times. Let me give some examples of what I do so you can prepare for those times too. Christmas is the easiest for me because I am a giver. I just transfer my giving spirit that I would have used on my son to another person. Until my son's best friend from school went away to college, I gave him a Christmas gift. Also, I would have my children pick an extra wish item from the angel tree so we could give a gift in Wes's memory. I still do that at my church. I pick one gift wish to give from myself and another to give in Wes's memory. This gesture helps me to be happy during the holiday season.

Another seasonal event for me, which is probably remote to most of my readers, was kite flying. Wes and I would always fly kites every spring. We would choose a windy day, dress warm, go into our front yard, which is the size of a football field, and run with our kites until they flew high. Spring could bring a spiral time, but I have made it into an event to anticipate with excitement and joy. Every spring, I still fly a kite in his memory on a windy day of my choice. I usually spend a half hour or so just getting my kite in the air and watching it soar. The experience exhilarates me, and I feel close to Wes.

Places are still hard for me even after such a long time. However, I pick something out that contrasts the sorrow and showers the experience with joy. For instance, the elementary school planted a tree in Wes's memory. When I drive by the school, I look at the tree growing tall and strong and think that if he was alive today, he would be tall and strong too. I do the same when I pass the park in which he wanted to play on a regular basis. There is a tree planted there in his memory too.

Sometimes we may have a situation with another child that might present a representation of our earlier trauma with our dead child. Let me explain. I do have to admit that I had a spiral time recently when my daughter had a minor traumatic brain injury when she fell off a golf cart and was taken to the same hospital in which my son had his treatments. I had short moments of anxiety that propelled me back into the sights and sounds and feelings that I experienced with Wes. My daughter and I talked about it. I had to do some major processing at that time because her injury had to do with the brain, which was where Wes had his tumors. If it had been a broken leg or a broken arm, I don't think it would have had nearly the impact it did on me. Being able to recognize it as a twofold experience, as a moment in time with my daughter and also as a spiral time for me, was important to processing it in the present moment. Because I could process it on two levels, I was able to keep my spiral time to a minimum.

Sometimes I used journaling to help me prevent or minimize a spiral time. I remember when I was asked to attend the graduation to middle school of my son's fifth grade class. I did not know why I was asked at first, so I wrote in my journal about what I was thinking and feeling at the time. Later, I discovered that the school had dedicated their school yearbook to Wes that year and they wanted us there when they recognized Wes. Here is my journal entry about my spiral time.

Spiral Time

June 2, 1994

Today would have been Wes's graduation from fifth grade. I have mixed feelings about going to the ceremony. The principal asked us to be there. Whatever it is that they want to do special for Wes may not be worth sitting there for an hour, thinking about how much I really miss him.

I have no doubt that at each milestone such as this, I will feel sad, especially his graduation from high school. I'll look back on all the potential he would have had if his life circumstances had been different.

I am angry and have been for about the last month. I am oppositional at work and at home over small, trivial issues. That's why I know my true feelings are stemming from my anger over Wes's early death and not from the current situations. So I took off a week from work to try to correct my attitude and go through a spiral time, another part of the grief cycle.

I am angry that this happened to Wes. He was good and kind and loving and helpful. Why him? Why our family? Why me? Why? Why? Why?

I am angry that in my mind I led myself to believe that God was going to save Wes because he had a destiny for him. I believed that God was preparing him for a special purpose and would let him live to grow up to make a difference in our world. At the same time, I am thankful I had that delusion for eight years. I guess without it, I would not have had the strength to get through all the horrible times. With my eye on the future, I could stand the present no matter how awful it was.

I am scared, too, that my memory of him will grow dim and that I will forget him. That is why my mind keeps holding little pieces of him and shoots them at me when his image fades. My hope is that I am still able to do that, but with images of him in fun, happy situations, and not in those last days when he was dying.

That is why it is important that I organize my picture albums to reflect the fun times of his life. So when images come to me, they will be of his smile and his warm, giving nature.

I talked to Wes today. He told me he was a guardian angel, guarding a newborn baby. I know that seems crazy, but if it is not his voice, whose is it? The voice is in my mind and not out loud. I answer sometimes out loud, or ask a question out loud, but the answer comes from within me. I have this dialogue that I make up to help me cope with my loss.

Wes tells me that God wants me to write. I keep rebelling against it. I just cannot believe that is what God wants me to do. Why? I have tried to get published, but rejection after rejection. No one wanted a children's story. Perhaps it's not the right timing or the right story yet.

I know I need to write this story. I am torn because I hear this, and yet I have to work to make money, so I cannot just drop everything and write. When I tell this to Wes, he reminds me that God will provide. Where is my trust? Where is my faith? What path am I supposed to be on?

Today, I asked Wes to come to me. He did within my mind and body. He asked me to lay down on the daybed and just feel him within me. I felt heavy and my emotions made my heart swell up. I could tell he was there. I asked him to appear to me. He said he no longer had his body and that he is in the peace plant in his bedroom. The peace plant moves in the breeze as I sit and write and put photos in albums.

The next day, he was in the brown bear that was on the daybed. I asked him to come to me so I could hold him. He told me to hold and hug the brown bear. I did, and I could feel him within me.

He says he will always be around to guard and guide Ali and Tony. Whenever I need him, he told me just to call and he would be by my side, just as he would have done had he lived.

I am just so very, very, very sad. I miss him and I love him and I want him back. I know he had a good life, and he keeps making me reflect on that, and he tells me I helped him as much as I could to bridge the two states of being, but I still feel so inadequate to have made his last days here on Earth a preparation for heaven. I wish I could feel better about having prepared him to die. Yet, I know that all the Psalty tapes and my talking with him about God loving him the most was the preparation he needed in order to go to God.

I question whether I should have kept telling him to go to God when he stretched out his arms to him. Was it right to push him into God's hands? I just did not want him to suffer or think he had to stay with us when God was beckoning him to come to heaven.

I know I will love him forever and ever. It is hard to stay on Earth because I want to go be with him. Wes told me today, and I know in my own mind, "My place is with Tony and Ali, helping them to grow up and be good, productive people."

Today, as I go to his graduation ceremony, I hope I can be happy for all of his friends. They have had the opportunity to grow up for another year and to experi-

ence the joys that life can bring. I hope I do not resent that Wes did not have that opportunity.

I love him and I miss him, and he will always be in my heart, no matter how many years pass or how many memories fade. His love is an eternal light in my heart that will keep glowing forever.

Lord, help me to accept his death and move on to write what you want me to write. Help me to take the challenge that you give me to write from my experience. Give me the courage to leave my security and to do your will. Give me faith and love and trust. Help me to say yes to writing, and may it touch other people and make a difference in their lives. Amen.

Time does not negate spiral times. No matter how long your loved one has been gone, spiral times can still surprise you. I wrote the following passage on what would have been Wes's twenty-first birthday, ten years after his death.

Another Spiral Time

June 21, 2003

Each night, I would put the children to bed with a bedtime story and prayers. We would gather on my bed. Then each of them would go to his or her room so I could tuck them in and say good night separately.

I remember how I would go from room to room, making each child feel special. My pattern was to tuck them in, stroke their hair, kiss them on the forehead, and say, "Special boy" or "special girl," and they would respond, "Special girl." Then I would say, "I love you." For Wes, it was different. I would go into his room and make sure he felt safe with extra pillows around him. He thought pillows all around his bed would protect him from monsters. After talking with him briefly, I would do butterfly kisses on his cheek, and then he would do butterfly kisses on my cheek. I would then say, "Who loves you the most?" He would say, "God." And then I would say, "Who loves you second?" He would reply, "Mommy." I would say, "Special boy." He would say, "Special girl." Then I would say, "I love you." I would kiss him gently on his forehead, tuck the covers around him, turn on his soft, relaxing music, turn on his night light, quietly close his bedroom door, and my eyes would fill with tears because I loved him so much.

I know the real feeling of being heartbroken. My heart felt like it would break all three times he had his brain tumors that they operated on, and a fourth time when we were told he was going to die. No mother could have cried more buckets of tears than I have. I could cry today as long and as hard as I cried then. That must be a sign of true loving.

I remember his long, long lashes, when he had them, and how they grazed the tip of my skin so gently. His featherlike hair was so soft to touch as I kissed him gently on the forehead. He always said he had a third eye in the middle of his head. He did have a slight darkened indentation there. He could see things that we could not. He saw his journey, and he was okay with it. He never complained, ever. I am so amazed by him and by his everlasting strength. Even when I told him God was calling him to heaven, he just said, "Okay." He is my inspiration. He is my strength. He is my beautiful, wonderful, son that I miss so very, very much.

What did I do in my life to have to witness the most difficult thing in the world, seeing your child suffer? I think back on all the safe nights they were tucked into bed, and I am glad that I could provide that safety, especially for him. We never left him, except for that *first time when he was three, but never again did we let him experience his ordeal by himself. We loved him with all our hearts. We still love him even now, years later. He would have been twenty-one today, and I am sure very handsome with his beautiful, blonde hair. Why didn't he get a chance to grow up? Why, why, why? He had an amazing sense of faith and great wisdom for a child.*

So you see, even after ten years, a person can have a spiral time. It might be brief or last for a few days. The trick is to never get stuck in your spiral time. Learn to handle your inevitable spiral times.

Review

When a day, event, place, object, word, smell, or feeling sends you spiraling back to your sorrow or you are suddenly irritable and wonder why, you are unconsciously processing what was and what can never be.

Plan for these spiral times. When you know a day is about to arrive that has the potential for spiraling you back to your sorrow, plan what you will do on that day or journal about what you are thinking or feeling concerning the upcoming day or event. As you begin to do the planning around these times, you will be creating a response pattern to these spiral times that will allow you to respond in a healthy way. My way is only one way that works for me. Begin to try some things that may help you to respond with resilience. Remember that I had to try several things in some cases to be able to move past the intensity of a spiral time. Perhaps it will take you time to understand what pattern is best for you. It is not impossible, and you can do it.

When spiral times catch you off guard, try the following process. First, realize that they are spiral times. Second, acknowledge them as such. Third, grasp the experience for that moment in time. Fourth, take a deep breath. Fifth, spend some time, if you need to, just reflecting. Sixth, gently bring yourself back to the present moment. The trick here is not to spend an inordinate amount of time dwelling on the day, event, place, object, word, smell, or feeling from the past. Let it wash over you like a wave. Then let the wave go back out to sea.

You can handle these spiral times. Yes, it will be difficult. Yes, you will have emotions surrounding spiral times. Yes, you can handle these emotions. Yes, the spiral time will pass. Yes, there will be more; count on it. So be resilient. Plan for them, or let them wash over you like a wave. Remember that the wave always goes back out to sea. Learn to handle your spiral times to keep your heart mended. Believe in yourself. It's time to mend your broken heart.

Conceptual frameworks are hard to grasp. Getting started mending your broken heart is even harder. My hope in the final chapter of this book is that I can do two things. First, I give you some simple frame-of-mind ideas to help you start thinking in a new way so that you can let go of the negative thinking and begin to think positive. Second, I give you ideas to jumpstart the process. Reading a book is one thing. Taking the ideas from the book and implementing them in your daily life is another.

The Mind Mends the Heart

Collectively, many ways of thinking helped me to mend my broken heart. In this last chapter, I will share with you the major ideas that helped me to weather the storm of my son's death and allowed me to lead a happy life. Remember that you have control of both your behavior and your thoughts. You can choose to have thoughts that help, not hinder, your life satisfaction. From your thoughts come resultant behaviors that help you create life satisfaction, even when you have lost a loved one.

Second, I will also reflect on how the acknowledgement of others has led me to believe that the techniques I have shared with you have truly been successful in helping me to have a happy life despite my sorrow. When friends and children give me feedback that I have done an effective job at being a friend and a mother, then my thinking and resultant behavior must have been successful in mending my broken heart.

Third, I will help you jump-start the process of getting started. It is definitely time to mend your broken heart. Do not procrastinate. Yes, you read this book. Yes, it is not easy to begin. Yes, it will take time. Yes, it will take effort. Yes, it will take mindfulness. Yes, it will be painful. Yes, you can do it.

Life as a Pathway

First, the idea that "life is a pathway upon which I journey with people for a time" allows me to put all relationships in perspective. With some people, I might journey for only five minutes, and with others, five years or even fifty years. No matter whether it is a short journey or a long journey, I value each. I valued the airplane ride of three hours getting to know a young man from Costa Rica whom I taught to do Sudoku puzzles as much as I valued the relationship I had with my graduate students whom I taught for sixteen weeks. I valued the relationship I had with the nurse who took care of Wes for six weeks at the hospital in the east as much as I valued the relationship I had with the nurses who took care of Wes for eight years. I just learned to accept the fact that I could value a person no matter how many minutes, hours, days, weeks, months, or years that person was in my life.

Thus, on my pathway of life, many other pathways crossed over or paralleled my pathway. I enjoyed each journey for as long as our paths crossed or paralleled. I accepted the fact that sometimes another person's pathway would go in a different direction than mine. With this idea, it was easier to let go of Wes and still value the time I had with him. So I would like to offer you a concept to consider as you mend your broken heart. A satisfying life is a matter of how you embrace the journey and those who cross your path. Contemplate this idea and then choose to live it every day.

The Butterfly Concept

Second, the caterpillar to butterfly concept was a tremendous help in mending my broken heart. This was the image I gave myself in order to become anew without Wes. You have often heard the saying, "What a caterpillar thinks is the end of life the butterfly knows is the beginning." I took this idea that Wes's death was not the end of my world. It was only a new beginning. To hold this concept in mind, I constantly wore butterfly jewelry or hair clips. I did this so that I would be constantly reminded to change my thought process and take a new perspective of my son's death. The butterfly concept helped me to emerge from the darkness of grief and be like the butterfly flitting from flower to flower, enjoying the amazing colors of life.

The point here is to take something in life that can act as a symbol for your healing. You can consider many items for symbols of healing. You could get a marble and always carry it in your pocket or purse to symbolize the circle of life. You could choose a flower that represents your healing. For example, I use the lilac as a symbol for my personality. It has many facets, yet is one flower. A bunch of grapes composes the same idea. You could pick up a stone from a stream and identify it as something that gets smooth only as the water rolls over it, and it tumbles over the riverbed, much like life. So brainstorm a symbol that can help you mend your broken heart.

Believing in Choice

Third, the idea that I can choose to change my thoughts and my behaviors allows me the freedom to be who I want to be. In March 2004, I wrote the following:

As I watched the March wind blow the leaves outside my sunroom window and knew that the season was beginning to change from the snows of winter to the chaotic wind of spring, I reflected on our own ability to change. Like the wind, we want to be free to change … After all, behavior is something we can change any time we want.

I have the power to choose to do exactly what the titles of my chapters emphasize. I can choose to prepare my children. I can choose to survive. I can choose to be happy. I can choose to manage my emotions. I can choose to change my perceptions. I can choose use my strengths to face adversity. I can choose to draw on fantasy to give me the freedom to be who I want to be. I can choose to listen to music to create courage in me. I can choose to handle the spiral times. I can choose to let my mind mend my broken heart.

So immerse yourself in the idea of choice. One

way to do that is to go to my Web site at www.yesyoucanchoose.com. On the left-side margin, there is a menu. Choose the item named "Articles on Choice." Click on it. You will be directed to a page with the current monthly article on choice that I have written. On the right side margin of the article page, there is a list of the last six articles I have written. Down at the bottom of that column it says, "Article Archive." Click on it. A list of all the articles I have written on choice will be in view. Peruse those article titles and see if any appeal to you. Try to read an article a day for at least twenty-one days. You will notice yourself thinking more in terms of choice.

Realizing the Gift

Fourth, thinking that I was very lucky to have experienced such an incredible, unforgettable, little boy with a mind that was wiser than his years allowed me to rejoice in knowing him. The quote I had put on Wes's gravestone was: "Little boys' pockets hold amazing things: fish worms, apple cores, a mess of string. But this treasure is nothing to the wealth one finds in little boys' hearts and little boys' minds."

I don't think that I was the only one that felt lucky to have known him. He created a special memory in the hearts of those who knew him. The following is an e-mail that was sent to me by a good friend on what would have been his twenty-fourth birthday. Lisa and Wes both share June 21 as their day of birth.

This day never goes by without me thinking of Wes and of all your family—remembering all those fun and busy days when the kids were little and how, despite the coming and going of Wes's illness, he lived a very full life for his short years.

I'm sure you wonder what he might be like today—a grown man. It's hard to imagine him as such!

He was such a sweetheart of a kid. I think the world is a better, more tender place for his having been here. And in time we might all be lucky enough to be like him—stardust, shining, golden.

He was an inspiration to many. The most profound example of this is how he impacted his elementary school teacher. I asked Mrs. Lock to reflect on her experience with Wes. When she gave me the following reflection, she shared several things that I believe show the impact he had on her. She told me that even after fifteen years, she still has the photograph of Wes I had taken just weeks before his death. She stated, "He is as much a part of my life as my family." As she considered how she now reaches out to others to help them because of his inspiration, she added, "That little stinker is still at work. His spirit is still around." Here is what Mrs. Lock wrote about her experience with Wes and why she considers him an angel in her pathway.

Wes

Bald head, little boy. This was my introduction to Wes Esterly. I couldn't help but notice this little boy in a long line of first graders coming up the stairs. While I obviously noticed the difference in that little head being bald, what struck me in those moments was that I really didn't think he felt he was any different than any of the other kids—he was bouncing along in line just like everyone else! Welcome to my world, Wes Esterly!

I continued to teach school, and Wes continued to attend school, our paths meeting here and there. When I would see him in our school building, he consistently seemed to be carrying on; doing what any typical school kid should or would be doing at the time. This made him intriguing to me because I was aware that he had a serious medical problem. I could only imagine what he had to deal with in regard to treatments for his illness. Yet, he seemed to be taking it so in stride!

Time continued marching on, another school year started, I received my fourth grade class list, and there was Wes's name! Well, needless to say, I came to know Wes very well throughout that year. I came to know that, yes, he did take his situation in stride, and yes, he just dealt with it. I've chuckled many times when I recalled how he really did not like hydrating after a chemo treatment. His mom would bring the water in that he should consume, and he and I would go round and round getting that water down. Little did I know that this particular activity would have a personal impact on me some time later.

In his own quiet way, he had an impact on the entire class. He wasn't a whiner or complainer; he just tried to do whatever I asked of him. Since he had attended our school since first grade, most of the kids knew him and knew of his health issue. With that in mind and given his positive attitude, the other kids would meet challenges with a "do my best" attitude like he did. After all, if Wes could do it or at least try, the others could too. They loved him. That was plain to see!

Another school year followed, I was assigned a fifth grade position, and Wes was to be in my class again! This was a joy for me! This little boy had managed, in his quiet way, to model for me patience and perseverance by the attitude he displayed in dealing with his own personal health issues. For me, it was a breath of fresh air to have the opportunity to work with and get to know better this unique individual. We did not physically end that year together, but in spirit, Wes was always with us! When Wes passed away at the beginning of that school year, the class did not want to move his desk. The children decided that we would leave Wes's desk in its place and when the time was right, whenever that would be, we would decide as a class, what to do next. The children let him go physically, but his spirit was truly always with us!

What was so special about Wes was that he impacted people in such a subtle way. He wasn't a tremendously demonstrative person, but he was powerful through his calm, positive perseverance. If ever there was a role model, it was Wes.

People come and go in your life. Some have more impact on you than others. Sometimes you wonder why a person passes your way. I found out about two years after Wes passed away. I was diagnosed with breast cancer. My course of treatment included chemo and radiation. Hydration! Déjà vu! My mind went back to fourth grade, and Wes and I trying so hard to down the prescribed bottles of water after his chemo treatments! Well, if he could do it, so could I. After all, he was just a little boy, I was a grown woman. I was scared, but I remembered how he carried on, and I thought if he could, so could I. So, I did. I went about my business, taught school, and just carried on just like Wes did.

Wes was my inspiration!

He was a gift in the lives of many. When I think of him as a time-limited gift, I still value him as a gift. Think of getting concert tickets for your birthday as a gift. You anticipate going, you enjoy the two-hour experience, and you have fond memories of how much you enjoyed the concert. The concert tickets were a time-limited gift. If you had received a picture to hang on your wall, that would have been a lasting gift. Both are valued in different ways. Realizing the value of the gift of time with your loved one and appreciating that gift can help you mend your broken heart.

Evaluating the Outcome

Using these concepts as well as all the other ideas in this book has helped me to mend my broken heart. How has my life been using these ideas? One never knows how one is perceived in life, but I had a chance to really find out. I was in a class that asked us to write our life summary by doing the following. Get three friends to answer the question "What do you know about me that would make you want to hire me as your friend?" Get your children to answer the question "What do you know about me that would make you want to hire me as your mom?" Take your signature strengths and add those to the mix. From the answers I got and from my signature strengths, I wrote my life summary.

Rita's Life Summary

I remember Rita as a friend with whom I loved to spend time. She was intelligent, visionary, ambitious, creative, independent, trustworthy, helpful, tenacious, generous, loving, kind, and forgiving. She helped me see the world in a clearer way. I trusted her with my deepest secrets and knew she would not share them with others. She helped me to be a better person. She had a great sense of humor. When I left her company, I always felt enriched physically, psychologically, and spiritually.

I remember my mom as a motivated, timely, task-oriented, hard-working person who was at the same time thoughtful, considerate, nurturing, generous, and kind-hearted. She was always there for me, no matter what I had done or how busy she was. She molded me into a person that I am proud to be. She tried to understand what was important to me in my life, even if she did not think it should be a priority. She taught me to be well rounded. She always loved to spend time with me. She would do anything for me. She was an excellent role model because she cared deeply about people, their lives, and how they chose to live.

Above all, she loved God and believed that God was directing her life. All that she did came from her belief that God had given her talents to use in this world to make it a better, more harmonious place. She was always true to herself and strove to be authentic and congruent with her inner values and what she did in life. Her greatest strength of persistence was also her greatest weakness. She loved beauty and the arts, whether it was the performing arts or the visual arts. She could see beauty in a blade of grass, or in the sparkle of the ripples on a lake. She had great energy and *enthusiasm for life. She was humble about what she did for others, and she was always grateful for what others did for her. She was genuine with everyone and always presented herself honestly to others.*

You saw her as she was with one exception, and that was she hid her deep sorrow and longing for her son Wes, not because it was a secret, but because it was private. She chose to keep it private. She realized that being stuck in her sorrow would only stand between friendship and her, between success and her, and between happiness and her. So although she missed Wes, she did not let that block her from creating a satisfying life. She chose to be the happy person she was. She will always remain someone whom I was proud to call my friend and my mom.

The reflections of my friends and my children show that despite the sorrow that Wes's death brought, I was able to live a productive and happy life. I guess I said it best when I answered the question I was asked when I was nominated for a woman of achievement award. In my city, a woman's organization honors sixteen women who have been successful. I was nominated by my service sorority. At first, I told the woman who asked my permission to be nominated that I did not believe I had done enough to be honored. She told me to think about it. That weekend, I read a book that changed my mind about accepting their nomination. So I said I would accept being nominated. In the process of picking two of the sixteen among those who were to be honored to be the women of achievement for the year, I was asked to describe my major achievements. I described what I had done over the past thirty years and ended with the following passage.

However, none of these achievements compare to the

major accomplishment that I consider to be the success of my life. What my true accomplishment has been is not my work as a psychologist with clients, nor my volunteer work, nor my academic achievements, but parenting a chronically ill child, who after eight years of brain surgeries, chemotherapy, and an autologous bone marrow transplant, died at the age of eleven. During this time, I never gave up hope. I always thought positive, and I never allowed the circumstances of his illness to take the joy from my life. The one thing this child taught me was to always be present to the moment, because every moment counts. My efforts continued after his death to raise my other two children to be productive despite the loss of their brother. I am proud to say that both my son who is graduating from pharmacy school and my daughter who is graduating from journalism school have become successful young adults. So despite the worst tragedy that a woman can endure, the loss of a child, I have maintained a cheery, positive attitude about life. I have not let tragedy stop me from meeting my potential for parenting productive children, for service to others in this world, and for interacting joyfully with friends to create amazing meaning in my life. My perspective of life has allowed me to be who I am and to achieve what I have.

You Getting Started

I want to share with you my journal writing from 2003. It was the last reflection that I wrote about Wes until I started this book.

No one knows the experience of what he lived through. I marvel at how strong he was, not only in his attitudes towards life, but also in his courage to endure.

What he must have suffered with the headaches, pressure on his brain, the trauma of the surgeries, the assault of the radiation, and the torture of the chemo, no one will ever know. One cannot know the experience of another. One can only imagine at a distance the reality of the pain and suffering. Yet he endured. Perhaps that's all he knew. He did not know what it was like to be without pain. He had probably endured it since his birth. I think how incredible he was, how much I wish I could have brought more comfort to him when he was in pain. All I could do was just be there for him, love him, hold onto him, and stroke his beautiful, feather head.

And thus, that is the only thing that I can do for you too. I can write this book and through the writing, I can be there for you. I can identify with your loss, identify with the feelings you have, identify with the struggles you endure, identify with the grieving process you go through, and identify with the chaos that comes with losing a loved one. But more than that, I can give you some effective techniques that, if you choose to apply them, might allow you to smile again, to laugh again, and to be interested in life again. More than anything, I wish for you a satisfying life, even without your loved one. So the choice is yours. You can apply these techniques you have read about or put the book down and do nothing.

Here is what I suggest you do after reading this book. It's the psychologist in me helping you to operationalize this book. I just cannot help taking you to the implementation phase. It is in my nature as a teacher and as a psychologist. So here goes.

Write down these chapter titles:

Prepare Siblings
Learn to Survive
Choose to be Happy
Manage Emotions
Change Perceptions
Use Your Strengths
Draw on Fantasy
Listen to Music
Handle Spiral Times
The Mind Mends the Heart

The first chapter is just identifying with you and what you might feel. The next three chapters are just my story and how everyone has a story. Chapters five through fourteen are suggestions of techniques you might try to actually mend your broken heart.

Take each chapter and identify one thing that you want to begin to either do or think (remember you are in control of both your behavior and your thoughts) to make your life more satisfying even when you have lost a loved one. Let me give you some examples.

From the chapter "Prepare Siblings," you might choose to be flexible and adaptable and not get stuck in tradition. Your strategy might be to talk with family members about what new idea they might have for celebrating a holiday. You invite them to a meeting a few months before that particular holiday, and you bring the issue up and everyone brainstorms. You find a new tradition, and although it might be awkward at first, the family adapts.

From the chapter "Learn to Survive," you might choose to begin basing your expectations on yourself and not on others. Your strategy might be for the next two weeks to first notice when you are disappointed in the behavior of others and then stop yourself. Then think about how you only have control of what you do. Ask yourself, "How did my thinking about how others should behave lead me to being disappointed?" Change your thought to expect yourself to do something about the situation.

From the chapter "Choose to be Happy," you might choose to use the idea of getting more excited about your life by being present to the moment. Your strategy might be that for the next month, you are going to focus on directing your mind to what you are doing at the time you are doing it. You decide not to wish you were somewhere else doing something else. You choose to be mindful of and honor the present moment.

From the chapter "Manage Emotions," you might choose to learn the technique to create relaxation so you can begin to take three deep breaths when a feeling begins to overwhelm you. Your strategy might be to take five weeks to do the program to learn relaxation. You decide to take six minutes of your busy day to learn a technique that will help you choose to manage your emotions.

From the chapter "Change Perceptions," you might choose to revise your dream. Your strategy might be to take Monday, Wednesday, and Friday of the following week to recreate your dream using the suggested exercise in that chapter. You schedule it, you follow through, and you let your mind create a picture of a satisfying life without your loved one in it.

From the chapter "Use Your Strengths," you might choose to go to the Web site to take the survey to learn all about your strengths. Your strategy might be to spend an hour on Monday evening completing the survey. You learn your strengths, and you choose one of the top strengths to help you weather the loss of your loved one.

From the chapter "Draw on Fantasy," you might choose to write a story. Your strategy might be to spend two hours on Sunday afternoon at your computer, writing a story to help you heal. You write, and you experience freedom from some emotions that have previously overwhelmed you.

From the chapter "Listen to Music," you might choose to adopt a song to help you mend your broken heart. Your strategy might be to spend more time listening to a radio station or to take a half hour each evening searching titles of songs to see what lyrics fit for you to gain the courage to heal. You find a song and play it over and over. You experience renewed courage to create a happy life.

From the chapter "Handle Spiral Times," you might choose to plan for an upcoming day that might be difficult for you to face. Your strategy might be to take off from work on the anniversary of your loved one's death and to write a letter to your loved one to get your feelings out. Getting your feelings out will help mend your broken heart.

From the chapter "The Mind Mends the Heart," you might choose to pick a symbol to help you heal, similar to what I did with the butterfly. Your strategy might be to incubate items to discern a symbol to represent your healing. So you look at a four-leaf clover and ponder it as having meaning in your life as a symbol for healing. You look at a frog as a symbol for healing. You look at a rose as a symbol for healing. Then you choose one that fits to help you mend your broken heart.

Of course, you cannot do all of these at once. Commit to doing one strategy from a chapter over the next ten months. That way you will have used ten strategies in ten months. Remember: it is combining many strategies that help you to mend your broken heart. Without making a commitment and a strategy, healing will not happen. Life will get in the way of your healing. You will stay stuck in your grief.

This is just a suggestion about how to operationalize what you have read in this book. The point is get started on doing something to mend your broken heart. You can choose to take just one strategy from all the chapters and use it. Work with it. If it works for you, then obviously it is getting you to your goal of mending your broken heart. If it gets you to your goal, then choose another one to implement, because obviously the techniques are working for you. If it did not work for you, then try another technique. Maybe another one will lead you to the goal of mending your broken heart.

The whole point is that unless you take pause to consider what you need to do as a result of reading and to actually build a strategy, it will never happen. So when you are done reading this book, take the next step.

The next step is to actually take some action as a result of reading this book. That, as always, is your choice. If you do choose to take an action, you have the potential to mend your broken heart. My hope is that you do have the courage to take an action to make your life more satisfying.

It is time for you to mend your broken heart. I believe that something in this book will work for you. I believe that you will begin to apply behaviors and thoughts that will help you mend your broken heart. I believe that you have the choice to create satisfaction in your life. I believe that you can choose to increase your happiness. I believe you truly desire to make your life successful. I believe you can do it because now you have the tools to help you succeed. I believe it is time for you to mend your broken heart, and I believe you can make it happen.

Forever Smiles

Rita Esterly, Ph.D.

About the Author

Rita Esterly, Ph.D. is a psychologist in private practice and a strengths coach. She established Choosing Wellness Eagerly, Inc. in 1995, on what would have been her son's thirteenth birthday. She used his initials, CWE, and chose words that fit her mindset. She believes that we have a choice in developing mental well-being. Additionally, she believes we have a choice in being enthusiastic about our mental wellness. She also has a coaching practice called YesYouCanChoose. Her Web site, www.YesYouCanChoose.com, reflects the same theme of choice.

Dr. Esterly was an avid reader as a young girl. Two characters from books she read had a large impact on her life. When she was about nine, her godmother, also named Rita, let her borrow *Gone with the Wind* and *Little Women*. Scarlett and Jo were strong, independent, passionate, enthusiastic women. These two fictional role models, along with the caring, loving, nurturing, generous role modeling of her mother, Bertha Cardetti, shaped the strength of character Dr. Esterly exhibits as an adult. She wonders if her own role modeling for her son helped him face the adversity he endured in his life.

When Dr. Esterly is not helping people have more satisfying lives or writing for her Web site, you can usually find her at some performing arts venue relishing the acting, dancing, singing, or musical ability of talented artists. Musical theatre holds a special place in her heart, as she sees it as an avenue for children to gain confidence by performing. This confidence carries over to other contexts of their lives. She appreciates that her children had the opportunity to participate in musical theatre when they were young, due to the generosity and teaching of their acting coach, director, and friend Wyn Riley. She credits their participation in the performing arts for the confidence her children have in themselves.

Because of her belief in choice, her ability to vividly role model a positive perspective and her passion for building confidence through the performing arts, she manifests a unique perspective with which to help people. She takes her clients from hesitation to action by helping them believe in themselves, no matter what journey they choose to take. You can contact Dr. Esterly through her Web site at www.YesYouCanChoose.com or by e-mail at coachrita@yesyoucanchoose.com.

Bibliography

Csikszentmihalyi, M. (1990). *Flow: The Psychology of Optimal Experience*. New York: Harper & Row Publishers, Inc.

Peterson, C. and Seligman, M. (2004). *Character Strengths and Virtues: A Handbook and Classification*. New York: Oxford University Press, Inc.

Schutz, W. (1958). *FIRO: A Three-Dimensional Theory of Interpersonal Behavior.* New York: Rinehart & Company, Inc.

Schwartz, B. (2004). *The Paradox of Choice: Why More is Less.* New York: HarperCollins Publishers, Inc.

Scofield, C. (ed). (1967). *Oxford NIV Scofield Study Bible.* New York: Oxford University Press.

Thurber, J. (1942). My World and Welcome to It. *The Secret Life of Walter Mitty.* Orlando, FL: Harcourt, Brace and Company.

listen|imagine|view|experience

AUDIO BOOK DOWNLOAD INCLUDED WITH THIS BOOK!

In your hands you hold a complete digital entertainment package. Besides purchasing the paper version of this book, this book includes a free download of the audio version of this book. Simply use the code listed below when visiting our website. Once downloaded to your computer, you can listen to the book through your computer's speakers, burn it to an audio CD or save the file to your portable music device (such as Apple's popular iPod) and listen on the go!

How to get your free audio book digital download:

1. Visit www.tatepublishing.com and click on the e|LIVE logo on the home page.
2. Enter the following coupon code:
   047b-2bba-220b-53ae-c46b-c464-d041-12ed
3. Download the audio book from your e|LIVE digital locker and begin enjoying your new digital entertainment package today!